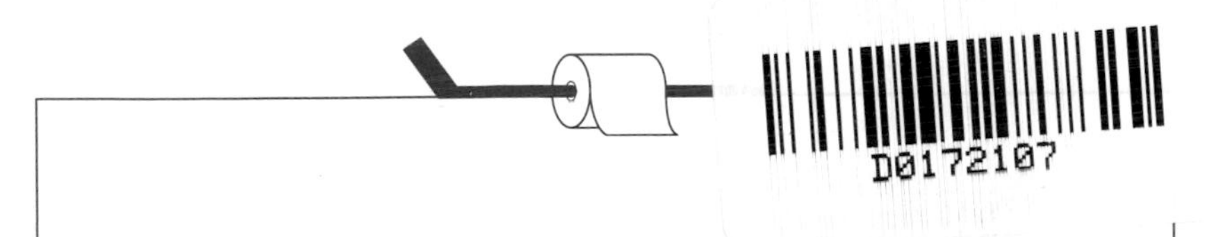

Uncle John's

BATHROOM READER®

SHOOTS AND SCORES!

BY THE BATHROOM READERS' INSTITUTE HOCKEY CLUB

RAINCOAST BOOKS
VANCOUVER, BC

BATHROOM READERS' PRESS
ASHLAND, OREGON

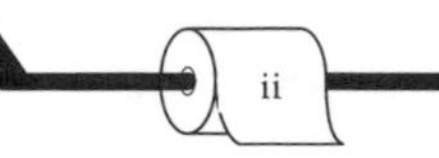

Raincoast Books gratefully acknowledges the ongoing support of the Canada Council for the Arts, the British Columbia Arts Council and the Government of Canada through the Book Publishing Industry Development Program (BPIDP).

Edited by Derek Fairbridge and Silas White
Cover design by Michael Brunsfeld
Typeset by Teresa Bubela

Library and Archives Canada Cataloguing in Publication
Uncle John's bathroom reader shoots and scores.
ISBN 10: 1-55192-849-3
ISBN 13: 978-1-55192-849-4
1. Hockey—Miscellanea.
GV847.U53 2005 796.962 C2005-902490-9

Raincoast Books
9050 Shaughnessy Street
Vancouver, British Columbia
Canada V6P 6E5
www.raincoast.com

The Bathroom Readers' Hysterical Society
Portable Press
5880 Oberlin Drive
San Diego, California
USA 92921
unclejohn@advmkt.com

Printed in Canada by Friesens
First printing: September 2005

05 06 07 08 09 10 9 8 7 6 5 4 3 2 1

CONTENTS

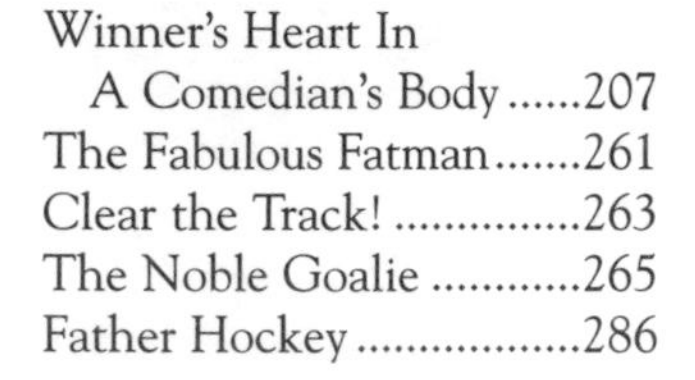

OFF-ICE PERSONALITIES

THE WORLD STAGE

UNSUNG PIONEERS OF THE GAME

UNDERDOGS, UNDERACHIEVERS & UNLIKELY HEROES

ACCESSORIES OF HOCKEY

LAW & ORDER

BLOOPERS AND MISCUES

THE BUSINESS OF HOCKEY

CEREMONIES & SUPERSTITIONS

CONGRATULATIONS!

The Bathroom Readers' Institute would like to congratulate the members of the BRI AllStar Shinny Team for their tremendous effort and great sportsmanship, and for making this book possible.

THE "WRITE" LINE

The journalists and writers who scouted the rinks and went into overtime in their quest for the most interesting hockey facts and stories.

Frank "Faster than Bobby" Orr (Captain) — Center
Mark "The Fog" Weisenmiller — Right Wing
Rob "Emmy" Adler — Left Wing
Kevin "Pappa" Woodley — Defense
Lucas "Barbershop" Aykroyd — Defense
Jeff "The Human Highlight Film" Rud — Rover
Adam "Suitcase" Schroeder — Goalie

BEHIND THE BENCH

The editors and designers who pulled the team together and made a book out of it.

Derek "Golf Pants" Fairbridge — Head Coach
Silas "Roadrunner" White — Assistant Coach
Alexandra "The Hammer" Wilson — Equipment Manager
Teresa "Boom Boom" Bubela — General Manager
Michael "Miracle" Brunsfeld — Team Mascot

... AND THANK YOU!

THE FANS

Everyone else behind the scenes who helped to pull together this "miracle on ice"

Michelle Benjamin
Allen Orso
Jennifer Thornton
JoAnn Padgett
Gary Lloyd
Sydney Stanley
Jennifer Browning
Mana Monzavi
Connie Vazquez
Dylan Drake
Antonia Banyard
Cindy Connor
And all our great friends at Raincoast

Thanks to all of you,
from all of us at Raincoast and the BRI!

Want to see the rest of the Uncle John's Bathroom Reader Hall of Fame?

Visit www.bathroomreader.com or www.raincoast.com/bathroomreader.

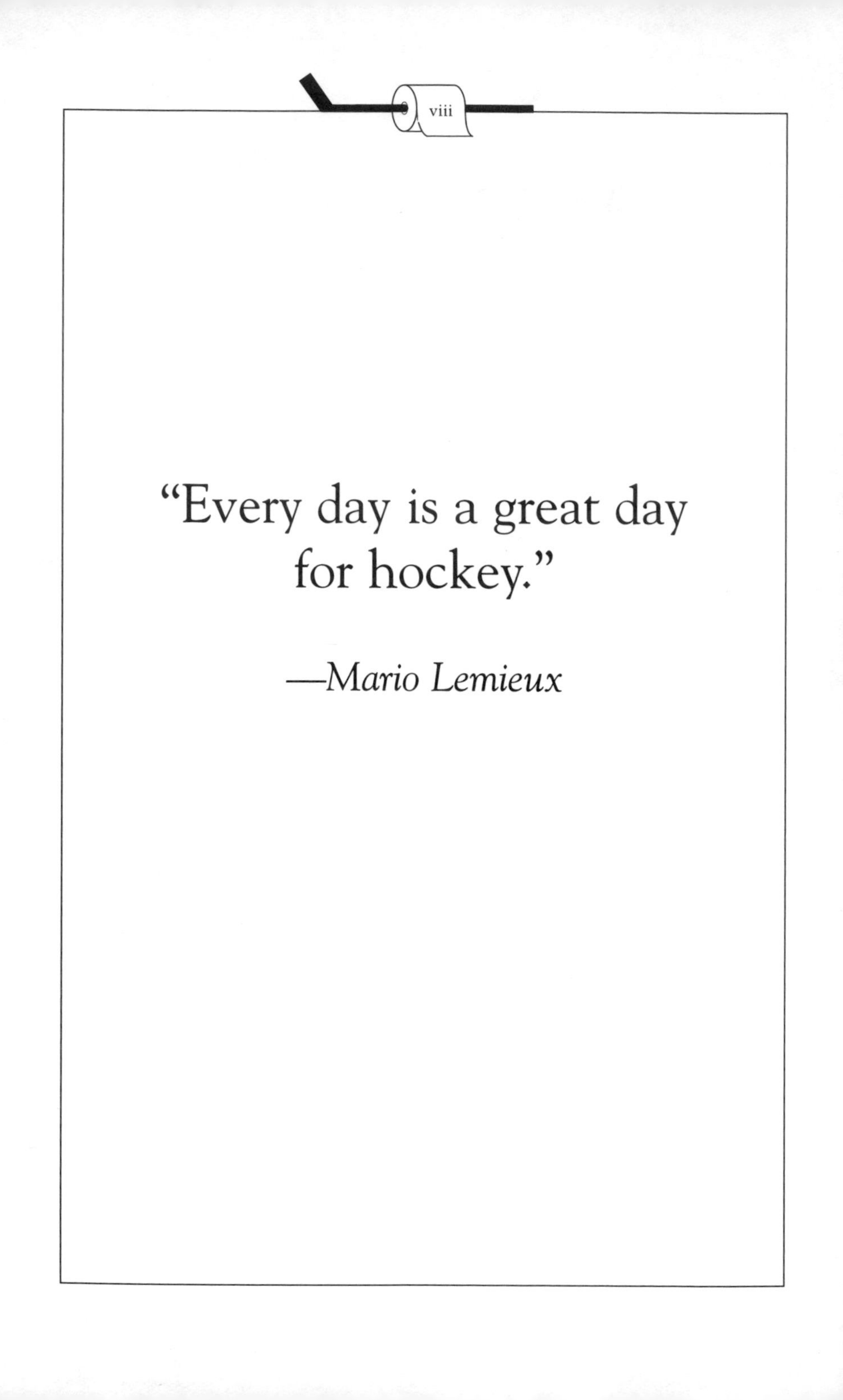

“Every day is a great day for hockey.”

—Mario Lemieux

INTRODUCTION

Hey there sports fans! Welcome to Uncle John's Wonderful World of Hockey!

So what did you do every Saturday night last winter, when the National Hockey League players were fighting with the team owners instead of with each other? Well, here at the BRI, we replaced the Saturday night hockey ritual with something new. Instead of sitting back and watching hockey on the tube, we decided to get out there and *play* a little hockey—road hockey, that is—known as "shinny" in most parts of North America. We headed out to the frozen concrete with taped-up sticks and a bright orange ball (an old tennis ball will do), and two old boots for goal posts. We put up with those annoying vehicular interruptions ("CAR!"), while impersonating our favorite on-ice heroes on our ultimate dream teams: "***Gretzky passes to Lemieux, Lemieux streaks past Orr, Cournoyer races in and steals the puck, he passes to Wickenheiser who HAMMERS it at the net, Roy reaches for it...SCOOOORES! Wickenheiser from Cournoyer, they win the Stanley Cup!***"

After the games, the BRI AllStar Shinny Team would get to talking, and we wondered if there was enough hockey trivia out there to fill a book. Well, imagine our surprise! We consulted our friends in Canada (they think they know a few things about hockey up there...), and together we drafted a dream team of hockey writers. They came up with an entire highlight reel full of interesting stories, hilarious hockey history, fascinating quotes, and some entirely useless facts about the weird and wonderful game of hockey.

Well, the strike's over now so we have to get back to our regular routine. But look—we got a book out of it! So sit back, and get ready for the puck to drop. There are no refs in this game (although we mention a few in the book...) and way more than three periods. There are a couple of quizzes, too, and a whole hockey sock full of trivia—enough to get you through to next season, anyway.

Enjoy, and try to stay out of the penalty box!

Game On!

If you're already an Uncle John's bathroom reader, skip this Introduction, turn to any page of this book, and start reading. You will be rewarded with some new insight or fascinating story about hockey that most likely you did not already know.

If you're a new to the world of Uncle John, welcome. We are best-known for our annually produced readers, which cover a range of topics. We have 18 numbered annual editions with over 5 million in print. These books are so popular that our readers begged us to publish more than one new title a year. So over the last few years we expanded our publishing program to include single topic bathroom readers on popular subjects. To see all we have to offer, visit us at www.bathroomreader.com

Uncle John's Bathroom Reader Shoots and Scores is our second foray into the world of sports. If you're a sports fan, especially a golfer, don't miss *Uncle John Bathroom Reader Tees Off on Golf.* Our Canadian partner, Raincoast Books, was so excited about the golf book, they proposed that we follow it up with their country's favorite sport—hockey. They were so enthusiastic, we asked them to author it under our auspices.

Hockey has a long and colorful history, not to mention larger-than-life personalities, time-honored traditions, and interesting idiosyncrasies. The editors had to make some hard choices. This may not be the most comprehensive hockey book, but it definitely is the most entertaining. We packed the best of what we uncovered into *Uncle John's Bathroom Reader Shoots and Scores*. Here are some of the fun stories inside:

The Origins
The Rinks and the Equipment
The Best, Worst and Weirdest
The Basics
The Competitions
But best of all, the Personalities.

I hope you will enjoy this book as much as you do the sport of hockey.

Sit back and enjoy. And, as always, remember to go with the flow.

Uncle Al

WHERE IT ALL BEGAN

Hockey's longest running and often most-heated argument concerns the site of the game's origins.

One of the liveliest hockey battles—as energetic as the scrappiest of scraps for the puck in any NHL rink corner—is waged by the game's historians. The contentious subject of debate is where and when the primitive forms of this wonderful game actually originated.

LET THERE BE ICE

Combine ice—a frozen pond or river—and narrow, steel blades attached to one's feet, and you will find that quick movement over the slippery surface becomes possible. Throw in sticks and something to hit while moving on the ice—a ball, a wooden disc, frozen horse manure—and a game is born. While there are reports of stones being kicked or hit back and forth with sticks after the Norman invasion of Britain in the 11th century, and while Chinese and Russian folklore document stick-and-ball games on ice 500 years ago, the earliest form of what *really* became ice hockey was most likely played in the Canadian province of Nova Scotia. And probably in the town of Windsor...

EARLY HURLEY BURLY

That Windsor would be among hockey's earliest sites shouldn't come as much surprise. It can get damn cold there! But also, Windsor was one of Canada's first towns, settled in 1684, and the location of the country's first college. Anglican Church members working in the New World as executives of steamship, lumber and fur trading companies did not want to send their children all the way back to England for a decent education, so instead they imported British professors to form King's College School. And the professors brought their games with them: Cricket, rounders (the forerunner of baseball) and Irish hurley (a form of field hockey) were field games that were modified for the snow and ice of the Canadian winter. Mention of "ice hurley" around 1800 is the first written reference to a stick-and-ball game on a frozen surface.

COLONEL HOCKEY

One story claims that a Colonel Hockey (a common English name at the time) had British troops based at Windsor play the game for winter exercise and Hockey's game became, simply, hockey. A ball struck in hurley was said to be "pucked," and the first wooden disc used in the game became known as, simply, the "puck."

OTHER CLAIMS TO THE GAME

For many decades the original site for hockey was thought to be Kingston, Ontario, because the first written report of the game was published there in 1855. Soldiers at the British Garrison, wearing primitive skates clamped to their shoes, used field hockey sticks and a lacrosse ball to play on a large area of Kingston harbor cleared of snow. In 1903, a Kingston newspaper brashly declared the town "the birthplace of hockey."

In 1941, an elderly Montreal resident recounted stories from his father about a primitive game of hockey in that city in 1837. In the 1870s, a group of students at McGill University in Montreal invented a game played on ice using a combination of rules from field hockey, lacrosse and rugby. A definitive seven paragraphs in the 1877 *Montreal Gazette* recorded the first set of printed rules for hockey as devised by these clever students.

WHOOPIN' IT UP IN WINDSOR

Although extensive research has provided evidence of the game in Nova Scotia from 1800 on, historians have been unable to agree on a precise locale and date. The area had long winters and abundant ice, students and soldiers with plenty of time on their hands, and keen sporting spirits in quest of diversion from the cold, cold season.

The much-quoted author Thomas Chandler Haliburton was born in Windsor and attended King's College. He had arts and law degrees and became a distinguished judge and writer, often called "the father of American humor." A paragraph in an article Haliburton wrote for a British magazine in 1844 about his days as a student at King's College has caught the eye of many a hockey historian: "The boys let out racin', yellin', hollerin' and whoopin' like mad with pleasure, and the playground, and the game at bass in the fields, or hurley on the long pond on the ice, or campin' out at night at Chester Lakes to fish…." Haliburton had graduated from King's in 1810 and his mention of "hurley," the early name for hockey, indicates the game was played before that year. Newspaper stories were discovered that discussed hurley on Long Pond at Windsor before 1816.

FROM IRONWOOD TO SHERWOOD

Windsor was enjoyed as a resort by wealthy residents of Halifax, some of whom owned luxurious estates in the town. They would come to fish, hunt, race horses (on the track and on ice), and to attend cultural events at the college. Thus, word of the most exciting game on ice was spread across the province and soldiers based in the Halifax-Dartmouth area also started to play. As the game grew, a loose set of rules was established—a sort of "sporting code" rather than a written rule book—to govern how the game was conducted.

The Mi'kmaq natives of Nova Scotia, who had a field and ice game of their own, supplied the first "pucks": slices of black cherrywood with tight, dark bark, making it easier to find in the snow. They also carved strong one-piece hockey sticks from ironwood trees with roots still attached: the root used for the blade, the stem carved into the handle.

THE FIRST ROAD TRIP

When the army moved west to Montreal and Kingston, the game went with them. An 1846 entry in a diary belonging to the father of a Kingston historian reads, "Most of the boys were quite at home on skates. They could cut the figure-eight but 'shinny' was their delight." The word "shinny" had come from the Scotch stick-and-ball field game of shinty, and is used today to describe a loosely structured game of pickup hockey. A British army officer wrote in his diary in 1843, "Began to skate this year, improved quickly and had great fun at hockey on ice." Supporters of Kingston as the game's birthplace used these lines to back their contentions.

BULLIES PROVIDE ORDER

One major development in hockey's growth from a "mad-scramble" sport, with as many players as the size of the available ice surface would hold, to a more organized game was the publication of the famous "*Gazette* rules." Those seven paragraphs, printed in the Montreal newspaper on February 27, 1877, supplied a basis for the game that exists to this day, defining offsides, fouls against opponents, and how plays were to resume after the ball or puck went off the ice. A faceoff in those rules was called a "bully." The rules slowly expanded over the years, the number of players on the ice for one team being reduced from 15 to seven.

SHALL WE TAKE THIS INSIDE?

By 1880, several cities in Canada had indoor arenas, built first for pleasure skating with no hockey allowed. Gradually the game moved indoors, the lacrosse ball bouncing out of play so often that some enterprising soul sliced it to produce a flat piece of rubber that would slide on the ice. As shooting skills improved, various pieces of primitive equipment were introduced to protect shins. Goalies wore padding, and skates evolved from the blades that were strapped to the boots to "skate boots" with blades permanently attached. But going all the way back to the chilly outdoor days, there is no doubt hockey is a *very* competitive sport—both on the ice and in the minds of many professional and amateur historians.

* * * * *

Howie Morenz was a center who played much of his hockey career with the Montreal Canadiens, amassing 270 goals and 467 points during the 1920s and 1930s. However, did you know that his grandson Shea Morenz was a collegiate quarterback who played at the University of Texas?

GOAL(S) HEARD 'ROUND THE WORLD

Paul Henderson scored the goal "heard around the world." Mike Eruzione's rates right up there, too.

To Canadian hockey fans, even the generations of them born since it happened, Paul Henderson's 1972 goal remains the greatest ever scored. It came 34 seconds from the end of game eight in the fabled Summit Series, giving Team Canada the slimmest possible edge over the national team of the old Soviet Union in the first meeting between the Soviets and top professional players from the National Hockey League.

Many U.S. fans, however, would rate it second best. To them, the greatest goal ever was scored by Mike Eruzione to give the young, underdog U.S. Olympic team a 4–3 victory over the Soviets in the key game of the Americans' gold medal win in the 1980 Games at Lake Placid, NY.

YEAH, ACCORDING TO WHOM?

Of course, many hockey fans have their own favorite tallies that rate the "greatest" tag, goals that locked up a playoff spot or won a Stanley Cup, set a record or ended a long overtime. But high placings on sheer numbers of "great goal" lists, the Henderson and Eruzione markers are in a class by themselves, stamping the scorers as heroes for life. That the two men who produced the grand goals, Henderson and Eruzione, were not superstars added to their luster. They were from the ranks but they produced when the ultimate crunch was on, a huge prize at stake, giving them the glory and the status that accompanies such feats. In both cases, the "damned Russians," as teams from the former USSR often were called, were viewed as the major enemy of North American hockey. The "us vs. them" quality produced by confrontations between Canada and the USSR in hockey, the U.S. and the Soviets in every area, thrived during the Cold War.

TAKING GOLD FOR GRANTED

Through close to 40 years of international hockey, Canada could send senior amateur teams of no great distinction to the World Championship and the Olympics and win with little trouble. But on a Sunday morning in 1954, Canadian fans woke to bad news: The country's representatives, the East York Lyndhursts from a Toronto senior league, were whipped 7–2 by a Soviet national team in its first try at the world "amateur" championships. Even those Canadians who had paid little attention to the world event through its history complained that the country should send a better team overseas. The Canadian entry was upgraded to top-notch senior clubs over the next seven years and won four times but after 1961, the country's best amateurs could not match the Europeans, especially the Soviets.

TAKING IT FOR GRANTED (AGAIN)

But as Canada lost, including a valiant but futile six-year attempt by a national team of young players through the 1960s, Canadians smugly said that the best 400 or so players were involved in pro hockey and NHL players would defeat the Europeans, including the "commies," as the Soviets were known, easily. After several years of negotiations, the series between the Soviets and Team Canada, comprising the best NHL players, was set for 1972.

Only a handful of Canadian observers familiar with international hockey predicted that the Soviets would be competitive with the glittering array of NHL stars. Not even the absence of two great players from the Canadian lineup, defenceman Bobby Orr, who had a knee injury, and Bobby Hull, who had jumped from the NHL to the rival WHA, dampened the Canadian optimism.

TEARS FOR JEERS

The series received a huge buildup, opened on a Saturday evening in late August at The Montreal Forum and, in one of the biggest shocks in hockey history, the Soviets skated to a 7–3 victory after falling behind 2–0 early in the game. The mastery of the quick, meticulously conditioned and highly skilled Russians was dazzling. The Canadians rebounded to win the second game at Toronto, then the clubs played a tie in Winnipeg. In the last game in Canada, fans in Vancouver booed the home side in a 5–3 loss, prompting star center Phil Esposito to make an impassioned plea on national television for support because the players were trying their utmost.

GREAT WHITE NORTH STRIKES BACK

After a ten-day break, the series resumed in Moscow and the Soviets won the first game there for a commanding 3–1–1 edge in the series. Even a tie in one of the three remaining games would give them the series. Through the series, a strong factor for the Canadians was the forward line of young center Bobby Clarke, two years into his excellent career with the Philadelphia Flyers, flanked by good but not top-level Toronto Maple Leafs wingers Ron Ellis and Paul Henderson. The line had played solid two-way hockey in every game, the trio's speed of much value on the larger ice surface in Moscow. With Esposito playing magnificently and emerging as the team leader, the Canadians slowly gained good conditioning and in the energetically played, bitterly contested competition, battled back to win the sixth and seventh game, Henderson scoring the winning goal in both.

AND FINALLY, THAT GOAL...

But his best was still to come in game eight. Canada trailed 5–3 entering the third period but tied the score by the 13th minute on goals by Esposito and Yvan Cournoyer. The game and the series appeared certain to end in a tie as the teams hit the final minute. Responding to Henderson's urgent cries from the bench, Pete Mahovlich came off to allow Henderson to rush headlong towards the Soviet goal, take a shot at goalie Vladislav Tretiak and fall into the endboards. Esposito snared the puck when a defenceman mis-handled it and shot just as Henderson was scrambling for the front of the net. Tretiak stopped Espo's shot and one by Henderson on the rebound. Then Henderson snared his own rebound the fired it past the valiant Soviet goalie to win the series.

JUST COLLEGE KIDS

Many of the players from the 1972 Summit were with the Soviet team for the Lake Placid Olympics eight years later. The U.S. team of college players, coached by the hard-driving Herb Books, was given a shot at a medal but the Soviets were considered a lock for the gold. However as the tournament progressed, it was obvious that the swift, skilled American kids had a chance to win.

A NAME YOU'LL NEVER FORGET

The key game was against the Soviets, a team that seemed to have lost its fine edge built up over the years. Coach Viktor Tikhonov made a puzzling decision when he pulled Tretiak after the first period with the score tied, 2–2, inserting Vladimir Myshkin. That seemed to give the Americans a shot of adrenaline and with U.S. goalie Jim Craig excelling, they were in a 3–3 tie halfway through the third period. Eruzione, the one non-college player on the U.S. roster (he played minor-pro), snapped home a 25-foot shot that led to broadcaster Al Michael's famous line: "Do you believe in miracles?" The U.S. Team clinched the gold medal by defeating Finland 4–2 in their final game to join the ranks of the most-revered sports heroes in American history.

* * * * *

COME AGAIN?

For those who thought that baseball legend Yogi Berra cornered the market on puzzling sports double-talk, consider Jean Perron, former coach of the Montreal Canadiens and Quebec Nordiques:

"I think that we took care of the issue at the beginning of the end of last season."

"The day when the Nords will stop losing, they'll win much more often."

"The Nordiques should trade to get some rookies with experience."

"This type of injury is very painful. Especially when it hurts."

"When Stephane Richer plays as per his talent, he could play with both eyes tied to his back."

"We're finally starting to see the train at the end of the tunnel."

A FUNNY THING HAPPENED ON THE WAY TO THE RINK

A few hockey men have taken a funny look at the game's serious side to remind us that it is just a game.

Former NHL head coach Harry Neale is a man who can see a funny side to most situations in hockey and life, and give it a verbal spin to make others chuckle. Little wonder that Neale has been among the best analysts of televised hockey, a mainstay of *Hockey Night in Canada* for a couple of decades since his NHL management career.

NEALE'S KNEE-SLAPPERS

During his coaching days, Neale became the media's favorite interview because of his countless one-liners. During a losing stretch when he was coach of the Vancouver Canucks, Neale originated a line used by many coaches over the years: "We're losing at home and we can't win on the road. My failure as a coach is that I can't think of any place else to play." When Canucks goalie Curt Ridley dove out of the net after a loose puck, injured both knees and had to be taken off the ice on a stretcher, Neale was asked if he seen such an occurrence before. "No, I never have," Neale said with a deadpan expression. "It's pretty good, too, because the NHL record is three."

Other memorable Neale descriptions of his team:

"Our best system of forechecking this season is shoot the puck into the other team's zone—and leave it there."

"We have too many guys who are small but slow."

"We have a couple of defencemen with really bad hands. We can let them rush once a game—then we have to replace the pucks."

QUIPS FROM THE CREASE

That goalie John Garrett logged time with the Canucks during Neale's regime is appropriate; their discussions had to be side-splitting. Garrett was a handy man with a quip and it's no surprise that he, too, has had a post-playing career as a television commentator. In reality, Garrett had a serious side and had completed university credits while playing junior hockey, studies he continued by correspondence and summer school while a pro. After all, his father was a high school principal.

After landing good marks in high school Latin, Garrett studied it at the college level. When he was questioned about the usefulness of a dead language, he replied, "It will be handy to have it if I ever meet an ancient Roman because we'll be able to have a great conversation." Garrett also studied Hebrew briefly while playing with the Quebec Nordiques. His goaltending partner, Dan Bouchard, was a devout born-again Christian, which inspired Garrett to call them "the perfect tandem."

"Dan can make contact with all those biblical characters up above, then I can translate what they say for him."

AND THEIR FATHER WAS A BIT SQUIRRELLY

Then there were the Plager brothers, Barclay, Bob and Billy, three tough, hearty, self-deprecating defencemen from northern Ontario who were serious about everything on the ice, full-time laughers off it. The sons of longtime amateur hockey referee Gus Plager, Barc and Bob had long NHL careers with the St. Louis Blues, and Billy a shorter stint with three teams.

With Bob as the leading laugh-getter, the Plagers specialized in tales about growing up in hockey hotbed Kirkland Lake. "In Kirkland Lake, they called our father 'Squirrel' because he raised three nuts," Bob said. "If we had a disagreement, Gus would send us into the backyard to settle it. I would beat up Bob, Bob would beat up Bill, [and Bill] would go down the street and beat up our cousin, who never could quite figure out why he was always getting pummeled when he hadn't done anything."

BEAM ME UP, SCOTTY

In junior hockey, Barclay (with Peterborough) had a fight with Bob (with Guelph) that is part of hockey folklore. They used sticks, fists and even tried a few kicks. They fought on the ice, in the arena corridors and the dressing rooms. Both were cut and bleeding at the finish. When they had a post-game meeting in a restaurant, everyone expected the furniture to fly. "Barc just wanted to borrow five bucks and tell me that our mom was complaining that I didn't write home enough," Bob said.

Bob's specialty was jokes about Scotty Bowman, who coached the Blues to the Stanley Cup final in the first three years of their existence and brought the Plagers to the team. "Scotty once told me that the higher up you are to watch a game, the slower it looks," Plager said, "and when I watch you, Plager, I figure I'm on the *Starship Enterprise*." Barclay best defined the hockey fighter's credo when he said, "It's not how many fights you win; it's how many you show up for."

COACH'S CHUCKLE

While not all coaches had Neale's wit, a few others overcame the tendency of the job to turn men dour. Another man who later found success in television was Don Cherry, who turned coaching the Boston Bruins into great fun in the 1970s. Cherry became a fixture on *Hockey Night in Canada* with his outspoken "Coach's Corner" segment. Cherry had an 18-season playing career, all in the minors except for one 1955 game with the Bruins. "When I was a kid, I prayed for enough talent to be a pro hockey player," Cherry said. "I forgot to say NHL, though, because they only gave me enough to make the minor leagues." Another coach who was always quick with the quip was Fred Shero, who guided the Philadelphia Flyers in their Broad Street Bully days. Once asked what it was like to live life in the fast lane, Shero replied, "I don't live in the fast lane; I live on the off-ramp."

WAS THE MAJOR A KERNEL?

Through history, many NHL team owners have been off-the-wall characters but few were as eccentric as Major Frederic McLaughlin.

Conn Smythe, founder and longtime owner of the Toronto Maple Leafs, supplied a strong assessment of Major Frederic McLaughlin, owner of the Chicago Black Hawks for their first 18 NHL seasons: "Where hockey was concerned, McLaughlin was the strangest bird," said Smythe, himself a unique personality. "In fact, he was the biggest nut I met in my entire life."

SPELLING NOT A STRONG POINT AT HARVARD

Son of a wealthy coffee importer, McLaughlin was a Harvard grad and a top polo player who commanded the 33rd Machine Gun Battalion of the U.S. Army's 85th Blackhawk Division in World War I. Purchasing the Chicago franchise during the 1926 NHL expansion into the U.S., he picked that name, the Black Hawks, for his team. The two-word spelling was used until research in the 1990s revealed that the army division employed the one-worded Blackhawks, and the official name was adjusted. Through his days as Hawk owner—he often doubled as general manager—McLaughlin fought never-ending skirmishes against the other owners.

GOODNIGHT IRENE

A tall man of almost regal bearing, McLaughlin was a major figure in Chicago society in the Roaring Twenties. He had married Irene Castle, the widow of Vernon Castle, her partner in a popular dance team featured in Broadway shows and nightclubs. Irene designed the black and white uniforms worn by the hockey team, and the aboriginal head crest resembling Chief Black Hawk, a Sauk tribal leader in the Illinois region during the early 1800s. The uniform outlasted Irene. In a 1937 divorce action against McLaughlin, Irene claimed that their palatial suburban home was chilly and her three dogs had to wear sweaters in the house.

THIS TEAM STINKS!

Tex Rickard, the legendary New York promoter behind Madison Square Garden and the NHL Rangers, sold McLaughlin on hockey as a good investment. McLaughlin bought the players, including stars Dick Irvin and Babe Dye, from the Portland Rosebuds and Vancouver Maroons of the defunct Western League for $125,000, making his Chicago club competitive quickly. Home arena for the Hawks was the 6,000 seat Chicago Coliseum that smelled of another big attraction—cattle shows. When the Norris family, an NHL ownership power for decades, applied for a second Chicago franchise, McLaughlin refused to share the market. That set off a long, bitter feud between two rich entities—the Major and the Norris clan.

BACK AT THE RANCH

When the $7 million Chicago Stadium was completed in 1929, James Norris founded the Chicago Shamrocks of the American Hockey Association for his new building. But when that league folded, McLaughlin moved the Black Hawks into the new house on a three-year lease. When the Stadium was deep in debt, Norris bought it plus another money-losing hockey house, the Detroit Olympia, and a big share of the Madison Square Garden Corporation. With his arch-enemy Norris owning the Stadium, McLaughlin took the Hawks back to the Coliseum to open the 1932–33 season. Despite small crowds, McLaughlin was adamant against threats from Norris that he honor his Stadium contract. Finally, the NHL ordered the Hawks to play in the Stadium.

FOUR OUT OF FIVE NHL PRESIDENTS SAY...

That season, Norris purchased the bankrupt Detroit Falcons, changed the name to Red Wings, and had a seat on the NHL Board of Governors. McLaughlin's boardroom scraps with Norris were legendary, but he also found time to clash with Art Ross of the Boston Bruins, the Rangers' Lester Patrick and Smythe of the Maple Leafs. "Instead of thinking of ways to make the league better, the governors' meetings were mostly the rest of us trying to straighten out the latest lunatic idea from that guy in Chicago," Smythe said years later. "He didn't know a damned thing about hockey but still shot off his mouth."

A TRAIN OF COACHES

The coaches of the team seemed among his favorite foes. In his 18 seasons as owner, McLaughlin changed coaches 18 times, involving 13 men. The Major was involved in what surely is the NHL's most unusual coach-hiring. In 1932, he was on a train from Minneapolis to Chicago and he chatted with seat-mate Godfrey Matheson, a Winnipeg native with assorted theories on hockey. Before the train arrived, McLaughlin had hired Matheson to coach the Black Hawks.

When the players arrived in Pittsburgh for training camp that fall, they found Matheson on the ice in his suit and tie, elbow pads over his coat, knee pads over his trousers. Instead of wearing skates, he was on all fours in the corner of the ice with a pail of pucks, sliding passes by hand for the players to shoot at the net. To keep the team's great goalie Charlie Gardiner from any risk of injury, Matheson had a stuffed figure in full goaltending equipment stationed in front of the net.

Matheson's coaching stint lasted for two games (both losses), then he was replaced by Emil Iverson, another unknown, who had the job for 23 games. Veteran NHL coach Tommy Gorman finished the season as Hawk coach, then guided the team to its first Stanley Cup victory in the 1933–34 season. Of course, McLaughlin's response was to fire Gorman.

MAJOR FRED WANTS YOU TO JOIN THE HAWKS

McLaughlin often sounded off about the domination of Canadian players in the NHL and wanted a full roster of U.S. talent. Late in the 1936–37 season, he added five Americans to the four already in the lineup, the team missed the playoffs, and the Major earned derision from rivals for not using the best possible talent at a time when league competition was tight. In the 1937–38 season McLaughlin had a new coach, Bill Stewart, who had been a hockey referee and a big-league baseball umpire in the offseason. The low-scoring team made the playoffs by two points, then eliminated the Montreal Canadiens, New York Americans and the Maple Leafs to win the Cup. Again extraordinary goaltending, this time by Mike Karakas, was a big factor in the victory. Not only did McLaughlin have the satisfaction of nosing out archrival Norris's team for the last playoff spot and claiming the Cup from his strongest critic, the Leafs' Smythe, but the winning roster also contained eight U.S. players.

AS AN UMPIRE YOU HAVE THE LUNGS, OF COURSE...

Fired early the next season, Stewart had a long, distinguished career as a major league umpire. He later told of McLaughlin pressuring him to coach the Hawks from the balcony for a better view of the ice. "The Major wanted me to be like a puppet master, running the team from the balcony with strings, the way he wanted to run me as coach," Stewart said. "It's not that nothing the Major said was a surprise because he had so many goofy ideas."

When McLaughlin died in 1944, his son William, aged 16, inherited the club. The family finally sold it to the Major's long-time enemies, the Norris and Wirtz families, in 1952.

* * * * *

MORE MONEY IN BASEBALL

Tom Glavine, major league baseball pitcher. He was drafted in 1984 by the Los Angeles Kings with the 69th overall pick in the fourth round. That was 48 picks ahead of the 117th pick in the draft who turned out to be future Hall of Famer Brett Hull. It was also 102 picks ahead of another Kings draft pick that season, Luc Robitaille. The number one overall pick that season was Mario Lemieux by the Pittsburgh Penguins. Glavine was the 1995 World Series MVP with the Atlanta Braves and won the National League's Cy Young Award in 1991 and 1998. In 2005, he was set to make over $10 million in salary.

Kirk McCaskill, major league baseball pitcher. He was elected to the Canadian Baseball Hall of Fame in 2003. Long before that, he was drafted in 1981 by the then-Winnipeg Jets with the 64th overall pick in the fourth round. This was eight picks ahead of John Vanbiesbrouck and 43 picks before Gerard Gallant. The Jets' first overall pick that year was franchise player Dale Hawerchuk. McCaskill was a runner-up for the Hobey Baker Award as top US college hockey player in 1981.

YOU ARE GETTING SLEEPY, VERY SLEEPY

The Vancouver Canucks of the early 1970s were once so desperate that they hired famed hypnotist Reveen to break a player out of a serious scoring slump.

Such a spectacle would never occur in today's comparatively buttoned-down big leagues. But 30 years ago, NHL general managers still understood that a little Barnum and Bailey went a long way when it came to promoting their sport.

"I WILL SCORE GOALS...I WILL SCORE GOALS..."
Vancouver Canucks boss Bud Poile was crazy like a fox when he commissioned "The Man They Call Reveen" to snap "Cracklin" Rosaire Paiement out of a 35-game goalless funk. Poile invited Vancouver's sports media to the Hotel Georgia in 1972 to watch the famed hypnotist attempt to induce the tough veteran's "superconscious" state—whatever that is. Paiement had scored 34 goals in the Canucks' inaugural NHL season but was shooting blanks in the team's sophomore year. And Poile was willing to try anything to generate a little more offence, not to mention publicity, for his fledgling hockey team. In a scene straight out of *Slap Shot*, Poile called on the powers of the mysterious, bearded man who billed himself as "The Impossiblist."

"You know, I told Reveen, 'I don't believe in this stuff,'" Paiement recalled three decades later. "The funny thing is, just two games later, the puck bounces in front and I had an empty-net goal. That's how the slump ended."

AND FOR MY NEXT TRICK
But Reveen couldn't work long-term miracles. Paiement never again reached the lofty scoring heights of the previous season and he finished with only 10 goals that winter, 24 fewer than in the 1970–71 campaign. He then skipped to the World Hockey Association where the goals came much easier, with or without his superconscious state. Just a suggestion: Next time, the Canucks brass might want to take a different approach and think about hypnotizing opposing goaltenders instead.

A WOMAN'S GAME

One of the greatest rivalries in hockey has become Canada vs. the USA in international woman's competition. The most intense and defining showdown so far has been the 2002 Olympics.

At the turn of the 20th century, Canada could legitimately say it had the best women's hockey team in the world. It had won the Women's World Championship every year it was held: 1987, 1990, 1992, 1994 and 1997. In 1999 and 2000, teams in the WWC tournament were divided into "A" and "B" sections; Canada was at the head of their respective divisions these two years as well. In the 1998 Winter Olympiad held in Nagano, Japan, Team Canada faced Team USA for the gold medal in the biggest game in women's ice hockey played to that date. Team USA's Karen Bye, Colleen Coyne, captain Cammi Granato, Lisa Brown-Miller and especially goalie Sarah Tueting overwhelmed Team Canada all game long. Final score: USA 3, Canada 1.

BEHOLD THE LUCKY LOONIE

Hell hath no fury like women scorned, and this loss to the Americans made the players for Team Canada bound and determined to win the gold medal in the 2002 Winter Olympics. The Americans would have home ice advantage, as the Olympics were held that year in Salt Lake City, Utah. This time the Canadians had a lucky talisman about which, until the end of the tournament, they never knew. The members of the ice-maintenance crew at the E-Center arena in Salt Lake City had secretly hidden a Canadian "loonie" (Canada's one dollar coin) below the center-ice faceoff circle for good luck, for both the men's and women's teams.

LES FEMMES

From the beginning of the 2002 Olympic tournament, it was clear that Team Canada head coach Danièle Sauvageau had the club thoroughly prepared. In the first two games, "Les Femmes" trounced Kazakhstan and Russia in 7–0 wins for Canada. The Canada-Russia rivalry in men's hockey does not extend to the women's game, which is far more advanced in Canada. Team Canada out-shot Russia by an incredible 60–6. Building on their momentum, Canada next beat Sweden 11–0, then prevailed over the tough Finnish team 7–3. This game was actually closer than the final score indicated. At the end of two periods, Finland was winning by a score of 3–2 on incredible goaltending from Finland's Tuula Puputti. But Canada exploded in period three on goals by Hayley Wickenheiser, Jayna Hefford, Vicky Sunohara, Cassie Campbell and Therese Brisson.

Meanwhile, Team USA was pulverizing *their* opposition. They beat Germany 10–0, China 12–1, Finland 5–0 and Sweden 4–0 to set up an Olympic gold medal rematch, between America and Canada.

GOLD MEDAL GAMERS

From the opening faceoff, it was obvious that Team Canada had to face another obstacle in the game—whistle-happy referee Stacey Livingston. In the first period, four penalties were called against Canada and two against the U.S.; by the time the game was over, Team Canada had 13 penalties and Team USA had six. Killing off penalties for much of the first, Canada still managed to get out ahead on an early goal by Caroline Ouellette. Early in the second, Katie King tipped in a shot to even the score, 1–1. Wickenheiser pushed Canada ahead again before Hefford knocked in her own rebound on a breakaway to make the score 3–1. Team USA pressured hard in the third—with Karen Bye bringing them within one on a hard slapshot from the point—but Canada's defence held out for a final score of Canada 3, USA 2.

O CANADA

Many fans at the E-Center were Canadians and proudly cheered as the country's national anthem was played during the gold medal ceremony. Wickenheiser was named most valuable player of the tournament. Mario Lemieux, Theo Fleury, and other Canadian men's players were in the stands for the game; three days later, it was Canada's female players in the E-Center, cheering the men on to their own gold-medal victory over the U.S., 5–2. Yes, the secret loonie *did* bring luck. It is now in the Hockey Hall of Fame in Toronto.

AND THE AWARD GOES TO...

The NHL's trophy collection, covering a wide selection of categories, is the most impressive in professional sport.

Each June, the NHL hands out an array of beautiful trophies to its best. No other professional sports league has as impressive a group of silverware as hockey's big league.

In addition, several team trophies, headed by the Stanley Cup, are awarded on the ice at conclusions of games in which they are earned. The donors of the original trophies range from Canada's Governors General to fabled hockey executives and players, and many individual laurels carry a cash prize. Most individual awards are selected by members of the Professional Hockey Writers Association.

THE TEAM HONORS

The Stanley Cup: The oldest trophy contested by North American professional athletes was donated in 1893 by Frederick Arthur, Lord Stanley of Preston, the Governor General of Canada. The trophy, purchased for ten guineas ($50 then) was to be presented to the amateur champions of Canada. Since the National Hockey Association, forerunner of the NHL, took control of the trophy in 1910, it has indicated supremacy in professional hockey. Only NHL teams have competed for it since the 1926–27 season.

Presidents' Trophy: Awarded annually to the club with the best overall record during the regular season, the trophy was presented to the NHL by the Board of Governors in 1985 and has a cash award of $350,000.

Prince of Wales Trophy: His Royal Highness The Prince of Wales presented the trophy in 1924 and it is now awarded to the playoff champion in the NHL's Eastern Conference.

Clarence S. Campbell Bowl: NHL teams placed the award in competition in 1968 to honor Campbell, president of the league from 1946 to 1977, and it now goes to the playoff champions in the Western Conference.

INDIVIDUAL AWARDS

Hart Memorial Trophy: Awarded to "the player adjudged to be the most valuable to his team," the trophy was donated to the NHL in 1923 by Dr. Dave A. Hart in honor of his father Cecil Hart, manager-coach of the Montreal Canadiens. The original trophy was retired to the Hockey Hall of Fame in 1960.

Conn Smythe Trophy: The trophy to "the most valuable player in the playoffs" was presented to the NHL by Maple Leaf Gardens Ltd. in 1964 in memory of the late Conn Smythe, the founder of the Toronto Maple Leafs, builder of the Gardens, manager, coach and owner-governor of the team at various times.

Art Ross Trophy: The trophy to the player who leads the NHL in scoring points during the regular schedule was donated in 1947 by Ross, the GM of the Boston Bruins from 1924 to 1954.

Calder Memorial Trophy: The award to the player "selected as most proficient in his first year of competition" honors Frank Calder, NHL president from 1917 to 1943. From 1936 until his death in 1943, Calder purchased a trophy for the top rookie, then the NHL presented a permanent Calder Trophy.

James Norris Memorial Trophy: To the defenceman "who demonstrates the greatest all-round ability in the position," the Norris Trophy was donated by the Norris family in 1953 in memory of the late James Norris, former owner-president of the Detroit Red Wings.

Vezina Trophy: The general managers of the 30 NHL teams select the winner of the award as "the goalkeeper adjudged to be the best at his position." The owners of the Montreal Canadiens in 1926, Leo Dandurand, Louis Letourneau and Joe Cattarinich, donated the trophy in honor of Georges Vezina, who had appeared in 325 consecutive games for the Canadiens from 1917 to 1925. He collapsed during a game in November, 1925 and died of tuberculosis a few months later. Until 1981–82, the Vezina went to the goalkeeper(s) on the team allowing the fewest number of goals during the season.

William M. Jennings Trophy: In the 1981–82 season, the NHL Board of Governors donated the trophy in honor of the late William Jennings, longtime president of the New York Rangers and an important booster of hockey in the U.S. It is awarded "to the goalkeeper(s) having played a minimum of 25 games for the team with the fewest goals scored against it."

Lady Byng Memorial Trophy: Originally donated by Lady Byng, the wife of Canada's Governor General in 1924, the award is "to the player adjudged to have exhibited the best type of sportsmanship and gentlemanly conduct combined with a high standard of playing ability." When Frank Boucher of the Rangers won the Byng in seven of eight seasons, he was given the original trophy and Lady Byng donated another in 1936.

Maurice "Rocket" Richard Trophy: Given to the league by the Montreal Canadiens in 1999, the award goes to the NHL's goal-scoring leader during the schedule, honoring the great star of the Canadiens, the late Rocket Richard.

Frank J. Selke Trophy: Awarded "to the forward who best excels in the defensive aspects of the game," the Selke Trophy was presented by the NHL Board of Governors in 1977 in honor of Frank J. Selke, the great GM who built powerhouse franchises and winning teams in Toronto and Montreal.

Jack Adams Award: The NHL Broadcasters Association presented this award—and annually votes on the winner—made to "the NHL coach adjudged to have contributed the most to his team's success." It honors the late Jack Adams, GM of the Detroit Red Wings from 1927 to 1962, coach from 1927 to 1947.

Bill Masterton Memorial Trophy: Under the trusteeship of the PHWA, the award is to "the NHL player who best exemplifies the qualities of perseverance, sportsmanship and dedication to hockey." It honors Masterton, a player with the Minnesota North Stars who died from head injuries suffered in an NHL game in January, 1968.

Lester Patrick Trophy: Honoring the late Lester Patrick, the longtime boss of the Rangers after first being an all-star player and then building the Pacific Coast Hockey League, the award is made "for outstanding service to hockey in the United States," and has gone to players, officials, coaches, executives and referees.

King Clancy Memorial Trophy: Francis "King" Clancy spent close to 70 years in the NHL as a player and executive, mostly with the Maple Leafs, plus a long stretch as a referee. A tireless worker for various charities, the NHL board honored his memory in 1988 with a trophy in his name "to the player who best exemplifies leadership qualities on and off the ice and has made a noteworthy humanitarian contribution to his community."

Lester B. Pearson Award: The trophy honors the late Lester Pearson, former Prime Minister of Canada and Nobel Peace Prize winner, and is given to the outstanding player in the NHL as selected by the members of the NHL Players' Association.

Bud Light Plus-Minus Award: First awarded in 1998 by Anheuser-Busch Inc., the trophy goes to the player who has the highest plus-minus in a minimum of 60 games. Plus-minus is the difference between goals for and against the team when the player is on the ice in equal manpower situations.

Roger Crozier Saving Grace Award: A strong NHL goalie in a 14-season career, Crozier worked for the MBNA American Bank when he retired. After his death in 1996, the bank donated the award, which goes to the NHL goalie with the best save percentage in a minimum of 25 games.

NHL/Sheraton Road Performer Award: A donation is made to the charity of choice of the player with the most points in road games of his team.

THE VERSATILE DIT

Bruin great Dit Clapper was the only player to be an NHL all-star at both forward and defence…just not in the same year.

The statistics covering the achievements of Aubrey "Dit" Clapper in his splendid career with the Boston Bruins do not list some of his best attributes. At 6-foot-2 and 195 pounds, Clapper was among the strongest and toughest players in pre-expansion history. His endurance and athleticism allowed him to have what some have called two distinct hockey careers, as both a forward and a defenceman.

ONE MORE DECADE AND HE'D BE A GOALIE

Clapper had the first 20-season NHL career from 1927 to 1947, serving the opening ten years as a winger (twice an all-star), then playing the latter half as a defenceman (four times an all-star, three as a first-team selection). "Dit was as good a player in all areas of the game as I saw in my time in the NHL," said Milt Schmidt, who spent more than 60 years with the Bruins as player, coach and executive. "He had such size and skill that he could play tough hockey without fouls, and he was such a good fighter that through most of his career, very few challenged him to fisticuffs."

NO ALL-STAR SELECTIONS FOR COACHES

Clapper played junior hockey in Oshawa when he was 13 and earned a spot with the Bruins when he was 20. In his second season, Clapper helped the Bruins win their first Stanley Cup crown and the next season he scored 41 goals in 44 games.

When the Bruins had a splendid group of young forwards for the 1937–38 seasons, they shifted Clapper to defence as partner to the great Eddie Shore. That year Clapper and Shore swept First Team All-Star honors on defence. The Bruins won the Stanley Cup the next season and, with Clapper and Flash Hollett as a strong backline pair, once again in 1941. After retiring, Clapper coached the Bruins for four seasons, then left hockey to operate his sporting goods store in Peterborough, Ontario. He coached the AHL Buffalo Bisons for the 1959–60 season, his last hurrah in hockey.

EDDIE, YOU'RE OUT!

The NHL was formed when the other owners had had enough of Toronto's aggravating Eddie Livingstone.

To say that spite against one team owner inspired the creation of the National Hockey League is not hyperbole. The other four team bosses in the National Hockey Association were fed up with the nonstop arguments of Eddie Livingstone, owner of the Toronto Blueshirts. Livingstone had waged long boardroom battles, never-ending debates over the rules, lawsuits, injunctions, and even a threat to form a rival league.

HOW TO FORM A ONE-TEAM LEAGUE

In November 1917, representatives of the other four NHA teams—the Ottawa Senators, Quebec Bulldogs, Montreal Canadiens and Montreal Wanderers—plus a new Toronto team, the Arenas, met at Montreal's Windsor Hotel and solved the "Livingstone problem" by forming the NHL with newspaperman Frank Calder as first president. "We didn't throw Eddie Livingstone out because he still has his team in the NHA," an NHL team owner said. "His only problem is that he's playing in a one-team league. We should thank Eddie. He solidified our new league because we were all sick and tired of his constant wrangling."

BE SUCCESSFUL AND I'LL SUE

The NHL's start was not smooth. The bankrupt Quebec team didn't open the season and after six games the Wanderers left hockey forever when their home rink was destroyed by fire. The remaining three teams, still determined not to ask Eddie back, carried on with the Arenas beating the Canadiens in the first NHL final and then winning the Stanley Cup against the Vancouver Millionaires. Predictably, Livingstone launched a lawsuit against the new league. But he lost the case and vanished from hockey.

HOW (NOT) TO FORM A ONE-MAN ARMY

Earlier, Livingstone had even waged war against the Canadian Army. During World War I, several star hockey players had joined the 228th Battalion, based in Toronto, including Duke Keats and Archie Briden from Eddie's Blueshirts. When the 228th formed a strong club to play against the pro teams, Livingstone staged a noisy battle, claiming that Keats and Briden had signed contracts with his team. The players eventually returned to the Blueshirts and played in three games against the army club, two of them won by the 228th, which rank among the most violent matches ever played. The battle was ended when the battalion was shipped overseas to fight with guns, not hockey sticks.

* * * * *

PUT UP YOUR DUKES

"Two people fighting is not violence in hockey. It might be in tennis or bowling, but it's not in hockey."

—Gerry Cheevers, former NHL goalie/coach

"It's not who wins the fight that's important, it's being willing to fight. If you get challenged and renege, everyone wants to take a shot at you."

—Barclay "Barc the Spark" Plager, former St. Louis Blues defenceman

"Either you give it right back or the next thing you know everyone and his brother will be trying you on for size."

—Doug Harvey, former Montreal Canadiens defenceman

"What are you, the fight doctor now or something? You've never been in a fight in your life, so what are you talking about?"

—Rob Ray, former Buffalo Sabres forward, to a reporter after Ray was pounded by Edmonton's Georges Laraque

THE FABULOUS NINES

Rocket Richard and Gordie Howe were two great stars in a glory era of NHL history.

They were as different as two men could be in approach, temperament and style but Rocket Richard and Gordie Howe remain to this day etched in the memories of most hockey fans—even those who never watched them play. The legends of the two fabled number nines are familiar to everyone with even a faint interest in the game, the way Babe Ruth and Mickey Mantle are to baseball devotees. Comparison of the two is one of hockey's most intense arguments, ranking with baseball's Ted Williams or Joe DiMaggio. Wayne Gretzky and Mario Lemieux inspired similar discussions for a later generation but while Gretzky broke Howe's goals and point records, Lemieux's career was hindered by a lengthy list of injuries.

ROCKET IS BETTER

Richard was the electric performer, high-strung and seemingly ready to explode with a dazzling goal or violence at any second—perhaps the NHL's most mercurial performer ever. His ability to produce goals, both on slick, deft skating and stickhandling moves or using his strength to get to the net, especially in crunch situations, was remarkable.

GORDIE IS BETTER

Howe took a relaxed approach, executing the most difficult moves with ease and grace. His natural instinct allowed him simply to show up where the puck was most likely to appear. His toughness was legendary, his retribution for fouls against him swift and hard, especially those delivered with his famous elbows. The game appeared easy for Howe, who really was a hard worker but always appeared nonchalant on the ice because of his great physical talent and ability to read the play and react to it much more quickly than others.

WHAT RED SAID

Referee Red Storey, who officiated many meetings between the two great players in the 1950s, offered perhaps the most-quoted analysis of the two exceptional right-wingers. "I don't think there's much doubt that the Rocket vs. Gordie argument was the busiest in hockey history," Storey said. "I was asked for my opinion often and I told everyone who asked that Rocket Richard was the greatest goal-scorer and most exciting player the world has seen. Then I would say that Gordie Howe was the greatest player in history. They were two very different people and no one had the talent of Howe and no one had the scoring ability of Richard. I don't think I pleased everyone, but that was how I felt."

A KING'S RULING

The great general manager of the Montreal Canadiens, Frank Selke, was careful in assessing the two great wingers, treading carefully because Richard had led the team to extraordinary success. But after Richard retired, Selke discussed them in an interview. "Gordie Howe is the finest all-round player in hockey history," Selke said. "That takes absolutely nothing away from the Rocket or any other player. King Clancy (in the NHL as a player, referee and executive for 70 years) said it well: "If there were two rinks in Montreal offering games at the same time with the Rocket and Howe as box office rivals, Richard would do more business. Richard was the game's greatest crowd pleaser, the most spectacular goal-getter but Howe could do more things than any player ever. And I know the Rocket thinks the same way."

NUMBERS DON'T LIE

Their career statistics can be used to make a strong case for each man. Howe's durability was unmatched: He played 32 seasons of big-league hockey, 26 in the NHL with the Detroit Red Wings and Hartford Whalers, and six in the World Hockey Association with the New England Whalers and Houston Aeros, which included his sons Mark and Marty as teammates. In his 32 seasons of pro hockey—Howe insisted that his WHA numbers should be included in his career total—Howe played 2,186 games, scored 975 goals, 1,338 assists for 2,358 points plus 96 goals, 135 assists for 231 points in the playoffs. In the 26 NHL seasons, Howe played 1,767 games with an 801-1,049-1,850 during the schedule, a 68-92-160 points mark in 157 games.

Richard was a Canadien for 18 seasons, producing 544 goals, 421 assists for 965 points in 978 games, a strong 82 goals and 126 points in 133 playoff games. Richard took great pride in his ability to produce in the pressure of the Stanley Cup playoffs. Of his 82 postseason tallies, 18 of them were game-winners, a record six of those in overtime.

IF ONLY HE WERE AS GOOD AS ME

Richard and Howe were involved in the extremely intense rivalry between the Canadiens and Red Wings in the 1950s when the Canadiens won six Cups, and the Red Wings four in an 11-season stretch. While Howe said little of his opponent, Richard could praise and criticize Howe in the same sentence. "Howe is a great player, the best I ever played against, but he should hustle more," said Richard, late in his career. "He doesn't seem to be trying as hard as he could. He was a better all-round player than I was, maybe the best ever. But I think he should have scored more big goals, like in the playoffs." Howe offered only praise for Richard: "The NHL never had a more dramatic player than the Rocket, nor one more dangerous in the clutch."

THE ODD COUPLE

At Richard's funeral in 2000, Howe admitted that he knew little about Richard personally and seldom had talked with him over the years. "I never knew that the Rocket had seven children," Howe said. "I certainly never knew what he was thinking. He was quiet man. A few times on the ice, I said 'Hi Rocket,' and he just growled at me."

In the 14 seasons Richard and Howe shared in the NHL, they dominated the right wing position on the NHL all-star team, Howe with seven first team and four second team selections while Richard had six first team and five second nominations. Little wonder the argument continues.

DOWN IN THE EH, EH?

The Eastern Hockey League managed to operate for most seasons from 1934 to 1974, providing the inspiration for the movie Slap Shot.

It all started in the 1933–34 season with the Baltimore Orioles, Hershey B'ars and Bronx Tigers and ended for good after the 1972–73 playoffs with the Long Island Ducks, Syracuse Blazers, Charlotte Checkers and Greensboro Generals. The Eastern Hockey League—it had the word Amateur in its name until 1953—was the bottom-ranked minor-pro league but no circuit is mentioned more in hockey's folklore.

NEWMAN'S GOONS

Even today when a group of old-time hockey men are telling yarns and spinning fables, the Eastern League invariably pops into the conversation. The EHL had an abundance of "goons" long before the NHL had discovered the word to describe its toughest players. It had high scorers and goalies who went onto big-league careers, too, but the EHL is in the history books—either written or imaginative—for its violence: the hard-nosed guys who, long after the league was gone, inspired the Paul Newman movie *Slap Shot* that became a cult favorite.

THE REAL REGGIE DUNLOP?

The player who perhaps represents the Eastern League best was John Brophy, a defenceman with several teams (Baltimore, Charlotte, New Haven, Long Island, Philadelphia) whom many rate as the toughest man in hockey history. Brophy was the EHL's penalty king, earning from 230 to 350 penalty minutes a season over his close to 20 years in the league. Brophy spent another 35 years as a coach at various minor-pro levels, becoming one of the few coaches to win more than 1,000 games—including 64 during a frustrating three-season NHL stint with the dismal Toronto Maple Leafs.

Brophy brushed off requests to reflect on the days when many referred to him as a "dirty" hockey player. He preferred to talk about the quality of the league and how much effort was required to excel in it. "Sure it was tough hockey and the salaries were not very high—guys knocking themselves out for $125 a week with some hideous travel," Brophy said. "But quite a few players earned a living for a long time in the Eastern League and used it as a springboard up the ladder as players, and into pro coaching like I did. You had to really want to play the game to stick it out and that's how I was."

WHO DOUBLED AS THE MECHANIC?

The teams operated on a sparse budget with small rosters, at one time dressing only 12 players for games. That meant a goalie, four defencemen and seven forwards, including one who could play defence if needed. For years most teams did not travel by bus. The dozen players plus the manager-coach—often teams had playing coaches—and the trainer traveled in two old limousines, one of them towing a trailer loaded with the equipment. The coach drove one and the trainer the other in a small convoy on long highway hauls from Clinton, New York, to Nashville, Tennessee.

PRE-DATING THE PREDATORS

Through many seasons, especially in the years after World War II, the league was often down to four teams with the New York Rovers and Boston Olympics as mainstays. The Rovers played most home games on Sunday afternoons in Madison Square Garden, the home rink of the NHL's New York Rangers. Eddie Giacomin and Gilles Villemure, who had fine NHL careers with the Rangers, apprenticed in the EHL with the Rovers and other clubs. Through the late 1950s and 1960s, the EHL flourished with between eight and 12 teams in two divisions, pushing as far south as Tennessee. Smaller cities such as Johnstown, Pennsylvania; Clinton, New York; and the Long Island Ducks, based in Commack, were league mainstays.

A "CHARACTER-BUILDING" EXPERIENCE

John Muckler spent many years in the EHL as a player, then as manager and coach with the Ducks, and is perhaps the league's best historian. He slowly worked up hockey's ladder as NHL scout, minor league coach and executive, associate coach with the Edmonton Oilers for four Stanley Cup championships, and finally head coach for a fifth Cup in 1990. Muckler has since been general manager of the Buffalo Sabres, New York Rangers and Ottawa Senators. "The

Eastern League was like no other hockey league ever, the game played as hard and tough—yes, dirty—as it has in any league," Muckler said. "It took special players to tough it out with the small rosters, the hard travel, the hard hits and fights on the ice. Every team had a couple of truly tough players and some of the fights between them were simply scary, especially if they went at it with the sticks."

THE INSPIRATION FOR ZORRO, TOO??

Muckler had a special relationship with Brophy, whom he calls "the best friend I ever had in my life. Brophy was very hard, in extraordinary physical condition because he worked as a laborer in the off season," Muckler said. "Remember that TV character Zorro, who could cut the 'Z' mark on guys' shirts or skin with his sword? Well, I think they got that from what Broph could do with a hockey stick. He would test every new player in the league and while many were very afraid of him because of what he could do, if they stood up for themselves, he wouldn't bother them again."

EHL TITLE PUTS BROPHY ON TOP OF THE WORLD

In all his years in hockey, Muckler is hard-pressed to recall a scrappier player than John Brophy: "No one who ever played the game—showed up as many nights tired, injured and underpaid—and gave it all he had [like Brophy did]. In my time in the league I traded Brophy three times and got him back twice. One year when I was GM-coach of the Ducks, we had a club that could win it all—winning the EHL playoffs earned a $1,200 per player bonus and that meant you didn't have to get a summer job—but we faced a major problem. Brophy was with the New Haven Blades and many of my players were scared out of their minds to play against him. So I did the only sane thing I could do: I made a bad trade for him, got him on our side and we won the title. Two days after we won it, Brophy was high above New York City working as a steel-rigger on some new skyscraper, a job he often did in the summer."

EHL ERA ENDS

In 1973, the Eastern League's days ended. It was split into a pair of pale imitations, the Southern Hockey League and the North American Hockey League; but there are no great tales about those two loops.

THE TEN-CENT-BEER-NIGHT CAPER!!

Having John Brophy on the Long Island Ducks with Don Perry—rated by many as the best fist-fighter ever seen in the sport—produced one of former Ducks coach John Muckler's favorite EHL yarns: the ten-cent-beer-night caper.

The Ducks were playing the New Haven Blades at the Commack Arena, and lured fans in with beer at ten cents a glass, one of the first-ever such promotions. On the night before, the Ducks played upstate in Clinton, hopping into their two limos right after the game for the trip home that, under normal conditions, would end at four in the morning. But this time the Ducks drove into a mammoth northeastern blizzard. All through the night and the next day, they plugged along through deep snow and poor visibility. As evening neared, the Ducks still had a distance to travel. With no way to check in with Commack (this was years before cell phones), they figured the game would be cancelled. But the beer had flowed, and the crowd in the old rink was loud and angry.

CRANKY DUCKS BLADE THE BLADES

The Ducks, tired to the bone, arrived at 9:30 P.M. and to their surprise were told to get into uniform and start the game or the fans, full of suds, might tear the arena apart. "Our equipment was frozen in the trailer behind one limo but our guys put it on and went on the ice," Muckler said. "In the first minute, Brophy cut the mark of Zorro on a couple of New Haven guys with his stick and Perry punched a couple more in the face. The New Haven team went to the dressing room, saying that they didn't want to risk their players against 'those lunatics.' That really whipped up the fans, and all indications were that there was going to be a riot if the Blades didn't come back. The owner of the Ducks, who was getting heat for the beer promotion, went into the New Haven dressing room with a handful of $100 bills and offered one to each player if they would continue the game. Now this was a league where $150 a week was a big salary. The New Haven players said they would if Perry and Brophy didn't play. The game continued, Brophy and Perry sat on our bench and we played with ten guys."

LITTLE BIG MEN

Some of the best in a big man's game have been half-pints with speed and skill.

When Theoren Fleury buzzed onto the ice for the warm-up, it appeared his club had allowed the stick boy to participate in the pre-game activities. Surrounded by many teammates more than six feet in height and 200 pounds in weight, Fleury, at 5-foot-6 and 155, surely had to be the club mascot. But when the game started, the smallest skater was often the biggest man on the ice.

CARRYING A BIG STICK

Fleury's physical dimensions were the antithesis of his statistics and accomplishments. In a 15-season NHL career with Calgary, the New York Rangers, Chicago and Columbus, fiery Fleury played in 1,084 games, produced 455 goals and 633 assists for 1,088 points and paid for his pestilent approach with 1,840 penalty minutes. In the pressure of the playoffs, Fleury was at his best with 79 points in 77 Stanley Cup games, and he also excelled for Canadian teams that won the World Junior and Olympic gold medal championships.

"From the start in kids' hockey, I had to show that just because I was small didn't mean I wouldn't mix it up with anyone, no matter how big he was," Fleury said. "If I had ever backed up from bigger guys' challenges, I could have gone home and forgot about having a hockey career. I worked really hard on my skating, especially my quickness and speed, and that allowed me to find as much open ice as I could."

EAT YOUR BROCCOLI!

Fleury's career from 1987 to 2003 stamps him as perhaps the "last of the great little men." The NHL's obsession with size has produced a modern game of giants: Rosters are now dominated by players over six feet and 200 pounds, a big change from the pro game's early days in the 1920s when the average size was 5-foot-8 and 160 pounds. But then, the size of humans in general has increased noticeably in the past century. Add to that improved diet and physical conditioning programs that athletes start at a young age, and the result is the biggest, strongest players in hockey history. In the NHL now, only the occasional small player—such as the stealthy Steve Sullivan, who is 5'9" and 155—sneak into the front ranks.

SHORT AND STOCKY PLAYING HOCKEY

Most players who are considered small might be short in height but carry much more weight than the vertically challenged of an earlier era. In the NHL's first three or four decades, many players between 5'5" and 5'9" often weighed between 140 and 155 pounds. The NHL's most valuable player in the 2004–05 season, Martin St. Louis of the Stanley Cup champion Tampa Bay Lightning, is considered short at 5'9" but not small because he weighs 185. The numbers of the Boston Bruins' highly skilled winger Sergei Samsonov are 5'8" and a surprising 194. Defenceman Francis Bouillon of the Montreal Canadiens appears out of place on the blue line at 5'8" but his 196 pounds make him a better fit.

KING FOR A DAY?

Reflecting on the measurements of a variety of players from earlier years makes one wonder about how players of such small stature might endure in today's league. King Clancy (5'7", 155) played front-line defence for Ottawa and Toronto for 16 seasons. The top goal-scorers of the NHL's early days, Babe Dye (201 goals in 271 games) and Joe Malone (143 goals in 126 NHL games), each weighed 150 pounds. Ken Doraty, whose overtime goal for the Maple Leafs against Boston in 1933 came in the sixth extra period, played at 133 pounds. Buddy O'Connor (5'8", 140) of the Rangers finished second by one point for the NHL scoring title in the 1947–48 season. Mush March, all 5'5" and 150 pounds of him, played 759 games for Chicago. Two of the finest forward lines ever carried total weights of 436 pounds—the elegant Howie Morenz, Aurel Joliat and Johnny "Black Cat" Gagnon trio of the Montreal Canadiens in the 1920s—and 460 pounds—the swift Pony Line of Chicago in the 1940s: Max and Doug Bentley with Bill Mosienko.

LITTLE NAPOLEON VS. KING RICHARD

The top goalies of the early NHL times had to be quick because their small bodies, skinny pads and gloves did not fill much of the net. George Hainsworth (5'6", 150) once had 22 shutouts in a 44-game schedule. John Ross Roach (5'5", 130) was called Little Napoleon and played in 492 games. Roy Worters (5'3", 135) excelled for three teams. Jumpin' Jake Forbes (5'6", 140) was a big star in the game's first venture into New York. Even the great Georges Vezina, who played in 325 consecutive games for the Canadiens (and was the father of 22 children) was only 5-foot-6. In the 1990s, another diminutive "King," Richard Brodeur (5'7", 158), led the Vancouver Canucks to the Cup final.

POCKET ROCKETS AND THE ATOM BOMB

Two economy-sized centers were elite all-round players in a later time. Henri (Pocket Rocket) Richard (5'7", 160) excelled in a record 11 Stanley Cup winners for the Canadiens in 20 seasons from 1956 to 1975. Dave Keon (5'8", 160) was a key man on the Toronto Maple Leafs' four Cup winners in the 1960s. These quick little stars would seem like mosquitoes if they shared the ice with Zdeno Chara of the modern Ottawa Senators. At 6'9" and 260, Chara is the biggest NHLer ever.

* * * * *

"[Jeremy Roenick] should be worried about playing the game, not innovating it. He thinks he's Brett Hull or something. You should remind him that he didn't go to college. He's a junior guy. So he's not that bright."

—Garth Snow, goaltender for New York Islanders

"It's not my fault [Garth Snow] didn't have any other options coming out of high school. If going to college gets you a career backup goaltender job, and my route gets you a thousand points and a thousand games, and compare the two contracts, it doesn't take a rocket scientist to figure out whose decision was better."

—Jeremy Roenick, former forward, Chicago Blackhawks

N-H-L-METS

For a game that is commonly thought of as the most violent major North American sport, it may come as a shock that the history of the helmet in the NHL is relatively short.

We begin in Boston when tough-as-skate-leather Bruin Eddie Shore hit Toronto Maple Leaf Ace Bailey from behind during a December 12, 1933, game—with the end result being Bailey sustaining a fractured skull. To raise funds for Bailey's expensive medical bills, the NHL played its first All-Star Game on February 12, 1934. After Bailey's retirement he became a coach and later an off-ice official in Toronto at his beloved Maple Leaf Gardens.

SHORING UP THE "D" (OF THE NOGGIN)

Seeing the damage that he did to Bailey and perhaps fearing for his safety from Leafs who had plans to retaliate, Eddie shortly afterwards began to wear a leather helmet during games. Looking at this contraption with a fresh 21st century outlook, it's difficult to see how Shore's head would have been protected if he had been clonked in the casaba. Shore's helmet more resembles headgear worn by a horse-riding jockey than a protective apparatus against pucks, sticks and falls to the ice.

CRAWFORD'S CRANIUM

For 12 seasons (1937–1950), Bruins defenceman Jack Crawford also wore a similar leather head covering, but much of this was due to vanity (understandable, in his case). In his teenage years, the crafty Crawford suffered a rare skin malady which left his scalp bald and scarred. So to cover his top, Crawford began wearing the leather helmet.

BILL MASTERTON: AN AMERICAN TRAGEDY

Very few NHL players wore helmets until one fateful night in Minnesota when the first (and still only) death of a player during an NHL game occurred. Not long into the first period of a January 13, 1968, game between the Oakland Seals and the Minnesota North Stars, rookie centerman Bill Masterton of the North Stars took the puck into the Seals' offensive zone. He passed to right wing Wayne Connelly, then skated toward the area in front of the Seals net to try to get a goal. Instead he got banged around by a few Seals, fell backwards, and cracked his head on the ice. Masterton began bleeding profusely from his ears and nose. He was immediately taken to Fairview Southdale Hospital in Minneapolis. On the way in the ambulance, Masterton lost consciousness and never woke up. Two days later, he died as a result of his head injury.

The North Stars retired Bat's (as he was nicknamed) No. 19 and shortly after Masterton's death, the NHL created the Bill Masterton Trophy, which is awarded annually to the player who is most dedicated to, and shows the most perseverance for, the sport of hockey.

MIKITA HEAD OF THE PACK

Interestingly, Clarence Campbell, then head of the NHL, did not immediately dictate that all players had to wear helmets during practices and in games. Yet slowly, very slowly, players began to wear them. One of the first was Stan Mikita, the great center and right wing from the 1960s Chicago Black Hawks. Wearing his coal-black-colored plastic helmet, Mikita was as easy to spot on the ice at that time as the remaining players *without* helmets were in the late 1980s.

SAFE IN SEVENTY-NINE

Mite and youth hockey leagues in Canada and the United States made helmet-wearing a must in the 1970s. In 1979 the NHL made helmets mandatory for any player signed after June 1, 1979. On April 29, 1997, grinder Craig MacTavish—the last NHL player to play without a helmet—announced his retirement, quietly rolling the percentage of NHL helmet-use up to 100 from there on in.

* * * * *

"There are two types of forwards. Scorers and bangers. Scorers score and bangers bang."

—Ken Dryden

MINER LEAGUE HOCKEY?

The first full-fledged professional hockey league was created to give Michigan copper miners some recreational activity.

Professional hockey's debut was not inspired by uplifting ideals or brilliant business plans. Instead, it grew out of a bonanza in copper and iron mining in northern Michigan and nearby Canada in the early 1900s, in towns with limited recreational possibilities. Hockey games gave the miners a Saturday night activity.

DOC HOCKEY

J.L. "Doc" Gibson was a dentist in Houghton, Michigan, who knew pro hockey well. He had played in his Ontario hometown of Berlin (now Kitchener), where his team was banned from the Ontario Hockey Association after players were given ten-dollar gold coins after an important win, in violation of amateur rules. Gibson graduated from college in Detroit and established a dental practice in Houghton, a town of 5,000 on the Michigan peninsula close to a productive copper mine. Gibson founded the Portage Lake hockey club in Houghton. To stock his team, he recruited amateur players, turned them into professionals by paying salaries, and his team dominated hockey in the area.

HOCKEY NIGHT IN HOUGHTON

Other teams, some backed by those with financial interests in the mines, formed to compete with Portage Lake. The result was the International Professional Hockey League in 1904–05, comprising Houghton; Calumet-Larium Miners; the Indians of Sault Ste. Marie, Michigan and Sault Ste. Marie, Ontario; and two teams in Pittsburgh, which had one of two artificial ice surfaces in existence at the time.

CYCLONE SIGHTING

Fred "Cyclone" Taylor, the brilliant 19 year old from Ontario, was playing senior hockey in Portage La Prairie, Manitoba for the Rat Portage [now Kenora] Thistles. He received room, board and $25 a month in spending money. "The Portage Lake team in Houghton made me an offer of $400 plus expenses for the rest of the season," Taylor said. "I took their offer and helped them win the championship that season."

STACKED LINEUP

When Taylor joined the Houghton team, he found himself in select company. The Portage Lake club had Riley Hern in goal, Barney Holden and Fred Lake at point and cover point (defence), and forwards Bruce Stuart, Joe Hall, Harry Bright and Grindy Forrester. Taylor, Hern, Stuart and Hall continued to put up big seasons even after the International League folded and were all inducted into the Hockey Hall of Fame.

The Houghton team played in the Amphidrome, located in the center of the town. It had 3,000 seats, all of them filled for the club's games. The fans were eager to see the team's new player and in his first game, Cyclone Taylor scored twice in an 8–2 win over Calumet.

NEWSY, THE CYCLONE & BAD JOE

Taylor faced another young player destined to be a big star, Newsy Lalonde – a tough player with great skill. Lalonde and "Bad" Joe Hall had a longtime feud that featured fist and stick fights over the years. Lalonde had the assignment of checking Taylor. "Newsy played a tough game and handling that caliber of checking prepared me for what I would encounter through my career," Taylor said.

Taylor returned for a second season in Houghton, 1906–07, won the scoring title and was named the league's outstanding player. A sweep of three late-season games in Pittsburgh clinched a second championship and the team returned to Houghton by train to be greeted by a band, a parade and a banquet in honor of their achievement.

RUBBED OUT BY RECESSION

But the future of the International League was in doubt. The U.S. economy was chopped down by a recession and the northern Michigan mining areas were the hardest hit. The next autumn, they announced that teams would not be able to afford players' salaries – the Houghton team's total payroll for the season was approximately $5,000 – and the league dissolved. "The International League was a great experience for many young players," Taylor said years later. "The hockey was good, very competitive, and physically tough, which prepared us well for anything we encountered later in our careers."

RENAISSANCE MAN

Frank Fredrickson had a multi-faceted life of music, flying and hockey glory at both amateur and professional levels.

The exploits of Frank Fredrickson read like the script for an Indiana Jones movie; he had a full life with a wide range of adventures and experiences both on and off the ice. The charismatic, flamboyant and handsome Icelander from Winnipeg excelled at any endeavor he tried from hockey to flying, coaching to music. Fredrickson was a star in senior amateur and Olympic hockey, then a fine player in both the Pacific Coast Association and the NHL, a violinist with concert potential, and a World War I fighter pilot whose ship was torpedoed in the Indian Ocean, forcing a 12-hour stay in a lifeboat before rescue.

FIDDLING AROUND

Fredrickson's family had moved to Winnipeg from Iceland, joining a community of their countrymen in the Manitoba city. He spoke no English until he started elementary school at six years of age, and was often teased and bullied by the other lads because he was different. "Luckily for me, I loved sports and played every game as hard as I could to gain acceptance," Fredrickson said years later. "Because Winnipeg had cold winters, ice surfaces for skating and hockey were plentiful. I was on them every chance I had and when I wasn't practising hockey, I was taking violin lessons and practising on the fiddle."

LIFEBOAT NEEDED SOME ENTERTAINMENT

Fredrickson played junior and senior hockey as a teenager in Winnipeg, then was captain of the University of Manitoba team while continuing in senior play. He left college after his second year and went to England with the Canadian Army's 196th Battalion, where he transferred to the Royal Flying Corps and, after training in Egypt, earned his pilot's wings. On the trip back to an active duty assignment in France, the ship he was on, the *Leasowe Castle*, was torpedoed by a German submarine in the Indian Ocean and those on board took to the lifeboats.

An oft-told story, which Fredrickson never denied, claimed that he scrambled to his cabin to rescue his prized violin before he left the sinking ship. They were rescued a half-day later by a Japanese ship.

FRANK'S FALCONS FLY HIGH

After a year of flying service in France, Fredrickson returned to Winnipeg, where he organized a hockey team called the Falcons, all but one of the players being of Icelandic descent. Refused entry by the Manitoba senior league, Fredrickson formed his own three-team league. After scoring 22 goals in nine league games, and another 22 in six playoff games, Fredrickson led the Falcons past the Manitoba league champions in a challenge game to advance to the Allan Cup final. The Falcons won the Canadian senior title by drubbing the University of Toronto Blues. This win sent the Falcons to Antwerp, Belgium, to represent Canada in the demonstration sport of hockey at the 1920 Winter Olympics. Led by Fredrickson's 12 goals in three games, they beat Czechoslovakia, Sweden and the U.S. to win the first-ever Olympic hockey gold medal.

PLAY HOCKEY, OR CONDUCT AERIAL STUDIES?

Because the newly formed NHL and the established PCHA were eagerly seeking players, Fredrickson was a much-prized commodity. Lester Patrick saw him as a star on the ice and a publicity-attracting figure because of his war exploits, and made Fredrickson a big offer. But Fredrickson took a different path. He signed a five-year deal to conduct an aerial study and make a report on the feasibility of air transport in Iceland, concentrating on fishing exploration and postal service in remote areas. His report showed that surveillance from air could locate schools of fish, something that quickly became standard practice. But his contract was cancelled after six months due to a lack of funds and Fredrickson returned to Winnipeg, where he joined the Canadian Air Force. In his spare time, he played the violin in a hotel orchestra and did concerts with his pianist wife Bea, a graduate of the Toronto Conservatory of Music.

PCHA ALWAYS GETS THEIR MAN

But needing a replacement for the aging Cyclone Taylor as the big star of his PCHA, Patrick was a determined recruiter. He signed Fredrickson to a contract worth $2,700 a season for the Victoria Cougars. Patrick mounted a large publicity buildup for the first meeting between the aging star, Taylor, whose career was in a decline, and the brilliant rookie Fredrickson. Fredrickson scored two goals in Victoria's win and even Cyclone had words of praise, calling Fredrickson "as fine a player as I've ever seen with a wonderful quick shot."

A GREAT PLAYER AGENT, TOO

Fredrickson spent six years with the Cougars, winning the scoring title in 1922–23 with 39 goals and 55 points in 30 games. In the 1924–25 season, Fredrickson led the Cougars to the PCHA title, then the Stanley Cup when they defeated the Montreal Canadiens and their great young star Howie Morenz in the final. When the PCHA was disbanded in 1926, most members of the Victoria team joined the Detroit Cougars of the NHL. Fredrickson made his own deal with the new club for $6,500 per season, more than double what the other players were paid. When they discovered his salary, they refused to pass the puck to him, forcing the Cougars to trade him to the Boston Bruins.

ROSS NOT AN APPRECIATOR OF FINE MUSIC

With the Bruins, Fredrickson's violin was joined by the saxophone of great young defenceman Eddie Shore and their music sessions on the team's train trips led Bruin boss Art Ross to ban all musical instruments. Fredrickson logged NHL time with the Bruins, Pittsburgh Hornets (he was playing-coach one season) and rejoined the Detroit club where a knee injury ended his career in 1931. He coached in Winnipeg, Canadian Air Force teams and the University of British Columbia and was named to the Hockey Hall of Fame in 1958. Hockey's Renaissance Man! That seems the best way to describe the Icelandic Icon from the 'Peg.

HOCKEY'S COLOR CHANGE

The NHL should have given black players a chance much earlier than they did but color barriers had to fall.

When Anson Carter of the New York Rangers scored the overtime goal for Team Canada that won the 2003 World Championship in Finland, he claimed he was happiest about one factor. "There was a big media conference after the game with press from all over the world," Carter said. "The great thing about those interviews was that nothing, no reference or question, was made about me being a black hockey player. I was just a hockey player who scored a big goal."

THOSE ALBERTA BOYS

Carter is one of the growing number of black players who are making their mark in the NHL. Jarome Iginla of the Calgary Flames has proven himself to be an elite NHL player: a scoring champ, twice winner of the Maurice Richard Trophy as leading goal-scorer, twice an all-star and winner of the King Clancy Memorial Trophy for community and charity service. Add the induction of former Edmonton Oilers goalie Grant Fuhr as the first black player in the Hockey Hall of Fame in 2003 and it's clear that black players are an integral part of the game.

SMYTHE MAKES US WRITHE

But it wasn't always that way. Herb Carnegie, now in his 80s, must often think of what might have been in a later time. He and his brother Ossie were the sons of Jamaican immigrants to Toronto and played pond and corner-rink hockey, becoming good players at the high school level. When Herb earned a spot with a Junior A team, the Toronto Young Rangers, in 1938, he was certain he was bound for the NHL. But the call never came and while debate exists as to why the Carnegie boys didn't make it, color definitely entered the picture.

Conn Smythe, the owner of the Toronto Maple Leafs, reportedly said while watching Carnegie practise with the Young Rangers,

"I will give $10,000 to anyone who can turn Herb Carnegie white." There's no definitive proof that Smythe made such a statement but some reliable hockey people insist the Leaf owner said it.

BÉLIVEAU & THE BLACK ACES

Even the player shortage during the years of World War II did not open the doors for the Carnegie brothers. They played in the Quebec League, a strong amateur circuit with Sherbrooke, where Herb was most valuable player for three consecutive seasons. The Carnegie brothers and Manny McIntyre played on a high-scoring all-black line called the Black Aces. Herb Carnegie joined the Quebec Aces as a teammate of the great Jean Béliveau, who had turned down the Montreal Canadiens to stay in Quebec for a big salary. Béliveau always said he learned a great deal from Carnegie whom he called "a beautiful skater and playmaker, a super hockey player."

CARNEGIE SPURNED

When he was 29, the New York Rangers wanted to sign Carnegie but told him that he would open the season on the American League farm team. He refused, figuring he would be buried in the minors for what remained of his career. An "ace" in financial businesses and founder of the Future Aces hockey school, Carnegie was a success in life but the bitterness still lingers on about the NHL door not opening for him.

O'REE AT LAST

The doors did open for Willie O'Ree, the first black man to play in the NHL when he joined the Boston Bruins for two games in the 1957–58 season and 43 in 1960–61. He was a fast skater who had a lengthy minor league career, spending the most time with Los Angeles Blades and San Diego Gulls of the old Western League where he was a high scorer. But not even the NHL expansion of the late 1960s gave O'Ree another shot at making it back to the bigs. He has worked for the NHL during the past few years as director, youth development, NHL diversity. O'Ree plays down the "pioneer" aspect of his brief NHL career: "There were a few racial slurs but I faced nothing even remotely close to what Jackie Robinson endured when he broke into big-league baseball."

UNDERGROUND HOCKEY

The post-Civil War "Underground Railroad" brought many black people to Canada to escape persecution in the U.S., where the freedom they had been granted didn't really mean that. Hockey was a growing game in Canada and the black community joined in. But as many former slaves drifted back south, the black population dwindled. Two black senior amateur players who made names in Ontario hockey in earlier times were Hippo Galloway of Dunnville and Charlie Lightfoot of Stratford. Bud Kelly was a star on an army team based in London, Ontario, during World War II and George Barnes stood out in intermediate hockey, a level for teams in smaller centers. In 1920, St. Catharines, Ontario, had an all-black team, the Orioles, playing against an all-white club.

RAMPANT RACISM

Arthur Dorrington, from Truro, Nova Scotia, the first black man in U.S. minor-pro hockey in 1950, faced heavy discrimination in both racial slurs from opponents and fans and barriers to accompanying his white teammates to hotels and restaurants. Mike Marson was a good junior, drafted by the expansion Washington Capitals in 1974, a talented and tough kid in an interracial marriage. He played 196 NHL games over six seasons but complained of racial slurs—even from his teammates—death threats by both phone and letter and having the tires of his car slashed.

TOUGH TONY MAKES WAY

Tony McKegney discovered early in his career in the late 1970s the sting of racism. He had been adopted by a white family in Sarnia, Ontario, and became a star junior with the Kingston Canadiens. Drafted by the NHL Buffalo Sabres in 1978, McKegney instead accepted an offer from the Birmingham Bulls of the World Hockey Association, which was in its final season. When Alabama fans threatened a boycott because of McKegney's color, the Bulls released him from his contract and he signed with the Sabres. McKegney played 912 NHL games with seven teams, scoring 320 goals. Several top stars—who just happened to be black—followed the McKegney lead and slowly the racism, both from rivals and fans, disappeared. Fuhr and Iginla are just two top-drawer black players who have contributed immensely to the modern game.

THE HOUSE THAT SMYTHE BUILT

In the midst of the Great Depression, Conn Smythe used his ingenuity to find financing and build Maple Leaf Gardens.

In 1931, the Great Depression had established its downward lock on North American financial markets, unemployment had reached record percentages and few trains in Canada ran without transients in the baggage car. To consider construction of a large arena to house a professional hockey team required a man with big vision, nerves of steel and the ability to get blood, in the form of money, from a stone (Canada's financial institutions and investors). Conn Smythe was precisely that man, and when Maple Leaf Gardens—for decades probably the best-known building in Canada—opened in November 1931, Smythe said, "I'm either a great visionary or the dumbest guy who ever lived."

A GUY WITH "GUILE"

But in a feat of incredible daring, guile and salesmanship, Smythe, aided abundantly by his assistant Frank Selke, raised the money in a dead market to build the living stage for his Toronto Maple Leafs hockey team. Smythe had scuffled hard to find the $160,000 to purchase the Toronto St. Patricks in the fledgling National Hockey League in 1927, a team that was a steady money loser in the elderly Mutual Street Arena.

HOW TO MOTIVATE A VENGEFUL HOCKEY MIND

Smythe was a college hockey player, served in the Canadian army in World War I, built a sand-and-gravel company and started his thoroughbred racing stable in the post-war years. He coached the U of T hockey team and was an investor in the Toronto Marlboros operated by Selke. The New York Rangers hired him to build their team when the NHL first expanded into the U.S. in the mid-1920s, and after he had assembled a strong team of mostly unknown amateur players—many who later went into the Hockey

Hall of Fame—the Rangers fired him. He returned to Toronto with $10,000 in severance pay, vowing to own a team there that would be better than *his* Rangers.

THAT'S RIGHT, KIDS, GAMBLING PAYS

Smythe increased his bankroll through winning bets on sports events, found backers through his persistence, then bought the St. Patricks. He quickly changed the team name to the Maple Leafs and the colors from green to blue and white and built a strong lineup around players from Selke's Marlboro junior team—augmenting it through trades and purchases until, by 1930, the Leafs had high potential. Turning a profit in the old Mutual Street building proved impossible, stoking Smythe's dreams for a big arena. But the stock market had crashed: The few investors who had money were clinging to it and construction of an expensive building did not appear to be in the cards.

LEAFS PROGRAMS GOOD BATHROOM READS

"It looked as if we would have to postpone the building," Smythe said. "Then early in the '30–31 season, Selke produced a special program to be sold at the games that boosted the need for a new arena. [Leafs radio broadcaster] Foster Hewitt mentioned on the air that the program was available for ten cents and we got 91,000 requests for it. Those 91,000 dimes convinced a few money guys and bankers that there was big interest in hockey and a new building." Folklore, much of it originated by Smythe over the years, includes the story of how in the spring of 1931 backers of the MLG project opened the bids from construction companies and found they were several hundred thousand dollars short of launching the building. Smythe claimed it was the bleakest moment of his life; he was certain the project was dead.

TAKING ADVANTAGE OF THE WORKING STIFF

The situation inspired a fine tale of how Selke, who was business manager for the electrical workers' union in his non-hockey job, jogged a mile from the bank where the fiscal backers' meeting was held to the building trades council meeting, where he persuaded the unions to accept 20 percent of their salary in shares of MLG stock. In reality, Selke made personal pitches to the 24 unions, his hard sell convincing the workers that 80 percent of their salaries in cash was better than the unemployment faced by many skilled trades in the depressed economy.

"Conn Smythe made it sound as if I ran up the street, made a pitch to the unions and ran back to tell the bankers that the workers went along with getting stock for part of their salaries," Selke said. "Mostly, it was a hard pitch to the union leaders that did it. When the unions agreed, the bankers gave us more money and, slowly, the construction money reached a level where we could go ahead. I think the unions were a little suspicious of the deal we offered and had the economy been strong and jobs more plentiful, they would have turned it down. But jobs were so scarce in '31, they went for our idea."

BUILDING FINISHED IN 80% OF EXPECTED TIME!
Smythe had acquired a choice piece of downtown land as a site for the building. On June 1, 1931, construction started and, in an incredible feat, Maple Leaf Gardens was completed in approximately five months. On November 12, 1931, the building's glittering opening night attracted a who's who of Toronto society and money to see the Chicago Black Hawks beat the Leafs 2–1. However, the Leafs went on to capture the Stanley Cup in the first season in their new home.

TODAY: SEASON'S TICKETS ON E-BAY FOR $250 Gs
Even from the start, sold-out houses for Leafs games were common and the owners like to boast that from the end of World War II until the demise of the Gardens (it was replaced by the Air Canada Center in 1999), every seat for a Leafs game had been sold. With Hewitt spreading the Maple Leaf gospel across Canada every Saturday night from the "gondola" high above the Gardens' ice, the Leafs filled Smythe's dream of being "Canada's team" (at least to that chunk of Canada that didn't worship Les Habs).

The controversial owner regarded the Gardens as Toronto's entertainment center, the way opera houses are regarded in European cities. The seats closest to the ice were filled with well-dressed folk in the building's first 30 years; old pictures show many women in those seats wearing snazzy hats. When Leaf games were televised in the 1950s, Smythe sent a letter to the box-seat holders, complaining that standards of dress had slipped and he hoped for an improvement.

THE FAT LADY SINGS...

A week after the first hockey game, the MLG ice was removed and a crowd of 15,000 packed the building to see a professional wrestling match in which Jim "The Golden Greek" Londos defeated Jumpin' Gino Garilbaldi. Pro wrestling became a regular weekly feature of the building. But Smythe also tried to pass off the big barn as a fine arts palace. Extraordinary ballerina Dame Margot Fontaine danced *Sleeping Beauty* in the Gardens, called the place a cavern, and never returned. Paul Robeson in 1942 and Maria Callas in 1958 also battled the building's horrific acoustics. Elvis Presley in 1957 and the Beatles in 1961 packed the place and with the rock era well underway, the sound system was upgraded and MLG hosted every major pop music group over the next four decades.

Conn Smythe sold his interest in the building to a group led by his son Stafford in the late 1950s and while he kept an office in the building, he often publicly expressed his distaste for the new regime's bids to increase revenue by adding advertising and seats to his sacred palace.

* * * * *

"The top three worst things I've seen in hockey? The invention of the trap. The invention of the morning skate. And the invention of the extremely ugly uniform."

—Brett Hull, former St. Louis Blues forward

"I don't know if I find Brett Hull funny. But I can tell you this: He sure thinks he is."

—Craig Ludwig, former Dallas Stars defenceman

BROTHERS-IN-TWINE

Match the brothers with the numbers of goals scored in the NHL:

1) Wayne and Brent Gretzky	a-902
2) Dennis and Bobby Hull	b-821
3) Maurice and Henri Richard	c- 666
4) Mario and Alain Lemieux	d-792
5) Brent and Brian Sutter	e-711
6) Peter and Frank Mahovlich	f-913
7) Peter and Anton Stasny	g-664
8) Marcel and Gilbert Dionne	h-764
9) Pierre and Sylvain Turgeon	i-702
10) Geoff and Russ Courtnall	j-895

* * * * *

"Yeah, I'm cocky and I am arrogant. But that doesn't mean I'm not a nice person."

—Jeremy Roenick, former forward, Chicago Blackhawks

Answers:

1-j, 2-f, 3-a, 4-e, 5-c, 6-b, 7-i, 8-d, 9-h, 10-g

STANLEY CUP STRATA

In its 100-plus years of history, stories ring around the Stanley Cup like the strata layers of the Earth. Uncle John would like to share some recent ones with you.

It is almost 36 inches high and weighs about 35 pounds. It has a top that bears a remarkable resemblance to a candy bowl (at one point, it was indeed used as a candy bowl, in Montreal in 1910) and below the bowl are silver bands—with hundreds of names engraved on them—that get larger as it grows older. "It," of course, is the Stanley Cup, awarded annually to the NHL team that wins the most games in a two-to-three-month-long series of playoff games.

LORD STANLEY THE GOOD

Initiated as the Dominion Challenge Cup in 1892, the award later known as the Stanley Cup was created by Governor General Stanley of Preston to be presented annually to the hockey team that won the most games in a season. One of Governor General (later Lord) Stanley's reasons for creating the trophy was to promote hockey as *the* sport of Canada. He has succeeded. Costing Stanley $48.67 in 1892, the first team to get the coveted prize was the Montreal Amateur Athletic Association in 1893.

THE DANGERS OF SKIPPING CHEMISTRY CLASS

Just as there are many chemicals interacting in the Earth's strata, certain chemicals do not mix well with Stanley Cup silver. The Pittsburgh Penguins found this out the hard way. After the Penguins won the Stanley Cup for the second straight year (1992), superstar Mario Lemieux invited his teammates to a party at his home. Booze was flowing freely, and in this alcohol-induced envelope of happiness, jovial Phil Bourque took the Cup to the top of Lemieux's manmade waterfall. When he was done, he pitched the prize into the swimming pool below. Lemieux, Bourque and friends learned quickly that chlorinated water is not good for silver; the Cup was badly tarnished.

WHY HE'S ONE OF THE SMARTEST IN THE GAME

It gets worse: Lemieux had to take the Cup to a victory parade the next day. He later told hockey sportswriters that he simply faced the blemished side of the Cup away from the people. This simple trick worked; nobody noticed that the Stanley Cup was discolored.

PLAYERS NOT TO LEAVE UNSUPERVISED

Lemieux was a two-time winner of the Cup, but goaltender Patrick Roy was a member of four Stanley Cup–winning teams (1986 and 1993 Montreal Canadiens and 1996 and 2001 Colorado Avalanche). The irrepressible Roy couldn't believe what had happened to the Cup a year earlier, so gave it a dip in his own pool in 1993. While conducting more experiments, the perpetually curious Roy wanted to find out what's inside the Cup. So he took a screwdriver, unscrewed the bottom, and found…nothing. The Cup is hollow.

TEAM TRAGEDY

Without question, the most tragic yet inspiring story of recent Stanley Cup memory involves the Detroit Red Wings of the late 1990s. Fans of the Red Wings waited a long time, 15,392 days to be precise, before they won the Cup in 1997. Previous to this—if you haven't made the calculation for yourself yet—the last time they won was 1955. On a celebratory summer day in 1997, some of the players hired a limousine to get them home safely from a golf course. That didn't happen. The limousine driver fell asleep and the car carrying three Russian Red Wings got into a severe accident. Hockey legend Slava Fetisov received a lung injury, team masseur Sergei Manatsakanov got a brain injury and star defenceman Vladimir Konstantinov became paralyzed, probably for life. The euphoria which had engulfed the Detroit area evaporated.

THIS ONE'S FOR VLADIMIR

Months passed and the Red Wings were determined to get back to the Stanley Cup finals. And they did, against the Washington Capitals. All of the team's personnel had but one goal: to repeat as Stanley Cup champions and devote the win to wheelchair-bound Konstantinov. The Red Wings won the first three games and, with five minutes played in the third period of game four, the attention of everyone during a play stoppage in Washington's MCI Center was diverted to a luxury box seating Konstantinov and his wife. As Konstantinov was raised to his feet by his wife and a friend, everyone cheered, including Capitals fans and players. After the

Red Wings won the game, Konstantinov was brought to the ice and the Cup was placed in his lap. Fellow Russian star Sergei Fedorov, Detroit captain Steve Yzerman, and other Red Wings pushed the smiling Konstantinov around the rink.

CAN THIS THING COLLECT AIR MILES?

During the summer months, each player of the winning team gets the Cup for 24 hours, to do with it whatever they wish. Red Wings Fetisov, center Igor Larionov (once called "the Russian Gretzky" by *The New Yorker*) and Slava Kozlov took the Cup to the Red Army Hockey School in Moscow and to their hometowns after the Red Wings' Cup win in 1997. Later, they took it on the streets of the Russian capital and curious onlookers touched the Cup the way a child first pets a cat—somewhat tentatively, yet with love and affection.

Besides Canada, Russia and the United States, the Cup has gone to the Czech Republic, Sweden and numerous other European countries. But contrary to popular belief, it has NOT been on all seven continents: never to Africa, Australia, Antarctica (naturally), or South America.

CANADA'S ANSWER TO LINCOLN'S TOMB

Lord Stanley's original Dominion Challenge Cup was retired in 1967. It now sits in a vault in the International Hockey Hall of Fame in Toronto. The vault door is open during business hours for all Hall of Fame visitors to peer at hockey's holy grail. A Hall of Fame employee is constantly with the Cup, both for its protection and to answer questions. These Stanley Cup guardians tell curious folk such gems as the fact that in 1971 Jean Béliveau of the Montreal Canadiens was the first team captain to circle the rink with the Stanley Cup, and that Wayne Gretzky came up with the idea of the Cup-winning "team photo" (where all players and coaches of the winning club gather at center ice to have their picture taken), after his Edmonton Oilers won it in 1987–88. These are just some of the Stanley Cup strata that will be passed down, from generation to generation, by lovers of hockey.

RISE OF THE UNION

Organizing the NHL Players' Association was a bitter fight that started with defeat on the first try, but finally found acceptance by the league.

That the NHL Players' Association had the strength to close down the league's operation for half the 1994–95 season and the entire 2004–05 schedule and playoffs was the result of a long, uphill climb over close to five decades—first to gain acceptance, then to acquire the solidarity to engage in labor war with the team owners.

IN BRIEF

The first try at organizing a players' association—the word "union" seldom was employed in the late 1950s—resulted in a bitter squashing of the workers' efforts by the league's old guard of owners, who operated the NHL as if the feudal system were still in vogue. But a decade later, with Toronto lawyer Alan Eagleson as the catalyst in several minor victories for individual players against the hockey establishment; the bright hope that Eagleson's main client Bobby Orr gave hockey; and the presence of a new group of forward-thinking owners—both with the established teams and the 1967 expansion clubs—the NHL agreed to accept the association.

PENSION PLANNERS

In the 1950s, the NHL governors, led by league president Clarence Campbell, a Rhodes scholar, lawyer and former NHL referee, had boasted frequently about the players having the best pension plan in professional team sports. At the same time, they claimed that the league's profits were, at best, very small. Detroit Red Wings star winger Ted Lindsay, as determined in his off-ice business efforts as he was in his gritty, abrasive playing style, and Doug Harvey, the mighty defenceman of the Montreal Canadiens, were named to the NHL pension board along with Campbell, New York Rangers president John Reed Kilpatrick and Ian Johnston, a Toronto lawyer and secretary of Maple Leaf Gardens Ltd.

BUM DEAL

The NHL pension was started in 1946 by a few players working with a Detroit insurance agent on injury benefits. Led by Maple Leafs owner Conn Smythe, the NHL quickly took over the pension plan and gave Campbell the job of stripping the players of any control. For ten years from the late 1940s, the players paid $900 per year into the plan, a large stipend considering that the average NHL salary was $5,000 a season. The owners added $600 per player, money gained from the all-star game gate and a surcharge on playoff tickets.

SMALL QUESTIONS, NO ANSWERS

When Lindsay asked pointed questions about the pension fund and its financing—the owners' contributions turned out to be very small—he was brushed aside. Never one to back away from a scrap, Lindsay persisted in his efforts to gain an accurate financial picture of the NHL's operation. Lindsay and Harvey, a lethargic-looking but mentally sharp man, did their own calculations and discovered that the NHL claims of losses or very small profits were false and all clubs made money, and some were very profitable.

CALL IN THE NEW YORK LAWYERS

Frustrated at the lack of answers, Lindsay, at his own expense, recruited the New York lawyers who had helped major league baseball players negotiate their first collective agreement. "I didn't want to start a union; I just wanted a few answers on the financial status of the league in regards to pension and benefits," Lindsay said. "We only went ahead when we were told that it was none of our business." The players' association formation was announced in New York in February, 1957, with Lindsay as president and Harvey, Fern Flaman, Bill Gadsby, Gus Mortson and Jimmy Thomson on the executive.

CAPTAIN COMMUNIST

But the NHL reacted quickly and harshly, led by Campbell, Smythe and Red Wings general manager Jack Adams. Smythe, who had fought in both world wars and had the rank of major, treated the players and team coach Hap Day, who suggested the association be allowed, as traitors. In a meeting with Thomson,

Smythe called his team captain a communist. “If Conn Smythe had fought the Germans as hard as he fought the players, World War II would have been over in about a week,” Harvey said years later. Adams was vehement in his opposition to the association. Years later, it was revealed that Adams was given a set amount of operating capital each season by the owners, the Norris family, and what he did not spend was his salary. One year, when several members of a Red Wing team that won the Stanley Cup signed contracts for the next season, their salaries were cut.

WHAT A COINCIDENCE

Within a year, most of the players involved in the association had been traded, several to the sad-sack Chicago Black Hawks. In the middle of a streak of five consecutive Stanley Cup wins, the Canadiens kept the great Harvey until the string was snapped in 1961, then traded him. Adams traded Lindsay, who had just finished his best NHL season (30 goals, 85 points) and sensational young goalie Glenn Hall, a Lindsay supporter, to Chicago. Adams' efforts led to the Wing players, minus Lindsay's leadership and determination, pulling out of the association and other teams, under extreme pressure from owners, buckled and the association folded, giving full control back to the owners. “Our effort was not a failure despite what happened because we did make some small gains in benefits and we paved the way for Eagleson and his bunch to form the union a few years down the road,” Lindsay said.

THE EAGLE LANDS

Eagleson had played lacrosse against Bob Pulford of the Maple Leafs, then their paths crossed again at the University of Toronto in the early 1960s, where Eagleson was a law school student and Pulford was working on a degree. Eagleson became involved in hockey when Bobby Orr's family asked him to look after the junior-hockey superstar's affairs. Then Pulford sought Eagleson's advice on a contract and other young Leaf stars of the 1960s such as Bob Baun and Carl Brewer consulted him, too. When Brewer left the NHL in 1965, Eagleson aided in the defenceman's successful fight to be reinstated as an amateur to join the Canadian national team. In 1966, Eagleson helped the players on the Springfield Indians of the American League gain some concessions against the cruel and unusual working conditions of team owner Eddie Shore. "A few of us had talked with Eagleson and his law partners for hours on forming a union," Baun said. "We talked about it with friends on other teams and there was positive response to the idea."

CAN'T SAY NO TO A ROOM FULL OF BRUINS

Eagleson negotiated the largest contract in NHL history for Orr when he joined the Bruins out of junior hockey in 1966. In Montreal to see his client, Eagleson was invited to a hotel room by several Bruins and when he arrived, the whole team was present. They suggested that a union was needed and Eagleson was the man to explore the idea. With the Leaf players encouraging him, Eagleson quietly talked with all NHL teams and set down the groundwork for the players' association. Pulford was the first NHLPA president and when the Board of Governors would not allow Eagleson, the association executive-director, to address their meeting, Pulford, accompanied by veteran players Norm Ullman, Bob Nevin, Eddie Johnston, Harry Howell and J.C. Tremblay, told the owners they had formed an association and the owners agreed to recognize it.

A SCANDALOUS SEND-OFF

Eagleson remained as the NHLPA's main man until the 1990s, negotiating several agreements that improved the players' conditions and benefits. He was replaced as executive director by Bob Goodenow, then Eagleson was convicted with theft and fraud involving association affairs. While his players' association time ended in disgrace, he did negotiate important gains for the players.

* * * * *

"Call them pros, call them mercenaries—but in fact they are just grown-up kids who have learned on the frozen creek or flooded corner lot that hockey is the greatest thrill of all."

—Lester Patrick, defenceman, coach and a founding member of the Pacific Coast Hockey Association

THE REAL MILLIONAIRES

The Ottawa Valley town of Renfrew once had the highest paid team with the most stars in hockey: the Millionaires.

The first decade of the 20th century was a great time to be a hockey player. Teams that paid players to play—the term "professional" was used sparingly—popped up across Canada with no structured administration to supervise the various circuits. As a result, players could sell themselves to the highest bidder and, for a few seasons, many did precisely that: sometimes changing teams in midseason or signing on for an important series.

DESPERATELY SEEKING CYCLONE

Fred "Cyclone" Taylor was an extremely fast, highly skilled attacker who was eagerly sought by several teams. "It was the best time to be a player because we could jump all over the country, going where the money was the best," said Taylor in a 1973 interview when he was 89 years old. "It wasn't like a later time, starting in the 1920s, when one team could tie up your professional rights for life. We knew we were lucky but we also knew that it wouldn't last. The costs of a competitive team were much more than the income produced by the small arenas. We players tried to get all we could before the owners got sick of losing money."

A SPENDING SPREE OF SILVER

The battle for playing talent was a mild one compared to the personal rivalries between team owners, including several very wealthy men who enjoyed sport as a diversion from their money-making businesses. M.J. O'Brien was a silver magnate, regarded as a "dapper dandy" right down to his pearl-buttoned spats. His son, J. Ambrose, talked his father into backing the Upper Ottawa Valley League, featuring teams in the silver-mining town of Cobalt; Pembroke; and Renfrew, the dairy town an hour north of Ottawa where O'Brien's team, the Creamery Kings, won five consecutive championships.

SICK OF HOCKEY? TRY LIVING IN MONTREAL IN 1910

The Eastern Canada Amateur Hockey Association had turned into the Canadian Hockey Association to squeeze out Sam Lichtenheim, who feuded with the other owners over gate receipts. The O'Briens, hoping for a shot at winning the Stanley Cup, applied for membership in the new league. When they were turned down, they found a strong ally in Lichtenheim. Together they formed the National Hockey Association and when it was obvious that the money behind the new venture gave it the edge, the NHA and the CHA merged. The new circuit had six teams: Ottawa, the Montreal Shamrocks, Montreal Wanderers, Renfrew, and the mining towns of Haileybury and Cobalt. J. Ambrose's idea to add one more club representing French Montreal, known as the Canadiens, received the backing of the other two Montreal clubs. Thus, the NHA opened the 1910 season with seven teams.

LOOT LURES LUMBER BARONS

Because the O'Briens wanted their Renfrew club to be the NHA's powerhouse, they spared no expense in assembling a team. Goalie Bert Lindsay, already a Creamery King, was rated the best in the game. The Patrick brothers were lured from the west, where they had combined hockey with the family lumber business: Lester for a top salary of $3,000 for a 12-game season and Frank for $2,000. This was big money considering many good players earned less than $1,000 per season. Renfrew forwards Larry Gilmour, Herb Jordan, and Bob Rowe had been top amateurs and Fred Whitcroft and Hugh Millar had been Lester Patrick's teammates with the Edmonton club that had lost a Stanley Cup challenge to the Wanderers the previous year.

LESSONS UNHEEDED BY THE PRE-LOCKOUT NY RANGERS

But Renfrew's big catch was Taylor, who had starred for the 1909 Cup-champion Ottawa Senators. "I was making good money with the Senators plus I had a civil service job for the other nine months of the year," Taylor said. "But the O'Briens offered me an incredible amount, $5,250 for a two-month, 12-game schedule. You have to remember how much money that was in 1908. My father was a salesman for a farm implement company and the most he ever made was $90 a month." The Creamery Kings, appropriately, were renamed the Millionaires, but were known in Renfrew as the Boarding House Gang because they shared lodgings in the same residence. The famous players became the focal point of Renfrew's social life and the rich O'Briens enjoyed spending time with the players. When the team was whipped 7–2 by the Wanderers to open the season, Lester Patrick summed it up well: "Unfortunately, the opening of the season interfered with our Renfrew social activities."

NOT EVEN NEWSY, ODIE AND SPRAGUE...

Despite the midseason addition of the great Newsy Lalonde from the Montreal Canadiens—he scored 22 goals in five games—the Millionaires finished third behind the Wanderers and Ottawa. The team made a postseason trip to New York for a three-game exhibition series against a club that combined Wanderers and Senators players, attracting attention for the game in the U.S. The Patricks left Renfrew for the 1911 season and were replaced by sniper Don Smith and another brother duo destined for big things, Sprague and Odie Cleghorn. But the result was the same. The Millionaires finished third and the O'Briens, who had lost $50,000 in the two seasons, decided that was enough hockey.

FOR A GOOD TIME, NOT A LONG TIME

"We had very good talent in my two years in Renfrew but, first, the Montreal Wanderers and then the Ottawa Senators were better teams," Taylor said. "But I had a great experience there. I got to know the Patrick brothers and listen to them talk about the game of hockey around the dinner table at the boarding house. Much of what they discussed there became the basis for the modern game." J. Ambrose O'Brien never expressed a single word of scorn about his failed efforts to win the Stanley Cup. "To have the chance to know well and watch that many great players on one team was worth whatever it cost us," he said.

THE RICHARD RIOT

A high-sticking incident leads to chaos in Montreal.

Most people think of March 17th as St. Patrick's Day, but in Montreal it is commonly remembered as the anniversary of the Richard Riot. 2005 marked the 50th anniversary of a black day for hockey fans. And it all stems from a suspension of a man know as "The Rocket."

HIGH SPIRITS AND HIGH STICKS

The week before March 17, 1955, the Habs were in Boston playing the Bruins. Even then, before the great Boston-Montreal rivalry of the 1970s, the Bruins had an inferiority complex when it came to the Canadiens. At this point of the 1954–55 season, the Bruins were in fourth place and had clinched a playoff spot. (The Habs would eliminate the Bruins in the playoffs later that year.)

During a game on March 13, Bruin defenceman Hal Laycoe, a former Canadien, walloped Montreal's star player Maurice "Rocket" Richard with a high stick, cutting his face. The Rocket could see the blood trickling down his face, and when he saw his own blood, the Rocket tended to go crazy. He responded in kind and gave Laycoe a lumber facial of his own.

YOU JUST PUNCHED THE WRONG GUY

Then, with sticks swinging all around, rookie linesman Cliff Thompson—who coincidentally once played for the Bruins—did something unprecedented for an official. He jumped on the Rocket's back. As a natural reaction, thinking that a player was on his back, Richard swung and punched Thompson. In any sport no matter the era, it has long been considered taboo to touch an official. It was known the Rocket was going to be punished, but for how long was yet to be determined.

GOD VS. SATAN, TONIGHT AT THE FORUM

According to Montreal GM Frank Selke Jr., "the owners told [NHL president Clarence] Campbell that you give him the proper penalty or your job is on the line." Three days later, the verdict came down. Rocket Richard was suspended for the final regular season game and for the entire playoffs. Famed hockey writer Stan Fischler once said of this sentence, "Now, that's like sentencing a pickpocket to the electric chair." The French hockey fans were outraged at this perceived (correct or not) indignity being thrown toward their hero. Campbell was suddenly in the forefront of an ethnic clash between Francophone and Anglophone—over, of all things, a hockey player, and if Richard was God, then Campbell was perceived as Satan. Then, Campbell sprinkled salt into an already-deep wound.

A PRESIDENT LACKING POLITICAL SAVVY

Saturday night, March 17, 1955. The Habs were scheduled to play the defending Stanley Cup champion Detroit Red Wings, with whom an intense rivalry had developed in the 1950s. President Campbell was a regular attendee at the Forum, and he was asked by the then-mayor of Montreal Jean Drapeau not to attend the game. The mayor did not want an already excitable situation to boil over into something calamitous. However, Campbell did not listen.

HABS HYSTERIA

Not only did Campbell show up at the game, Campbell showed up about halfway through the first period, as though to draw extra attention to himself. The crowd did not respond well. Fans booed, hissed, and threw things such as tomatoes at Campbell and his guest. At the end of the first period with the Canadiens trailing 4–1, a younger male reached to shake the president's hand, and as Campbell reached out his hand, the youth threw a punch at Campbell. Then, out of nowhere, a teargas bomb went off inside the Forum creating mass hysteria. Fans started stampeding toward the exits, and things spilled over to St. Catherine Street. Trolley cars were turned over. Newspaper stands burned. Shops were looted. Many shopkeepers lost everything. (Thankfully, no one was killed in the chaos.) The Habs forfeited the game to the Red Wings 4–1, but that was the least of the problems in downtown Montreal.

A VOICE FROM THE HEAVENS

There was only one person who could subdue the violence, and that person was none other than Richard himself. Richard, who was in attendance at the game, was stunned and appalled by the reaction of the rabid Montreal fans. Richard spoke on radio and television, both in French and English, to appeal to the citizens of Montreal to stop the rioting. Once they heard the pleas of their idol, the fans acquiesced and the violence soon ceased. According to the Rocket's son, Maurice Richard Jr., "maybe it was the first time my father realized that he was so important."

HOW COULD YOU BOO "BOOM-BOOM"?

Rocket Richard would end up losing the scoring title to his teammate Bernie "Boom-Boom" Geoffrion by the slimmest of margins. Geoffrion, also a Francophone, was hurt and stunned when the Forum fans booed him for passing the suspended Rocket and claiming the title. Also, the Habs and the Red Wings would indeed meet in the Stanley Cup Finals. The Red Wings would win in seven games, and it was widely thought that if the Rocket had suited up, the Red Wings would not have won the series.

ROCKET SPOOLING

The Rocket and the Habs went on to win an unprecedented five straight Stanley Cups from 1956 through 1960. The Rocket retired during training camp of the 1961 season. After his NHL career, the Rocket played on the old-timer's circuit, and then he had a major split with the Montreal Canadiens franchise over what his duties should entail. He attempted to become the head coach of the WHA Quebec Nordiques. He didn't even make it to the first game, and was replaced by Jacques Plante. He then had his own mail-order fishing and spooling business, but that didn't last for too long.

STANDING-O

Then, in the 1990s, the Canadiens got new owners, and they hired Richard as a goodwill ambassador for the team. On March 11, 1996, the final game in the Forum was played and all the great Canadiens were brought back. The fans showed they hadn't forgotten Richard by giving him a ten-minute standing ovation. Legendary broadcaster Dick Irvin said of the fans, "as the ovation went on and on, I looked around and thought to myself 75 to 80 percent of the crowd never saw him play. Never saw him score a goal even on television. He hadn't scored a goal in 37 years. And people were crying." The Rocket even signaled to the fans to sit down, but that was only to hide his own tears of knowing that he was still appreciated.

MODELS OF CONSISTENCY

Separated by more than 80 years, the Ottawa Silver Seven and New York Islanders sustained longtime excellence.

Their eras were a lifetime apart, their only common bond a consistent display of skill and grit.

The Ottawa Silver Seven was hockey's first "glamor" team from 1903 to 1906 when the embryonic sport was fighting to get indoors and from the outdoor rinks. The Seven won ten consecutive Stanley Cup challenges, the right to contest hockey's biggest prize granted to teams across the country.

The New York Islanders were part of NHL expansion from six to 21 teams in 13 years in a bid to make hockey a major U.S. team game. Brilliantly constructed from draft choices, shrewd trades and the wise employment of European players, the Islanders won four consecutive Cup crowns from 1979–80 to 1982–83. From the first playoff round in 1980 until a loss in the 1984 final to the Edmonton Oilers, the Islanders won an astounding 19 playoff series in a row.

McGREAT!

From a distinguished Ottawa family, Frank McGee had lost the sight in one eye when struck by a stick in a pickup game. But he became the dominant player of his era, playing the rover position for the Silver Seven. McGee scored 14 goals in a Cup challenge game, eight in a playoff game and had seven five-goal games in his brief four-season career totalling 71 goals in 23 schedule games, 63 in 22 playoff contests. His uncle, Thomas D'Arcy McGee, was a Member of Parliament and Father of Confederation, part of the 1867 meeting in Charlottetown, Prince Edward Island, when Canada was founded as four provinces. Frank's father, J. J. McGee, was Clerk of the Privy Council, a key position in the Canadian government.

WE'LL LICK YOU IN HOCKEY, FOOTBALL, POLO...
Like most of his Silver Seven mates, McGee was a fine all-round athlete, playing lacrosse in the summer, football in autumn, hockey in the winter. Goalie Bouse Hutton is still the only athlete to play on Canadian championship teams in the three sports in one year. Point (defence) Harvey Pulford was an exceptional football player, a classic stay-at-home defenceman for the Seven, who seldom scored but smothered the opposition. The Gilmour brothers—high-scoring Billy and Suddy—Harry Westwick, Alf Smith and cover point Art Moore rounded out the lineup. McGee, Pulford, Hutton and Billy Gilmour were among the first players inducted into the Hockey Hall of Fame and, in 1950, a poll of Canadian newspaper sports editors named the Silver Seven as the Country's Team of the Half-Century.

SEVEN NUGGETS...McGREAT!
The team name was conceived after the 1902–03 season when the "Ottawas," as they were known, won two-game, total-goals challenges from the Montreal Victorias and the Rat Portage (later named Kenora) Thistles. To commemorate the Cup victories, the club directors gave each player a silver nugget, inspiring the Silver Seven nickname. In the 1903–04 season, the Seven withstood three challenges (Winnipeg Rowing Club, Toronto Marlboroughs, Brandon) and a shortened series with the Montreal Wanderers. In 1905, the Dawson City Nuggets made an arduous 6,000 km, 23-day trip from the Klondike to lose 9–2 and 23–2, McGee scoring 14 times in the second game.

AND NOW "TUBE SKATES"?
The second Rat Portage challenge in March, 1905, was the toughest the Seven would face. With a top star in Tom Phillips and using the new tube skates, the visitors won the first game 9–3, a big shock for the Ottawa club, which was without the injured McGee. When the teams played the second game of a best-of-three series, the ice mysteriously was soft—rumors claim salt was applied the surface—making the tube skates ineffective. Ottawa won 4–2, with McGee scoring the winner in 5–4 third-game victory.

In 1906, the Seven won challenges from Queen's University and Smith's Falls, before their streak ended with a 12–10 two-game loss to the Montreal Wanderers. McGee retired after that season but continued to play football. A lieutenant in the Canadian Army in World War I, he was killed action in France at age 37.

OVERSEAS EXPANSION

Having joined the NHL in a 1972 expansion, the Islanders were based on Long Island, a huge bedroom community for New York. Bill Torrey was named general manager and while half the players claimed in the NHL expansion draft signed with the rival World Hockey Association, Torrey did land goalie Billy Smith and forward Ed Westfall. In the team's first entry draft, Torrey claimed Billy Harris, Lorne Henning, Bob Nystrom and Garry Howatt, all of whom served roles in the team's success.

A BRILLIANT DRAFTSMAN

While the Isles won only 31 games in their first two seasons, Torrey made maximum use of the entry draft, selecting defencemen Denis Potvin and Dave Lewis in 1973, forwards Clark Gillies and Bryan Trottier and defenceman Stefan Persson (plus landing the NHL rights to winger Bob Bourne) in 1974, wingers Mike Bossy and John Tonelli in 1977, and Duane and Brent Sutter in 1979 and 1980.

Coach Al Arbour masterfully turned the young talent into solid NHL players and the team improved steadily through the decade. When it appeared the Isles were ready for serious Stanley Cup contention, they suffered two shattering losses to the Toronto Maple Leafs in 1978 and the New York Rangers in 1979. But management did not panic, assessing the losses as indicators of addressable team flaws, not of any lack of talent.

GORING TO THE ISLAND

During the 1979–80 season, the Islanders made the necessary changes, adding muscle in defencemen Dave Langevin and Gord Lane plus tough young draft pick Duane Sutter. Steady defenceman Ken Morrow joined after the 1980 Olympic victory by the U.S. team at Lake Placid. At the trading deadline, Torrey added the sparkplug the Isles needed in center Butch Goring, acquired from the Los Angeles Kings at a high price in Harris and Lewis.

OIL SLICK

With goalie Smith, defenceman Potvin and the line of Trottier, Gillies and 50-goal perennial Bossy leading the way, the Islanders were ready to start their run. They lost only six games in ousting the Kings, Boston, Buffalo and Philadelphia on their way to their first Stanley Cup. And they rolled on through the next three springs, taken to the seven-game limit only once in 12 series to capture three more Cups. After winning the first three rounds in the 1984 playoffs, they faced the Oilers, a team as smartly constructed as the Islanders had been, and led of course by the Great One, Wayne Gretzky. The Oilers ended the Islanders' remarkable run at 19 consecutive series wins, claiming the final four games to one.

* * * * *

HEAD GAME

"Hockey's a funny game. You have to prove yourself every shift, every game. It's not up to anybody else. You have to take pride in yourself."

—Paul Coffey,
former Edmonton Oilers defenceman

"Half the game is mental; the other half is being mental."

—Jim McKenny,
sportscaster, former Leafs defenceman

"Hockey is like a disease, you can't really shake it."

—Ken Wregget,
former Pittsburgh Penguins goaltender

"I don't like hockey. I'm just good at it."

—Brett Hull,
former St. Louis Blues forward

THE "OTHER" BIG LEAGUE

The World Hockey Association lasted only seven seasons but changed the financial structure of the game forever.

In reality, the World Hockey Association became a living, breathing entity with a million-dollar cheque and these words from a golden-haired lad: You rotten so-and-so! In a ritzy private club in St. Paul, Minnesota, on June 27, 1972, Bobby Hull—the National Hockey League's biggest star of the previous decade—received a cheque for $1 million from the fledgling league and signed a contract with the Winnipeg Jets that would pay him $1.75 million in salary over ten years—more than double what the Golden Jet had earned in any of his seasons with the Chicago Black Hawks. Surrounded on the small stage by his wife Joanne and two of the couple's four boys—Brett, who would score more NHL goals than his famous father, was left at home—Hull was signing the biggest deal in hockey history when one of the boys snapped a large elastic band and zapped his brother on the ear, drawing the loudly stage-whispered retort.

THE AMAZING RUBBER HOCKEY LEAGUE

Perhaps the elastic snap was symbolic for what would happen to the NHL's only serious rival over the next seven years. The WHA stretched every part of hockey, often to the breaking point—the player supply, the bankrolls of the team owners in both leagues and, especially, the wallets of all hockey players. It extended the careers of some veterans with the biggest paydays of their lives, gave minor leaguers and young junior players a chance to show their talent that would not have arisen otherwise, and paved the way for the influx of players from Europe.

A LITTLE BITTER, HAROLD?

"What the WHA did mainly with its crappy challenges in the courts to many of the NHL rules was to place a large number of lawyers and agents in expensive sports cars," said Toronto Maple

Leafs owner Harold Ballard, whose team was stripped bare of young talent when he refused to compete with the new league. Ballard and the Leafs had lucked into goalie Bernie Parent, among the best in the game, and could have retained him for a raise of $40,000 over two seasons. Ballard refused and Parent signed with the Miami Screaming Eagles (who transformed into the Philadelphia Blazers before their first season).

ENOUGH LOOT TO GO AROUND

The NHL had grown from its longtime six-team configuration with six new teams in 1967 and four more by 1972 while keeping costs in line with its monopoly status. Even signing precocious defenceman Bobby Orr to the biggest NHL contract ever by the Boston Bruins in 1966 had not changed the league's salary limits a great deal. But hockey growth in the U.S. and indicators that network television had interest in paying highly for game-packages gave promoters an idea that a second league might share in the wealth. By then, the American Football League had forged a merger with the established NFL, expanding and sharing the loot with the older circuit.

VISIONARIES: BIG IDEAS FOR SOMEONE ELSE'S MONEY

Young California visionaries Gary Davidson and Dennis Murphy had founded the American Basketball Association in 1968 to wage a serious war against the NBA. Their hunt for franchise sites for that league gave them a strong knowledge of North American sports markets: the cities where a new hockey league might flourish. Fortunately for Davidson and Murphy, they met three western Canadians with a long background in hockey, mostly at the junior level—Bill Hunter of Edmonton, Scotty Munro in Calgary and Ben Hatskin of Winnipeg. Hunter and Munro had hockey expertise while Hatskin had experience in the entertainment business, especially nightclubs.

BY "BAZOO" YOU MEAN "NOSE," RIGHT, BEN?

A booster of the star system, Hatskin loved to tell a self-deprecating "star" story. A New York agent booked promising young singers for Hatskin's Winnipeg club, and after the opening night of one young Manhattan thrush, Ben was on the phone the next morning. "I called the agent and said, 'What are you doing to me, sending me this young chick with the big chest and the big bazoo? She emptied the place last night. Get her outta here!' He did and I guess I'm in the history books as the only guy who ever fired Barbra Streisand."

A HULL OF A CATCH

Babs aside, Ben had an appreciation for stars, and told the young promoters that their league would only have a chance if it landed some of the NHL's biggest names. Bobby Hull, the biggest available, was having trouble getting a new contract from the rich but penny-pinching Black Hawks. Hatskin put his money where his mouth was, signing Hull to give his Winnipeg franchise and the whole WHA serious credibility. Few athletes have ever worked harder on the marketing and promotional side of their sport than Hull, who never stopped beating the drum for the new league in countless interviews in every city. Such NHL stars as Parent, Gerry Cheevers, Ted Green, Derek Sanderson, Johnny "Pie" McKenzie and J.C. Tremblay also made the jump. The league played the 1972–73 season with 12 teams: New England, Cleveland, Philadelphia, Ottawa, Quebec and New York in the Eastern Division; and Winnipeg, Houston, Los Angeles, Alberta, Minnesota and Chicago in the Western Division.

LEGALITIES, LEGENDS AND LARS-ERIK SJOBERG

The WHA always seemed a rather loosely operated league with an assortment of hockey styles. In its seven seasons, the league had teams in 24 different locations with an assortment of franchise moves, start-ups and failures. A few of the noteworthy characters who passed through, and around, the "other" league:

Judge A. Leon Higginbotham: When NHL legal challenges kept several stars, including Hull, on the sidelines at the start of the first season, Philadelphia Judge Higginbotham, in a complicated ruling, ruled that adherence to the NHL's reserve system would give it "a monopoly over major league professional hockey," and therefore could not allow it to destroy the WHA.

Maurice "Rocket" Richard: The mighty star of the Montreal Canadiens from 1942 to 1960 and a hockey deity in the province of Quebec lasted two games as the first head coach of the Quebec Nordiques. The Rocket learned quickly that the job would drive him batty.

Derek Sanderson: The Philadelphia Blazers signed the Boston Bruins' number-three center to a whopping contract but he played only eight games in the WHA before rejoining the Bruins. The Blazers promoted opening night in Philly by giving away pucks to the fans. However, when the "ice" proved to be all water and cracks after the warm-up, the game was cancelled. The Blazers sent Sanderson out to make a speech of apology, and he was pelted with the free pucks.

Anders Hedberg, Ulf Nilsson, Lars-Erik Sjoberg: The talented Swedes were sought by three NHL teams but joined the Jets because they wanted to make a mark on the style of a new team. Hull joined Hedberg and Nilsson on an extraordinary forward line; Sjoberg was a brilliant attacking defenceman. The Jets' free-wheeling formula inspired Glen Sather to build his NHL Edmonton Oilers with a similar approach.

Gordie, Mark and Marty Howe: The Houston Aeros lured "Mr. Hockey" Gordie Howe out of retirement but only when they agreed to sign his sons, too. Thus, Howe achieved a dream of playing on the same team as his sons, and achieved two WHA titles while doing so.

Vaclav Nedomansky: The first hockey star to defect from an Iron Curtain country (Czechoslovakia), Nedomansky bolted to the Toronto Toros after years as a top player in his homeland. He had big seasons for the Toros before taking his game to the NHL Detroit Red Wings.

Ken Dryden: The excellent goalie of the Canadiens took the 1973–74 season off to finish his law degree in Toronto and did some commentary on Toros' broadcasts. He was close to signing a contract with the Toronto team but decided against it while working a game in Haddonfield, New Jersey, where the New York Golden Blades played part of their schedule. The ice was dreadful—

a series of peaks and valleys—and when the point man on the power play held his stick high for a slapshot and the sliding puck jumped up from a dip in the ice and hit the defenceman in the face, Dryden decided the NHL was the better place to be.

Wayne Gretzky: Signed as a 17-year-old by the Indianapolis Racers, Gretzky was traded to the Oilers early in the 1978–79 season, the WHA's last, and the rest is history. When the elastic band snapped for good, Gretzky's Oilers, the Jets, the Whalers and the Nordiques joined the NHL.

* * * * *

BEHIND THE BENCH

"They say you're not a coach in the league till you've been fired. I must be getting pretty good."

—Terry Simpson, coach, Winnipeg Jets

"Coaches are like ducks. Calm on top, but paddling underneath. Believe me, there's a lot of leg movement."

—Ken Hitchcock, Philadelphia Flyers coach

"There are three things that are sure. You're going to pay taxes, you're going to die, and I'm going to change the lines."

—Pat Burns, New Jersey Devils coach

"Our system of forechecking is to shoot the puck and leave it there."

—Harry Neale, former Vancouver Canucks coach

"Coaching the Bruins is like going bear hunting with a butter knife."

—Pat Burns, New Jersey Devils coach

"I know my players don't like my practices, but that's okay because I don't like their games."

—Harry Neale, former Vancouver Canucks coach

BÉLIVEAU SAYS NO

The mighty Jean Béliveau forced the Montreal Canadiens to wait two seasons for his services as an NHL player.

The man who often is the example for the best hockey can offer—classy, stylish, dignified and intelligent—surprised everyone by telling the NHL and the Montreal Canadiens that they would have to wait for him to join the league. Jean Béliveau was one of the very few players to stand up to the traditional system during the league's six-team days.

HIGHEST PAID AMATEUR

When he emerged from junior hockey in 1951 as the most outstanding prospect since Gordie Howe, Béliveau became hockey's highest paid player with the senior "amateur" Quebec Aces. When the Canadiens finally appeased their disgruntled fans and signed Béliveau to the biggest NHL contract, consisting of a $10,000 bonus and $20,000 per season, managing director Frank Selke said, "I just opened the vault and told Jean to take what he liked."

DON'T YOU HATE GUYS WHO "MAKE IT LOOK EASY"?

Béliveau's NHL performances made the heavy buildup of his ability seem modest. In his 18 seasons as a Canadien, he played on ten Stanley Cup championship teams. He scored 507 goals, 1219 points in 1125 schedule games, and 79 goals, 176 points in 162 playoff games. Béliveau was First All-Star team center six times, twice winner of the Hart Trophy as most valuable player and once of the Smythe Trophy as MVP in the 1965 playoffs. Huge for his time at 6-foot-3 and 205 pounds, Béliveau was a strong, effortless skater who made the game look easy, an excellent scorer and playmaker and feisty competitor who did not accept fouls against him graciously.

BACKYARD-RINK PIONEER

Béliveau had the classic hockey development background. Growing up in Victoriaville, Quebec, he was an altar boy who spent countless hours on an outdoor rink flooded by his father. The long scrimmages, where controlling the puck was the goal, taught Béliveau his stickhandling skills. He played in a man's league when he was 15, moving quickly to the top junior level, first with the Victoriaville Tigers, then the Quebec Citadelle.

LA MAISON DE JEAN

The new 10,000 seat Quebec Coliseum opened in the 1949–50 season and Béliveau, already a gate attraction at 17, transformed it to the House That Jean Built. When he had 61 goals and 124 points in 46 games in the 1950–51 season, 45 goals and 85 points in 36 playoff games over two springs and showed well in a two-game hook-up with the Canadiens, Béliveau was hockey's most-discussed player. In his final junior season, Quebec friends and fans even presented him with a new car. While the Canadiens eagerly awaited the great young prospect's arrival in the NHL, Béliveau chose to join the Quebec Aces of the Quebec Senior League, considered an amateur circuit at the time. Béliveau was signed to a "B-form," which gave the Canadiens control of his professional rights. Had he signed the strongly scorned "C-form," the Canadiens would have had total control of his hockey career.

ALL A GOVERNMENT CONSPIRACY

"I had security in Quebec, I had married a Quebec City girl in my first year with the Aces, I had a free car and a salary as good as Montreal offered," Béliveau said. "I always planned to go to the NHL and it wasn't even a matter of trying to do it on my own terms. Playing senior hockey in Quebec helped me grow up as a man and a player so that I was much better prepared for the NHL than if I had joined the Canadiens directly from junior." That the Canadiens could not pry Béliveau out of Quebec City until he was ready was also due to financial and political ramifications. Years later, Selke revealed how the Canadiens were told by the Quebec provincial government that if Béliveau left before the Coliseum debt was paid off, the licence for the very lucrative tavern in the Montreal Forum would be cancelled and attendance at Canadien games would be reduced considerably by the enforcement of fire regulations.

WE LIKED HIM SO MUCH WE BOUGHT THE COMPANY

When Béliveau had a three-game whirl with the Canadiens in 1952–53 and scored five goals, three in one game, their supporters were sneering at management for failing to get such a big talent in Montreal. In his four Quebec City junior and senior seasons, Béliveau helped attract more than a million customers to the Coliseum, which wiped out the construction debt. He had decided to move to the NHL but to save face after not being able to outbid a senior team for a player, the Canadiens took the expensive step of "purchasing" all clubs in the Quebec League and the pro rights to all players in it, elevating the league to the professional level.

WORTH THE WAIT

Béliveau was an instant fit on one of the greatest rosters ever assembled with goalie Jacques Plante, defencemen Doug Harvey and Tom Johnson, forwards Maurice and Henri Richard, Dickie Moore and Bernie "Boom-Boom" Geoffrion. The club won five consecutive Cup titles from 1956 to 1960, then rebuilt the team around Béliveau and Henri Richard to win four more crowns in the 1960s. Béliveau, at 39, had a wonderful farewell as a player in the 1970–71 season, counting 76 points in 70 schedule games, then 22 points in 20 playoff games to lead the way to his tenth Cup title. When he retired, Béliveau moved into the team's front office as vice-president of corporate affairs, a post he held for 23 years.

* * * * *

"I'm going to look for opportunities to grab the puck by the hair and try to do something with it. I mean, it's not like I have to save the whole country with it, I just have to put it in the net."

—Sergei Fedorov, former Detroit Red Wing forward

"Some days, the sun even shines on a dog's butt."

—Wade Redden, Ottawa Senators defenceman, on Ottawa's come-from-behind 6-2 win over Toronto

"One road trip we were stuck on the runway for seven hours. The plane kept driving and driving until we arrived at the rink and then I realized we were on a bus."

—Glenn Healy, former New York Rangers goaltender, on his time in the minors

THE LONGEST ROAD TRIP

The Dawson City Nuggets' road trip may not have been a victorious one but it does take the prize for longest and most arduous.

In its early history when the Stanley Cup was a challenge trophy, hockey teams from unexpected locales played for the big prize against the champs at the time. Clubs from Rat Portage, Ontario (later Kenora); Brandon, Manitoba; Queen's University at Kingston, Ontario; and New Glasgow, Nova Scotia, challenged for the Cup. But the most unusual challenge came in 1904–05 when the Dawson City Nuggets met the hockey powerhouse of the time, the Ottawa Silver Seven.

BOATS, TRAINS AND BICYCLES (AND DOGSLEDS)

The Nuggets were based 4,400 miles from Ottawa in the Yukon's Klondike where the legendary gold rush of 1897 had produced millionaires (a few) and paupers (many). Financed by Colonel Joe Boyle, a rich prospector, four Nuggets "mushed" on dogsleds from Dawson to Whitehorse. Four rode bicycles and the stagecoach because of a December thaw. They continued onto Skagway, walking 40 miles some days, and hit a –54°F cold snap that reduced practice time to one brief session on a small outdoor ice surface and delayed their trip for five days. They took the *S.S. Dolphin* from Skagway to Seattle, then the train to Vancouver to catch the trans-Canada train to Ottawa. A telegram from Winnipeg requesting a series delay was turned down by Ottawa officials. The bedraggled Nuggets arrived in Ottawa on January 12, 1905, 23 days after they left Dawson City, and played the first game of the best-of-three series the next night.

THE GREAT ESCAPE

Led by the big stars of the era, the great Frank McGee, Harry Westwick and Harvey Pulford, the Ottawa team won the first game 9–2 before a packed house. Before the second game, the Nuggets said they were not impressed with McGee, who scored only one goal in the opener against 17-year-old goalie, Albert Forrest. In the second game, McGee impressed the Nuggets and everyone else by scoring a playoff record 14 goals in a 23–2 victory. However, series reports note that the Nuggets were not shattered by their wipeout. Most players, especially those from eastern Canada, agreed to make the trip to have their fare paid home because prospecting for gold had not been any more fruitful than their hunt for Stanley's silver.

* * * * *

THIS ORR THAT

Thoughts from and about the greatest defenceman ever.

"I've been gifted. The world is full of people who not only haven't been gifted, but have had some thing taken away from them. All I have to do is see one of them, some little girl who can't walk, and then I don't think I'm such a hero anymore. I think that compared to them, I'm a very small article."

—Bobby Orr

"If I can be half the hockey player that Bobby Orr was, I'll be happy."

—Ray Bourque,
former Boston Bruins defenceman

"I don't think you ever stopped Bobby Orr, you contained Bobby Orr, but you NEVER stopped him!"

—Larry Robinson,
former Montreal Canadiens defenceman

"Forget about talent; worry about results."

—Bobby Orr

THE BIG RED MACHINE

The Russians' seemingly quick ascent of the world hockey ladder was a carefully planned, government-backed try at domination.

It's true. The Russian national team is no longer the powerhouse of international hockey it once was in the "CCCP" days. But it isn't for lack of talent or personnel. In fact, when one thinks of goaltenders Nikolai Khabibulin and Evgeni Nabokov, defencemen Sergei Gonchar, Sergei Zubov and Darius Kasparitus, and forwards like Pavel Datsyuk, Alexei Yashin, Alexander Ovechkin, Alex Mogilny, Sergei Fedorov, Sergei Samsonov and Pavel Bure (if anyone can find him), it's quite conceivable that a lineup with such talent could compete with the accomplishments of the Big Red Machine of earlier times. The main difference being, of course, that in those days Soviet hockey's first and only priority was international domination—keeping and training the country's best players together for six to seven months every year. Boston Bruins president and keen USSR-hockey follower Harry Sinden classifies the thought of the Russians being able to follow the same steady, disciplined strategy with the amount of talent they have today simply as "frightening."

THOSE DAMNED REDS...

Of course during the Cold War period most North American fans resented the USSR for their hockey dominance; for the fact that we couldn't see their best players in the NHL; and also from a good number of political and surely stereotypical angles that we needn't get into. But in hindsight the Soviet determination to build the best team in the world (and build some patriotism while they were at it) is not only a project responsible for some of the most exciting moments in the history of the game, but is also something well worth looking back at.

LENIN POWER

The era of world domination for Russian hockey started on the scoreboard in 1954 when the comrades won the first World Championship they entered, whipping the ordinary senior team representing Canada 7–2 to give a huge jolt to Canadian hockey. But the sport has a lengthy history in that country, like the Russian approach to many other games featuring a government-backed development program to show that the Communist system produced top athletes.

BANDY WAS DANDY

For decades, the Russians had played a game called "bandy": in reality, field hockey on outdoor ice because the country lacked indoor arenas with artificial ice. Canadian-style hockey was first demonstrated in Russia in 1932 after the Olympic Games tournament in Lake Placid, NY, when a German team played a series of exhibitions against the Moscow clubs Central Red Army and the Selects. Commentators of the day called the "new" game a poorly played version of bandy.

SPORTS SUPREMICIST

But Joseph Stalin, the Soviet dictator, viewed sports like bandy as a handy propaganda tool in the Cold War against the U.S. in the late 1940s. Stalin's philosophy was that vigorously trained athletes winning global championships would best spread the word on the advantages and glory of the Communist system. A healthy population from participation in sports was another goal. Through a strong system of sports schools and clubs, elite Russian athletes received the best possible training from a young age, leading to many exceptional accomplishments in figure skating and a multitude of Olympic sports, and such team games as soccer, volleyball and hockey.

HOCKEY HANDBOOK BECOMES SOVIET BIBLE

When a concentrated effort under coach Anatoly Tarasov—known as the "godfather" of Russian hockey—produced the 1954 World Championship team, the era of the Big Red Machine was launched on the world hockey stage. Using *The Hockey Handbook*, a book written by Canadian fitness and sports guru Lloyd Percival, as his guideline, Tarasov devised on-and-off-ice conditioning programs, skill-teaching methods, and the "collective" approach to total team play that stressed skating and passing the puck. The NHL had ignored Percival's work, many of the pros scoffing that a man with a background in track and field had nothing to teach hockey experts.

BACK IN THE USSR

Over the next 35 years, the USSR produced three incredible national teams that dominated the World Championship and other tournaments, led by many of the highest skilled players ever to play the game. Their teamwork was honed sharply by the many months the national team trained as a unit. In addition, the core of the team was part of the perennial Russian major league champs, Central Red Army, who had the pick of the talent from all areas of USSR hockey. The first of those clubs grew out of the Tarasov scheme in the 1950s and won nine consecutive World Championships plus two Olympic golds from 1963 to 1971. Anchored by the sterling defence pair of Nikolai Sologubov and Ivan Tregubov plus brilliant forwards Anatoly Firsov, considered by many the greatest Russian player, Veniamin Alexandrov, Konstantin Loktev, Boris and Evgeny Mayorov, and Vyacheslav Starshinov, the Russians easily overpowered the world's amateurs.

STRONG IN THE SEVENTIES

That team slowly changed into another extraordinary club for the 1970s, a decade highlighted by the Summit Series when the Soviets finally agreed to meet a Canadian team stocked with the best NHL players. Goaltending long had been a weakness of the USSR teams, which was viewed by the NHL as the big reason why the Soviets declined opportunities to play NHL clubs, but when Vladislav Tretiak developed into an extraordinary goalie at age 20, the Soviets accepted the challenge.

The USSR's player development system through sports clubs had built a splendid new team with Starshinov, Viktor Kuzkin and large defenceman Alexander Ragulin the only holdovers from the previous decade. The forward line of center Vladimir Petrov flanked by Boris Mikhailov and the breathtaking Valeri Kharlamov plus Alexander Yakushev, Alexander Maltsev and Vladimir Shadrin gave the team a strong attack, and defencemen

Valeri Vasiliev and Sergei Liapkin were strong in front of Tretiak. Team Canada won the Summit by the slimmest of margins—Paul Henderson's famous goal in the final minute of the eighth game—and that Russian roster excelled on through the 1970s with five world and two Olympic titles and a win over the NHL All-Stars in the 1979 Challenge Cup. But they stuck with that basic lineup too long and lost the 1980 Olympics to the U.S. at Lake Placid.

THE FINAL HURRAH

Another brilliant cast arose for the 1980s, when the Russians won six world and two Olympic titles. Leading the way was the excellent "Green Unit" of forwards Igor Larionov, Sergei Makarov and Vladimir Krutov with defencemen Slava Fetisov and Alexei Kasatonov, named for the color of their practice uniforms. Perhaps that team's most memorable series was the 1987 Canada Cup tournament, the best-of-three final decided late in game three when Wayne Gretzky set up Mario Lemieux for the goal that gave Team Canada the crown. But the fall of the Iron Curtain and the breakup of the USSR and the democratizing of Russia around 1990 saw the entire Green Unit and many other Russian players jump to the NHL for their first big paydays. Since then, Russian players have flocked not only to the NHL but to Canadian junior hockey.

* * * * *

"He brings something special. I don't know what it is, but if you ask him, you couldn't understand his answer."

—Wayne Gretzky on Oilers linemate Esa Tikkanen

"They do a lot of talking, but I'm not sure they actually understand each other."

—Darren McCarty on Redwings teammate Vladimir Konstantinov and rival Claude Lemieux

"American professional athletes are bilingual; they speak English and profanity."

—Gordie Howe

HELPED BY A RED HORN

Hockey people are extremely superstitious, idiosyncratic devotees of rituals and habits.

In the slot directly in front of the opposition net with the puck on his stick, even with the defenders hacking, chopping and harassing him, Phil Esposito was among the most confident players in NHL history. He fought through maximum efforts to stop him from unloading the deadly accurate shot that made him one of the best pure goal-scorers ever to play.

In the dressing room before the game? A completely different Espo, a man full of superstitions, a creature of habit with a carefully crafted routine that had to be followed to the letter or he felt his game would disintegrate. This is something Esposito has shared with many players. Pro athletes are among the most superstitious people extant and hockey folks are in the front ranks.

WHAT WOULD HE HAVE TO DO FOR *THREE* GOALS?

Esposito's teammates with the Boston Bruins in the 1970s were in awe of his scoring feats but they enjoyed recounting the long list of his pre-game rituals. Center Derek "Turk" Sanderson was recruited by Espo to help ward off evil while preparing for a game. Sanderson would adjust Esposito's shoulder pads until they felt comfortable and put the suspenders holding up his mate's hockey pants in place. "Phil said that when I did it, there was chance he would score a goal or two in that game," Sanderson said.

BEWARE THE EVIL EYE

While suiting up for the game, Esposito would stand and wink at a red horn hanging on the shelf above his seat. His grandmother gave him the horn because she claimed it would ward off *malocchio*, the evil eye. Esposito always wore the same tattered black T-shirt inside-out and backwards and pinned a St. Christopher's medal to his suspenders. He would place his stick on the floor between his outstretched legs, then place his hockey gloves palms-up beside the butt end of the stick. That's when trainer Frosty Forristall would shake white power on the stick blade. "Phil would check the room for bad omens, such as an upside-down paper cup or crossed hockey sticks," said defenceman Bobby Orr. "We would leave them that way deliberately just to shake him up."

TOSSING THE COOKIES

Goalie Glenn Hall was a rock in the nets who played in a record 502 consecutive complete games for Detroit and Chicago and was sick to his stomach before them all. At first, Hall claimed that he vomited because of pre-game stress but slowly became convinced that his "cookie flipping" had a ritual value and if it didn't happen, he wouldn't play well. Late in his career, Hall gave the expansion St. Louis Blue great goaltending, vomiting all the way to the Stanley Cup final in the club's first three seasons. Before the seventh game of a 1968 playoff series against the Philadelphia Flyers, Blues' coach Scotty Bowman was very worried when Hall approached him with bad news.

"Glenn told me that he hadn't thrown up and if he looked shaky early in the game, I was to pull him out," Bowman said. "I had a moment of panic, then looked in the washroom and saw a pair of pads sticking out of one of the stalls, and I knew everything was fine. Glenn played a terrific game and we won the series." Hall had another ritual: He would not retrieve the puck from the net behind him when a goal was scored, saying, "I didn't put it there so why should I get it out?"

99 QUIRKS

Wayne Gretzky produced points at a rate so far above any other player that it seemed no superstitions should have concerned him. But No. 99 had his fair share of quirks. Gretzky's most visible hang-up was having half his team sweater hanging free, half tucked into his hockey pants. Through a big part of his career, Velcro was fixed to his pants and sweater to hold his favored arrangement in place. "I started tucking half the sweater into my pants in kids' hockey when it happened one game by accident and I had a good offensive night," Gretzky said. "I just kept doing it and started to think it brought me luck."

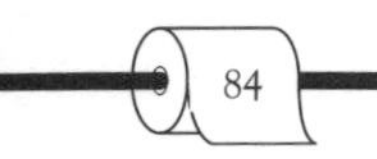

NO FEAR OF FLYING ON ICE

Gretzky had more than superstitions when he boarded an airplane for a road trip. What he had was sheer terror—a deep fear of flying—and a shirt soaked with perspiration, especially if even the slightest bit of turbulence was encountered. At one time, he had psychological help with his phobia. "It got better when I asked to see the cockpit and, on some flights, I was allowed to sit there for a time, watch how they were flying the plane even if I never understood it, and it helped me relax a little," Gretzky said.

HELLO LEFT POST

Other idiosyncracies and rituals:

Patrick Roy: The brilliant goalie often "talked" to the goal posts, standing a few feet in front of the net and chatting away to the metal. "The posts were my friends so I just said hello to them," Roy once said. "If I missed a shot, maybe it would hit them and stay out of the net."

Derek Sanderson: The Bruin center wore a piece of Italian ram's horn, given to him by a friend, on a chain around his neck, and had few injuries after he started wearing it.

Steve Shutt: If anyone touched the carefully prepared sticks of the Montreal Canadiens sniper before a game, he immediately changed to other "untouched" sticks. Asked why, Shutt had a simple explanation: "I just don't like anyone touching my sticks."

Mike Palmateer: The nickname for the Maple Leaf and Washington Caps goalie was "The Popcorn Kid," because he liked to eat a large box of freshly popped corn brought to him by the team's trainers just before the warmup.

Gordie Howe: The 32-season veteran felt that his pre-game preparation wasn't complete if his midday meal was not a steak with a coating of blue cheese and a baked potato. "No special reason," No. 9 said. "I just liked it that way."

A YOUNG MAN'S GAME

The Memorial Cup, awarded to the Canadian junior champs, is a competition with a history and tradition as long as the Stanley Cup.

Canadian junior hockey, a mainstay of the game as the leading producer of talent for the pro leagues, takes a multi-pronged approach to prosperity. The competition factor of the three leagues for young men between 16 and 20 is strong, the caliber of play at a high level and the deep rivalries have existed for decades. The development of prospects for the NHL, selected via the annual entry draft, provides a large discussion point for the juniors. Players are not only motivated to outshine their opponents in order to get ahead in the standings, but also to individually get a step up on the draft ladder.

BIG-LEAGUE PROSPECTS

Situated in many middle-sized cities, most teams are their town's "big-league" sports franchise, many attracting close to capacity crowds in arenas that have from 4,500 to 10,000 seats. The 2005–06 hockey season will see the Canadian Hockey League, the umbrella organization for the Western, Ontario and Quebec Leagues, operate with 58 teams stretching from St. John's, Newfoundland to Vancouver, British Columbia. Nine of those are in the northern U.S.—Erie, Pennsylvania; Saginaw and Plymouth, Michigan, in Ontario; Lewiston, Maine, in the Quebec League, and Spokane, Seattle, Everett and Tri-Cities in Washington plus Portland, Oregon, in the Western League.

ROUND-ROBIN RULES

Each spring, four teams play in the Memorial Cup championship tournament, an event that has national television exposure with strong audiences in Canada. A host city is selected several years in advance and the team in that town has an automatic berth in the Cup event. It is joined by the three league champions for the round-robin tournament. If the host team happens to be the league playoff champs, the other finalist from that loop is the fourth team. This tournament approach started in 1972, replacing the longtime east-west final for the trophy.

ULTIMATE SHOWDOWN: SCHOOLS VS. PATRICIAS

The juniors have been a strong part of Canadian hockey for more than 100 years. The Ontario Hockey Association, to oversee all levels of the game, was founded in 1890 and within a few years, the first Ontario junior champs, the Kingston Limestones, were crowned. When the Canadian Amateur Hockey Association was created in 1914, various provincial leagues were formed under its banner. The true Memorial Cup, in memory of those who had died in World War I, was first contested in 1919—won by the University of Toronto Schools in a two-game, total-goals series against the Regina Patricias. The Ontario junior league donated the OHA Memorial Cup Trophy for the Canadian championship. Originally, the trophy was donated by John Ross Robertson, one of the early OHA presidents, who is in the Hockey Hall of Fame as a builder.

WHO WOULD WIN: GRANITES OR LIMESTONES?

A member of that UTS team was defenceman Dunc Munro, who performed a unique feat in his hockey career. Not only was he part of a junior championship team, Munro won two Allan Cups (1922–23) and an Olympic gold medal with his senior amateur team the Toronto Granites, and the 1924 and 1926 Stanley Cups with the Montreal Maroons. To demonstrate the value the junior leagues, especially championship teams, could have in producing top players for the NHL, the 1920 Memorial Cup winners, the Toronto Canoe Club, were led by goalie Roy Worters, defenceman Lionel Conacher and forward Billy Burch, all Stanley Cup winners in the NHL and Hall of Famers.

JUST LIKE CANADIAN IDOL

A year later, the first team from western Canada, the Winnipeg Falcons, won the Memorial Cup in a two-game, total-goals series, 11–9 over the Stratford Midgets, whose star Howie Morenz was a teenager with dazzling skill and speed on his way to a splendid NHL career with the Montreal Canadiens. Thus, the tradition was established for just about every Memorial Cup final to provide a showcase for a future star, or sometimes several, some finals matching two teams with as many as nine future NHL players. The 1934 champion Toronto St. Michael's College Majors had eight players who became NHL regulars.

LOOKING UNDER EVERY ROCK

Until the first NHL expansion in 1966 when the universal draft was established to distribute talent, most junior teams operated as amateur "farm clubs" of the original six NHL franchises. The big-league teams' scouting concentrated on players younger than 16 years of age who were channelled to Junior-B teams as part of their education to top level junior play. NHL clubs often paid a sizeable sum of money to a town's minor hockey system to tie up all the players on those teams, often to land one or two outstanding prospects. The NHL teams engaged in serious pursuits of midget (16 and under) age players. Bobby Orr, a 13-year old star in Parry Sound, Ontario, was courted by all six NHL clubs before he joined the Boston Bruins' organization through their Oshawa Generals junior team. Wren Blair, the general manager of the Generals under the Bruins umbrella, joked that he spent so much time in the Orrs' Parry Sound home that the family considered adopting him.

TRIUMPH TORONTO

Because the Toronto Maple Leafs were perched in the area with the most registered minor hockey players anywhere and the team was a big favorite across Canada because of Foster Hewitt's Saturday *Hockey Night In Canada* broadcasts, the Leafs' junior teams, St. Mikes and the Marlboros, were perennial contenders for the Memorial Cup until the universal draft took the Leafs out of the teenage scouting business. In fact, Toronto teams, with 14 victories by five different teams, hold the one-city record for Memorial Cup titles. The Marlboros won the Cup a record seven times, their last triumph in 1975, before the team left Toronto to be become the Hamilton Dukes. Toronto was without major junior hockey until St. Michael's returned to the Ontario league in 1997 after dropping out in 1962.

LONDON GETS ON THE MAP

The 2005 Memorial Cup in London, Ontario, provides a splendid example of the tournament's clout. All seats for the May event at the new 9,200 seat John Labatt Center were sold by January 1. The combatants were an ideal combination of teams and with no Stanley Cup playoffs because of the NHL labor dispute, the tournament received significant media attention. Of course, that the host (and eventual winners) London Knights were the Ontario champions and the top-rated CHL team was a great start. The defending Memorial Cup champs, the Kelowna Rockets, represented the Western league and the Rimouski Oceanic, led by phenomenal prospect Sidney Crosby, provided a huge attraction. As Ontario League finalists, the Ottawa 67s coached by Brian Kilrea, a Hall of Famer for his more than 1,000 wins in junior hockey, were the fourth team.

OF COURSE, HIS OUTLOOK IS BIASED...

Dave Branch, the CHL president who doubles as head of the Ontario League, is one of the forward-thinking, marketing-oriented executives who has helped to lift the junior game to a high level. "Of course, my outlook is biased but I don't think any other sports competition in Canada matches the Memorial Cup," Branch said. "Our teams represent every area of the country and no other sport has such a sustained level of interest as the Memorial Cup over the nine days of the tournament."

17-YEAR OLDS TAKING OVER THE WORLD

The juniors have not lagged behind the big leaguers in their international outlook. The annual world junior championship in the Christmas-New Year holiday period now is a major global event with more than a half-dozen serious contenders every year. Canadian junior teams recruit players in the European countries, with players from Russia, the Czech Republic, Slovakia, Sweden and Finland raising the standards of play to higher levels every season.

A competition for teenagers? The Memorial Cup is that but those lads just happen to play the game at a grand level.

BIG, BAD AND BROAD

The Philadelphia Flyers dominated through grit, determination and just a little bit of stick-work.

When the Philadelphia Flyers started NHL play on October 11, 1967 (they lost 5–1 to the Oakland Seals), they were strictly a "pass-and-shoot" team. Two men—head coach Fred Shero and center Bobby Clarke—would lead a conversion from "pass-and-shoot" to "bump-and-grind." This, in turn, would evolve into a form of play where the Flyers would so thoroughly intimidate opponents that they would deservedly become remembered as the "Broad Street Bullies."

BROAD STREET BOBBY

Clarke was the dynamo and focal point of the Broad Street Bullies (Broad Street being the location of the Philadelphia Spectrum). He had both grit and talent and would do absolutely anything to win. Clarke's first full season with the Flyers, the only NHL team he ever suited up for, was 1969–70. A diabetic, he was skipped over by every team in the 1969 draft before the Flyers decided to sign him. In his rookie season, he tallied 15 goals, 46 points and 68 penalty minutes; all these figures would go up significantly.

PLUGGERS, GRINDERS & A NETMINDER

Freddie "The Fog" (he was always daydreaming about hockey) Shero became the head coach of the Flyers in 1971–72. A man who stayed around minor league hockey for most of his adult life, he was a rough-and-tough player in his younger days. As a coach, he instilled this win-at-all-costs feeling in his players. Goalie Bernie Parent and Clarke's former Brandon Wheat Kings linemate Reggie Leach—a natural goal-scorer who had a tendency to elevate his game in the playoffs—were the team's other genuine stars. But just as integral to Shero's system was the fact that left-wingers Bill Barber and Ross Lonsberry, center Rick MacLeish, right wing Don "Big Bird" Saleski, and defencemen Barry Ashbee, Ed Van Impe, and Joe Watson were not afraid of checking opponents and fighting to obtain the puck.

The word "fight" brings to mind Dave "The Hammer" Schultz, unquestionably the toughest hombre in this bunch of hockey desperadoes. In 1974–75, he managed 472 penalty minutes in 76 games (for those wondering, that's an average per-game of 6.26!).

OVERCOMING TRAGEDY

In 1973–74, the Flyers finally pulled all aspects of their play together. They swept past the Atlanta Flames in the semifinals, then faced the New York Rangers in what may have been the most exhausting and demanding playoff series the Broad Street Bullies ever played. There were bloody fights in almost every match of this seven-game series but the biggest loss for the Flyers was that of their best defencemen, Ashbee. He got hit over one of his eyes by a shot in game four, and never played another NHL game. He continued to contribute to the team as an assistant coach, but in 1977 Barry Ashbee would die of leukemia.

THE NOT-SO-SECRET WEAPON

At the Spectrum the Flyers won a hard-fought game seven over the Rangers 4–3. Now it was on to the Stanley Cup finals against the Boston Bruins and the Flyers had a not-so-secret weapon. Singer Kate Smith was selected to sing "God Bless America" before a Flyers game for their first home match of 1973–74. They beat the Toronto Maple Leafs 2–0, and owner Ed Snider quickly realized that Smith's rendition of the song before important home Flyers games could be a clever marketing gimmick. (Not to mention one more possible psyche-out for opponents about to face the Bullies of Broad Street.) Smith's rendition of "God Bless America" took the place of the U.S. national anthem whenever Snider felt it was time to pull out the team's good luck charm. And he had a damn good sense of it; the Flyers went 37-3-1 whenever Smith belted the song out.

INFUSED WITH INSPIRATION

The Bruins beat the Flyers in game one, but when Clarke scored in overtime in game two, it marked the first time that the Flyers won in Boston Garden since November 21, 1967. In game six, on May 19, 1974, at the Spectrum, Snider called for "God Bless America." If the Flyers won this game, they would be the first of the 1967 expansion teams to win the Stanley Cup. They did, and in typical Flyers fashion: 1–0 on a goal by MacLeish, relentless shut-downs of Bruins superstars Phil Esposito and Bobby Orr, and a shutout by Parent. The roly-poly, affable Parent won the Conn Smythe Trophy as best player in the playoffs. For his regular-season performance, in an ultra-rare tie-vote, Parent shared the Vezina Trophy for top goalie with Chicago Black Hawk Tony Esposito.

FREDDIE HERO

The main man responsible for the Stanley Cup was Shero, one of the most idiosyncratic coaches ever to take the helm of an NHL team. To get his players in condition at training camp, he had players push teammates seated in chairs up and down the ice. When he read a newspaper article about the special exercises that NASA astronauts were doing to prepare for the Apollo space flights, Shero incorporated some into the regime. For all of Shero's strange tactics, he was much loved and respected by his players. And appreciated, especially by Bernie Parent: "There is only one Freddie Shero. That's one reason why I gave him the Javelin car I won from *Sport* Magazine after the 1974 Stanley Cup playoffs. When I gave Freddie the keys, he said 'I've always said you have to be a little goofy to be a coach. But now I think my players are a little crazy, too.'"

BACK ON THE ATTACK

The Flyers reputation became so infamous that *Time* Magazine made the team and Parent the subject of a 1975 cover story. While giving the team and goaltender their due respect, *Time* reported that NHL hockey violence was "getting out of control." Parent responded to the attention by leading the league in wins (44), shutouts (12), and goals-against average (2.03) in 1974–75. The team won their division with 113 points, swept the Maple Leafs in the quarterfinals, took seven games to defeat the New York Islanders in the semifinals, and went on to battle the Buffalo Sabres in the Stanley Cup finals.

THE FOG VS. FOG

After winning the first two games, the Flyers played game three in Buffalo. It was late May and the outdoor temperature at game time was in the 70s (degrees Fahrenheit). Inside the arena, a more accurate estimate would be in the 90s. "On the ice, it felt 110, and inside the mask at least 130," remembered Parent in his autobiography. The heat caused fog to rise from the ice surface. With no air-conditioning in Buffalo's arena, the only proven method of dissipating the fog was to stop play and ask *all* of the players for both teams to skate around on the ice, which had to be done on more than one occasion. At the end of regulation play, the score was 4–4. In overtime, Rene Robert took a shot that Parent never saw, giving the famous "Fog Game" to the Sabres.

HAMMERING A COUPLE HOME

Still trying to find that Robert shot, Parent uncharacteristically let in four goals the next game, resulting in a 2–2 series tie. In game five Dave Schultz proved his hands were useful for more than just beating people's face to a pulp by potting two goals in a 5–1 win. Then for the second straight year, Philadelphia took the Cup on a game-six shutout win, this time 2–0. But the next year in the 1976 finals, the Montreal Canadiens swept the Flyers on their way to a new string of Cups based on finesse, speed and a bevy of star players. The Flyers reign of terror was over.

* * * * *

NO BRAIN, NO PAIN

"The guys tell me I have nothing to protect—no brain, no pain."

—Randy Carlyle, former Winnipeg Jets defenceman, on not wearing a helmet

"Bob Kelly was so dumb, they shoulda written his name on the Stanley Cup in crayon."

—Gene Hart, former announcer for the Philadelphia Flyers

"That's so when I forget how to spell my name, I can still find my #$%@& clothes."

—Stu Grimson, former defenceman, Detroit Red Wings, explaining why he keeps a color photo of himself above his locker

CURSE OF MULDOON

A famous hockey story involves the curse placed on the Chicago Black Hawks by fired coach Pete Muldoon.

The late Jim Coleman admitted he had a hangover, common during that period of his career, when he "discovered" the fabled Curse of Muldoon. At the time, the late 1950s, Coleman was a sports columnist for the *Toronto Globe and Mail* who was renowned for weaving fantasy into his breezy columns.

ONE SEASON TO WIN

A much-quoted part of hockey folklore, Coleman's tale concerned Pete Muldoon, the coach of the Chicago Black Hawks in 1926–27, their first season in the expanded NHL. The Hawks, owned by the erratic Major Frederic McLaughlin, joined the NHL in the big expansion into the U.S. In their debut, the Black Hawks finished third in the American Division, then lost to the Boston Bruins in the playoffs. McLaughlin, who changed coaches about as often as he did ties, fired Muldoon, telling him that the Hawks had the talent for a much better finish.

IRISH CURSE TO NEVER FINISH FIRST

"Over the years, writers covering the NHL ridiculed the many coaching changes with the Black Hawks," Coleman said. "I wasn't at my best after a night of partying and I had a column deadline without an idea. The Muldoon yarn was one I had been kicking around and, with nothing else to write, I went with it." In Coleman's column the next day, Muldoon's response to McLaughlin's firing was, "If you fire me, I'll put an Irish curse on your team that will last forever. The Black Hawks will never be first in the NHL."

COLEMAN PSYCHES OUT TEAM FOR 40 YEARS

The Black Hawks did not finish first over the next 40 years—they were last 14 times—until the club led by Bobby Hull and Stan Mikita won the pennant in the 1966–67 season. "The 'curse' story got big play then, much to my embarrassment," Coleman said. "I wrote a piece explaining my creation of the curse of Muldoon but it received little attention. The end of the 'curse' was too good a yarn." Coleman continued to write well into his 80s.

FROM RENFREW TO REPLAYS

Frank and Lester Patrick wrote the hockey rule-book in the early years of the 20th century.

Watching today's game in a theatre-style seat with large high-definition screens showing instant replays of action performed by superbly conditioned athletes wearing space-age equipment, it can be difficult to realize that many of the rules governing the sport were conceived almost a century ago. In fact, the formative discussions on how modern hockey should be played ensued around a boarding-house dinner table in the Ottawa Valley town of Renfrew, Ontario. Many of those ideas entered the rule book a few years later, but across Canada in British Columbia.

PATRICK PIONEERS

Lester and Frank Patrick were two early stars on the ice, and pioneers and financiers in hockey's development and growth into a true professional sport. Being in control of a league, the Pacific Coast Hockey Association, based in an area with little or no hockey heritage presented many wrinkles, but the Patricks applied their brilliant hockey minds to not only introducing the sport, but also to improving the sport. More than 20 rules and countless strategy ideas conceived by the Patricks remain in the NHL book today.

VALLEY BOYS

When silver mining magnate M.J. O'Brien bankrolled the formation of the National Hockey Association, he also signed several top stars for his own Renfrew team for high salaries. The team became known as the Millionaires, comprising the likes of the Patrick brothers, Cyclone Taylor, goalie Bert Lindsay, Sprague Cleghorn and Newsy Lalonde. Most players lived in the same boarding house, where post-dinner conversations often lasted well into the evening with hockey as the one and only subject. The Patrick boys suggested dozens of ideas they had on the game.

HOW TO STOP A CYCLONE

"Frank and Lester never stopped talking about ways to make the game better," said Taylor, one the top pure talents of hockey history. "They would throw out new ideas and wanted the other guys to shoot holes in them. The debates often became very heated." A Taylor habit inspired one NHA rule change. Because teams dressed no extra players, a fast-paced game over 60 minutes was exhausting. Especially for Taylor, for his rover position demanded that he cover the complete ice surface. So, to earn the occasional breather Taylor would flip the puck into the stands. Lester Patrick saw that as an unnecessary stoppage in play that interrupted the action. His suggestion of a two-minute delay of game penalty for deliberately shooting the puck into the seats was adopted by the league.

RULES TO LAST LIFETIMES

Using the family fortune from the lumber industry, the Patricks founded the PCHA and built arenas to house the teams in Vancouver and Victoria. When PCHA play started in 1912, the rule and strategy changes, many produced by Frank Patrick, came regularly.

Up to that point, offside calls were made for *all* forward passes and when a game involving quick skaters resulted in 15 such whistles in the first five minutes, the Patricks had had enough! Their long-discussed idea of using blue lines to divide the ice into three zones with unrestricted passing in the neutral zone, later in all areas of the ice, made the game much more exciting for players and spectators.

After a trip to the family's native Ireland, where Frank saw runners in a cross-country harrier race wearing easily visible numbers for quick identification, he placed numbers on his PCHA team's hockey sweaters. The numerals, plus the programs with names and numbers sold to fans, remain in place.

When Frank saw a polo match in Ireland where the referee awarded a penalty shot, he decided this, too, would be a good addition to hockey.

Lester felt a rule stating that goalies had to stand erect at all times and could not fall to the ice was absurd. Legislation that permitted goalies to stop the puck by whatever means they chose—except throwing the stick at the puck—was soon in place.

Goalie acrobatics (can you imagine a game without them?) were an immediate fan favorite.

In 1918 the Seattle Metropolitans were far in front of the PCHA, killing attendance in the league. Up to that point, the team leading the standings at the end of the schedule was declared champion. Frank Patrick's idea of a playoff between the top two teams revived interest in the remaining games and produced large gates plus concessions for the playoff series. Other sports leagues quickly saw the wisdom of having playoffs and copied Patrick's notion.

The PCHA had several excellent playmakers who received no official credit when their passes resulted in goals. The Patricks solved that by awarding assists on goals counting as one point, the same as a goal.

When stoppages of play anytime a player kicked the puck resulted in yet more aggravating halts to the action (and they say there are too many whistles today!), a PCHA rule allowed the puck to be kicked anywhere except into the net.

The Patricks decreed that PCHA games would have two referees and also that teams would play home games on the same night every week, a pleasing move to fans.

When the Victoria Cougars, with Lester Patrick as manager-coach, beat the Montreal Canadiens in the 1925 Stanley Cup final, their big edge was in changing forward lines on the fly. The PCHA had increased rosters from seven to 11 skaters and the quick line change was part of hockey in the west.

END OF AN ERA, BUT LEAVING A LEGACY

The PCHA could not survive the NHL's expansion into the U.S. in the mid-1920s, as several of the new clubs were to be stocked with players from the west. The NHL rule book also included a large number of rules from the PCHA; that many have not changed is a tribute to the Patricks' incredible hockey foresight.

MORENZ MONEY, NOT MORE MONEY

How the Montreal Canadiens landed one of the greatest players for what now seems a ridiculously small amount.

That Howie Morenz was not signed by an NHL team quickly remains a hockey enigma, still debated by folks in western Ontario where Morenz grew up. He was born in Mitchell and raised in Stratford, the railway hub in the early 1920s, and later the Shakespeare capital of North America. The teenage Morenz was a fabled amateur player with dazzling speed, superhuman puck control and enough toughness to handle any defensive tactic used against him. In what ranks among the worst recruiting errors in hockey, the scouts for the Toronto St. Pats were not enthusiastic about his pro potential.

I'LL BE WORKING ON THE RAILROAD

The Montreal Canadiens, who paid little attention to players outside the province of Quebec, did not look seriously at the "Stratford Streak," until he was 20 years old. Canadiens' boss Leo Dandurand asked referee Lou Marsh, who also was sports editor and columnist for the *Toronto Star*, to check on the kid who was attracting attention in Stratford. Marsh sent the Canadiens two letters of praise for Morenz, urging them to act quickly because the St. Pats were showing interest. Dandurand sent former NHL goalie Riley Hern to Stratford with a $2,500 per season contract to offer Morenz. But Morenz had a good job with the railway and liked playing intermediate hockey. While the Toronto club was preparing an offer, Marsh told Dandurand that Morenz and his family had a few small debts that he wanted to clear up.

CASH ONLY, PLEASE

Dandurand sent Cecil Hart, later a great coach with the Canadiens, to Stratford with a batch of small bills. When Hart spread the $850 on the Morenz kitchen table, Howie was wide-eyed, and his father signed the contract because his son was under

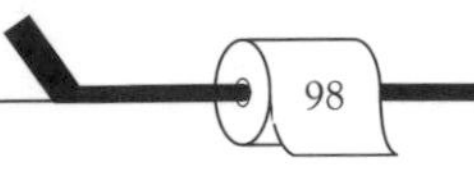

the legal age of 21. A negative reaction in Stratford led Morenz to send Dandurand a cheque for the $850 with regrets that he could not join the Canadiens. But Dandurand had learned that Morenz was paid $800 a season to play in Stratford, a violation of amateur rules, and threatened to expose the fact.

STAR POWER

When Morenz traveled to Montreal to plead with Dandurand for his freedom, the wily Canadiens' executive had an associate summon every Canadien player available at a restaurant where he took the downcast Howie for lunch. Such illustrious players as Sprague Cleghorn, Georges Vezina and Aurel Joliat treated Morenz as if he were a star, not a frightened kid. Morenz agreed to attend training camp for two weeks. The two weeks turned into one of the NHL's greatest careers, by a player who dominated his era enough to earn the title "the Babe Ruth of hockey."

* * * * *

HEY, GOOD LOOKIN'

"I was 14 when I lost them [his front teeth]. The main thing was we won that game, so I was the happiest. You hate to lose your teeth and the game, too."

—Bill Barber, forward and coach, Philadelphia Flyers

"Most people who don't know I play hockey think I was thrown through a plate-glass window or something."

—Theoren Fleury, former Calgary Flames defenceman

"We get nose jobs all the time in the NHL, and we don't even have to go to the hospital."

—Brad Park, former New York Rangers defenceman

"I had all my own teeth and I wanted to keep it that way."

—major leagues pitcher Tom Glavine, on why he decided to play professional baseball rather than hockey

HERO FOR A GAME

While the top stars usually produce in the crunch, a few modest workers have had big moments at important times.

The hockey cliché goes that in crunch situations, especially in the Stanley Cup playoffs, watch out for the "little guy": the fourth-line forward, little-used defenceman or backup goalie; the unlikely hero who jumps out of obscurity to make the big play when it counts the most. This outlook is more myth than reality—the big stars who usually produce are also most likely to score when the heat is on—but enough examples exist to illustrate that the little dogs can have their day in the sun. Perhaps the fact that they are not well-known threats means they can go unnoticed until they find the room for the big move.

MY NAME IS MUD

Mud Bruneteau and Ken Doraty are the NHL's two prized examples of the unlikely hero. They were fill-in forwards when they scored overtime goals that ended the two longest games ever played. Bruneteau, 21 at the time, had spent half the 1935–36 season with the Detroit Olympics of the International League. Promoted to the Red Wings when regulars were injured, he scored only two goals in spot duty over 24 games. In the Stanley Cup semifinals the Red Wings met the Montreal Maroons, at the time an NHL power. The opening game of that series started at 8:30 P.M. one night and ended at 2:30 A.M. the next morning. Not a goal was scored in the near-equivalent of three games until Bruneteau, used a little more through each period to give the exhausted big guns a breather, scored after 116:30 of overtime to give the Wings a 1–0 win. Bruneteau played another ten seasons for the Red Wings, was a member of three Stanley Cup winners and scored 139 goals. But Mud is mainly remembered as the guy who ended the longest NHL game ever played.

133 POUNDS BEFORE OR AFTER THE GAME?

The record Bruneteau broke had been set by Ken Doraty, an even more out-of-the-blue hero. He was a 5-foot-7, 133-pound winger who had played a few games with the Chicago Black Hawks in 1926–27, then made it back to the NHL in 1932–33 as the Toronto Maple Leafs' extra forward. In a semifinal game, the Leafs and Boston Bruins played 106:46 of OT before Doraty, who had played very little in the previous eight periods, scored to win the series for the Leafs. Doraty played only 37 NHL games over the remainder of his career but in oft-told tales of Maple Leaf history, his is one of the first names that pops up.

TALK ABOUT LEAVING IT TILL THE LAST SECOND

Only two of 20 Stanley Cup finals that have reached the decisive game have also gone to overtime. Both were won by the Detroit Red Wings of the 1950s, but even though they had an assortment of big stars at the time—notably Gordie Howe and Ted Lindsay—the OT Cup-winners were scored by two "foot soldiers," Pete Babando and Tony Leswick.

During the 1950 playoffs, when the Wings won a tough seven-game series against the Leafs, defenceman Leo Reise, who scored 28 goals in a nine-season career, twice won games with OT goals. Their seventh game against the New York Rangers was a dogfight, tied 3–3 after 60 minutes. At 8:31 of the second overtime, Babando, a journeyman winger who scored 86 goals in 351 NHL games and had a long minor league career, scored to give the Wings the Cup. It was the final playoff goal of his career.

In the 1954 final, the Wings and Montreal Canadiens split the first six games and were tied 1–1 after 60 minutes in the seventh. Leswick, who had a solid 12-season NHL career mainly because of his strong defensive play, fired a shot that struck the glove of Canadiens defenceman Doug Harvey and eluded goalie Jacques Plante at 4:29 of overtime to give the Cup to the Wings.

STICK IT TO 'EM, ALFIE

Alfie Moore was a skinny goalie who had spent 15 seasons in minor-pro hockey before he played 18 NHL games with the New York Americans in 1936–37. He had spent the 1937–38 season in the minors and was back in Toronto working his summer job with a dry cleaner when he received a call to report to Maple Leaf Gardens, where the Maple Leafs and Black Hawks were in the Cup final. Hawk goalie Mike Karakas had a broken toe and couldn't play and Leaf boss

Conn Smythe had refused the Rangers' Davey Kerr as a replacement, suggesting Moore for job. Moore told Smythe that he would win the game and he did, 3–1, with a brilliant display as the Hawks tied the series. Moore was barred by the NHL from the next game but Karakas, sore toe and all, returned to lead the Hawks to the Cup.

THE SONS OF SUDDEN-DEATH HILL

Sudden-Death Hill sounds like a hit man for the mob, but Mel Hill of the Boston Bruins earned the nickname when he scored three overtime goals in one series against the New York Rangers in the 1939 playoffs. Only one other player scored three OT winners in one spring: Rocket Richard of the Canadiens in 1951. The 2004 playoffs were a big time for the unlikely. Six players who had only one goal in postseason play saved the score for a big occasion —an overtime winner. Steve Montador (Calgary Flames), Marek Svatos (Colorado Avalanche), Nikos Dimitrakos (San Jose Sharks), Steve Ott (Dallas Stars), Mike Fisher (Ottawa Senators) and teenager Patrice Bergeron (Boston Bruins) produced at precisely the right time for their teams.

* * * * *

BY ANY OTHER NAME

Hockey has had some real doozies—players and their nicknames.

Chicoutimi Cucumber — Georges Vezina
The Dominator — Dominik Hasek
The Flower — Guy Lafleur
Golden Jet — Bobby Hull
Grapes — Don Cherry
The Great One — Wayne Gretzky
Grim Reaper — Stu Grimson
Mr. Hockey — Gordie Howe
Pocket Rocket — Henri Richard
The Rat — Ken Linseman
Russian Rocket — Pavel Bure
Stratford Streak — Howie Morenz
Super Mario — Mario Lemieux

SOPHOMORE JINX

Sure he's rookie of the year, but now what? How to live up to the reputation of being a Calder Trophy winner.

He makes a big splash in his professional sports debut, perhaps earning the award as best rookie to confirm glowing prospects for a splendid career. Occasionally, a funny thing occurs on the way to stardom: It doesn't happen. Maintaining first-season performance standards has proven to be difficult, leading to the cautionary words: Beware the sophomore jinx.

STATS COURTESY BATHROOM READERS' INSTITUTE

A check of the first 71 players (1933–2003) to win the Calder Memorial Trophy as top NHL rookie reveals that 38 of them more-or-less matched their rookie performance, 13 improved their work by a noteworthy margin, and 19 suffered from the so-called "jinx," a noticeable sag in their play the second time around.

"Rookie award winners sometimes figure they have it made and not step up their play enough to show improvement in their second season," said Scotty Bowman, the NHL coach with the most career wins and Stanley Cup victories. "Then, too, they're much better known in their second season and are watched more closely. Quite a few rookies learn their way around the league in their first season, then increase their effort to, at least, stay at the level they've established. Many players have used that consistent start as the springboard to a good career."

SECOND-YEAR SAG

The play of several top rookies declined noticeably in their sophomore seasons, giving credence to the jinx theory. The Toronto Maple Leafs had two Calder winners in the mid-1960s—defenceman Kent Douglas in 1963 and winger Brit Selby in 1966—and both spent large parts of their second seasons in the minors. Eric Vail of the Atlanta Flames scored 39 goals to win the Calder in 1974–75 but could manage only 16 in his sophomore term. Gus Bodnar of the Leafs had 22 goals and 62 points as 1942–43 Calder winner, then sagged to eight goals and 44 points in season two.

Kilby McDonald of the New York Rangers had 15 goals in his 1939–40 Calder season, five goals the next term.

OVER THE HILL AT TWENTY-ONE

Vail, Bodnar and McDonald were among eight Calder winners who never equalled the statistics of their first season, though several still had decent careers. Goalies Frank Brimsek of the Bruins (1.80 average in 43 rookie season games, 1.25 in 12 playoff games) and Roger Crozier of the Detroit Red Wings (40 wins, 2.52 average) had lengthy stays in the league but never matched their remarkable first-year numbers. Howie Meeker, Jimmy McFadden and Pentii Lunds were others with a first year as their best statistically.

GUMP DUMPED

Goalie Lorne "Gump" Worsley had perhaps the most unusual second-year experience. Worsley collected the Calder in 1952–53 when he had a 3.06 goals-against average in 52 games for the NHL's last-place team. But the next season, Worsley was demoted to the Vancouver Canucks of the Western League for the entire year, replaced by 28-year old "rookie" Johnny Bower. Worsley and Bower reversed jobs again for the 1954–55 schedule.

OUSTED BY ULCERS

Frank McCool was one Calder winner who was struck hard by the sophomore jinx. In 1944–45, McCool backstopped the Maple Leafs to the Stanley Cup, but only by gulping litres of milk prior to games and between periods to combat stomach ulcers. McCool played 22 games the next season before his stomach woes became so difficult to handle that he had to retire.

GREAT LEAPS FORWARD

Several large steps forward were taken in second seasons. Winger Pavel Bure of the Vancouver Canucks had an impressive Calder season with a 34-26-60 point mark in 65 games, then lifted his numbers to 60-50-110 in 83 games as a sophomore. The eagerly anticipated Mario Lemieux of the Pittsburgh Penguins did not disappoint as a Calder rookie with 43 goals and 100 points but that was just the appetizer. Lemieux produced 48 goals and 141 points in season two! Goalie Terry Sawchuk built a tough act for himself to follow as a freshman goalie of the Detroit Red Wings in 1950–51 when he had a 44-13-13 win-loss-tie record with 11 shutouts and a 1.99 average in 70 games. As a sophomore, Sawchuk again won 44 but had a dozen shutouts and a 1.90 average; in the playoffs, he allowed only five goals in eight games (four shutouts, 0.63 GAA) as the Wings swept to the Stanley Cup.

Winger Gaye Stewart made a splendid Maple Leaf debut in 1942–43, scoring 24 goals to win the Calder. But Stewart had to wait three years to test out the jinx: He entered the World War II Canadian Army after his rookie season and didn't return to hockey until 1945–46, when he led the league in goals with 37.

RINGER OF THE YEAR

The rules governing the Calder were changed after Sergei Makarov, 31 at the time and a veteran of more than a dozen years with the Russian national team, won the "rookie" award for an outstanding 1989–90 first season with the Calgary Flames. Legislation was passed that offseason to limit the Calder to players 25 years or under by September 15 of their eligible season.

* * * * *

"I wouldn't ever go into a season trying to re-build from scratch. You can't trade good players for high picks because the world ends at the end of each season. Live with the idea that the world is flat and you're coming to the edge."

—Neil Smith, former Rangers president–GM

"I don't want to talk about today's market anymore because nobody can make sense of what the market is. It's all over the map. There's a bunch of lunatics out there throwing money away. I'm sick and tired of it. It's lunacy. Punch me in the head and tell me I'm stupid, but that's the way I feel. There's no sense to it anymore."

—Kevin Lowe, GM,
former defenceman, Edmonton Oilers

DIRECT LINES

NHL history is dotted with threesomes that accumulated high point totals and dazzled with their moves.

There was the Production Line, the Punch Line and the Krauts plus the A-Line, the Pony Line and more than a few lines with the "Kid" handle. Try Million Dollar Line, the Scooters, the Triple Crown Line and the French Connection. And there were some good threesomes that simply defied being tagged with a snappy title.

LINES IN DECLINE

Through NHL history, when three forwards played strongly as a unit and had stayed together for a couple seasons, they were handed a nickname that became part of hockey folklore. The majority of the fabled lines played in the earlier NHL eras. Small rosters employed as few as a dozen skaters plus a goaltender, which usually meant two complete forward combinations that all but eliminated the coaches' opportunities to juggle lines. As the number of players used in games increased, up to the 18 skaters and two goalies in the new-millennium NHL, coaches could deploy the troops in differing combos on every change, lines tailored specifically to work against the trio the opposition tried.

"By the 1980s, the amount of line juggling had increased to the point where you never could predict the combination that would be used by the other team and a coach had to make quick changes—sometimes just one player—to try and nullify what the other team was trying," said Glen Sather, general manager and head coach of the Edmonton Oilers when they won five Stanley Cup championships from 1984 to 1990. "Since then, a pattern has been for two players to be linemates over the long haul with a variety of mates in the third slot, depending on the situation."

IN LINES OF TWO

The NHL's two great offensive stars in the 1980s and 1990s, Wayne Gretzky and Mario Lemieux, were not the wheel-horses of long-term lines. During his record-smashing days with the Oilers, Gretzky was partnered with right-winger Jari Kurri and while big

Dave Semenko often played left side in a protector role, a variety of Oilers worked that slot. Lemieux and left-winger Kevin Stevens were a powerful combo for the Pittsburgh Penguins in the early 1990s, including two Cup crowns, but no player staked a permanent claim on the their right flank.

LINES ON THE ICE

Punch Line: Goal-scoring genius Maurice "Rocket" Richard was right-winger on a line with slick center Elmer Lach and gritty Toe Blake. Richard specialized in placing the puck in the net on chances created by Lach, an underrated player who twice won scoring titles, and Blake, an efficient two-way winger. Richard later played on a splendid line with his younger brother Henri "Pocket Rocket" Richard and Dickie Moore when the Canadiens wore the crown in five consecutive seasons from 1956 to 1960.

Production Line: When Gordie Howe joined the Detroit Red Wings in 1946 at 18, he quickly took a spot on the right wing with center Sid Abel and Ted Lindsay. All three were all-star candidates with complete skills and toughness and because they could do it all, the line is rated among the most difficult ever to check.

Kraut Line: Milt Schmidt, Bobby Bauer and Woody Dumart all came from Kitchener, Ontario, an area with a heavy German ancestry (it used to be called Berlin), thus the Kraut nickname when they joined the Boston Bruins. When World War II started, the line was called the Kitchener Kids but that never took. Had Canadian military service not chopped four seasons out of their careers' prime, the Krauts likely would have registered more than the 1939 and 1941 Cup triumphs.

The Pony Line: Three brilliant little western Canadians, Max and Doug Bentley and Bill Mosienko, excelled for the Chicago Black Hawks for a half-dozen seasons in the 1940s. Ultra-quick and splendid at passing, they always looked like boys among men but their goal totals were strictly adult.

The A-Line: Named for the A-train subway that ran under the old Madison Square Garden in New York, the line of Frank

Boucher with Bill and Bun Cook is rated as the best ever by many old-timers, especially because of its passing. Owners of complete skills, they produced an average of more than two points per game from 1926 to 1937 and two New York Rangers Cup titles.

The Kid Line: The name has been carried by many young lines but the definitive "Kids" were the Toronto Maple Leafs trio of Joe Primeau, Charlie Conacher and Busher Jackson. They all came out of Toronto junior hockey to be key players in building a strong team to move into the new Maple Leaf Gardens in 1931, winning the Cup that season. All-star selections and scoring titles followed and all three became heroes across Canada because of Foster Hewitt's *Hockey Night in Canada* radio broadcasts.

The Espo Line: The Bruins' extraordinary line of Phil Esposito, Wayne Cashman and Ken Hodge produced more than 2,000 points in almost 700 games from 1967 to 1976 and earned two Stanley Cup wins. Esposito broke goal-scoring records galore, many on passes from his big linemates. Having the mighty Bobby Orr on defence didn't hurt their offensive cause.

The French Connection: Gil Perreault, Richard Martin and Rene Robert led the expansion Buffalo Sabres to quick prominence in the 1970s.

The Million Dollar and Scooter Lines: Big for the Black Hawks, the Million Dollar line of Bobby Hull, Bill Hay and Murray Balfour were a big part of the 1961 Stanley Cup. The swift Scooters, Stan Mikita, Kenny Wharram and Doug Mohns, stood out for six seasons later that decade.

The Triple Crown and Trio Grande Lines: Allow the fans to name things and these silly tags are what happens. Marcel Dionne, Dave Taylor and Charlie Simmer were an exceptional trio for the Los Angeles Kings while Bryan Trottier, Mike Bossy and Clark Gillies, also known as the Long Island Lighting Company, led the New York Islanders to four consecutive Stanley Cup wins in the early 1980s.

HOCKEY IN THE TRENCHES

During the two world wars, not all of hockey's battles were fought off the continent with tanks and guns.

The German tanks that twice rumbled across Europe, plunging the planet into World Wars I and II, shook the National Hockey League hard. But the NHL was founded in 1917 even as World War I raged on. And while World War II created an enormous challenge for the NHL to continue play, government officials felt that the games would provide some relief from the depressing headlines for the folks at home. Despite the loss of many players to the armed forces during the two conflicts, the competitive factor of hockey did not weaken during the much more serious battles. Team owners and management and even the military competed vigorously to recruit players from a diminished pool of talent.

YOU'VE BEEN DRAFTED! (NO, NOT TO THE NHL...)

Some old-timers claim that some of the finest hockey ever played was in the war years. In fact, various areas of the military tried all sorts of deals to land the best NHL players in their units, in order to build the strongest hockey rosters for competition in the service leagues. During the basic training periods, most bases iced teams. But during both wars, disputes often arose over which team had first call on players' services: the service club or the team back home. Training schedules and mobilization calls forced major lineup changes or even pullouts from competition.

DODGING BULLETS

World War I broke out in late 1914 and by the 1915–16 season as many as 17 service teams were in competition, most of them at the senior amateur level. With several military training bases in the area, Winnipeg was a hockey stronghold. The Winnipeg 61st Battalion team, led by future Hockey Hall of Fame inductee "Bullet" Joe Simpson, won the 1916 Allan Cup as Canadian senior champions. All players of age on the superlative Winnipeg Falcons senior club, including Hall of Famer Frank Fredrickson, enlisted as a group—training with the 233rd Battalion in Portage La Prairie and traveling to Winnipeg for games in the aptly named Manitoba Patriotic League. At the end of the 1916–17 season the entire battalion was shipped overseas.

DUKE DISPUTE

A wartime dispute over star player Duke Keats led to the formation of the NHL. A member of the Toronto Blueshirts in the National Hockey Association, Keats and other players enlisted in the 228th Battalion, which entered a team in the NHA for the 1916–17 season. Blueshirts owner Eddie Livingstone, who fought a never-ending battle with rival owners, won an appeal that forced Keats to play for the Blueshirts until the battalion went overseas in February 1917. Fed up with Livingstone's antics, the other owners then formed the NHL as a way to shed the troublesome Toronto owner.

HORRIBLE LOSSES

Winnipeg senior hockey was hit hard by the war as several players lost their lives in Europe. Frank McGee, the great star of the Ottawa Silver Seven, died in France in 1918 and Scotty Davidson, leading scorer with the 1914 Stanley Cup champion Blueshirts, was killed in Belgium in 1915. Hobey Baker, the top U.S. amateur player at Princeton University, where he was captain of both the hockey and football teams, became a fighter pilot. A member of the fabled Lafayette Escadrille fighter unit, Baker survived the war missions but shortly after the armistice was signed in 1918, he took a plane up for a "farewell flight" and died in a crash. The award to the top player in U.S. college hockey carries his name.

SMYTHE HEROICS

Among the first hockey men involved in World War II, which started in 1939, was Conn Smythe, owner of the Toronto Maple Leafs. As a player, Smythe was captain of the University of Toronto team that won the Ontario junior title in 1915, right before he and most of his teammates enlisted in the service for World War I. A strong NHL owner from 1926 on and builder of Maple Leaf Gardens, Smythe, who earned a Major ranking, formed the Sportsmen's Battery of the Royal Canadian Artillery with many sports stars in its ranks and took it overseas, seeing heavy combat himself in the anti-aircraft battery. He was badly wounded in 1944.

KRAUTS IN THE RCAF

A large number of players were drafted or enlisted for World War II, and the two top teams in the immediate prewar time—the Boston Bruins and New York Rangers—had their rosters depleted. As in World War I, service hockey teams were strong. The Bruins' brilliant Kraut Line of Milt Schmidt, Woody Dumart and Bobby Bauer enlisted and played for the Royal Canadian Air Force team based in Ottawa, winning the Allan Cup in 1942. A year later, the Ottawa Commandos army team, assembled by Frank Boucher of the Rangers, won the senior crown.

ON THE HOME FRONT

In the early years of the war, a draft for home defence with a 30-day training period gave players a chance to remain in the game. That changed as the war progressed, when training was lengthened and the athletes shipped overseas. Because Canadian military health standards were so high, many players with hockey injuries were rejected for service. Some scorn was heaped on players not healthy enough to serve but still able to play pro hockey. Because the Quebec government fought the compulsory draft, the Canadiens retained a powerful roster through the war years. Although many Maple Leafs enlisted or were drafted, the club stayed strong; the hockey hotbed of Toronto had many junior and senior players the Leafs could use to stay in contention. Some future stars, such as 17-year-old Ted Kennedy, made early starts to their NHL careers.

COMING HOME TO A DIFFERENT NHL

The New York Americans folded after a 1941–42 season and the other U.S. teams, especially the New York Rangers, Boston and Chicago, struggled, often filling their lineups with whatever players were available. The Rangers used Saskatchewan senior goalie Steve Buzinski for nine games in the 1942–43 season, in which he surrendered 55 goals. He became known as Steve "The Puck Goes Inski" Buzinski. Overtime in schedule games was ended to allow teams to catch trains on time and the introduction of the center red line allowed the use of long clearing passes. When the war ended, the veterans returned and combined with a big crop of young players who had had a chance to play in their absence. The NHL entered a period of prosperity.

HOCKEY HERO

The award to the top U.S. college hockey player honors the first great American puckster and flying ace Hobey Baker.

Hobey Baker could have been a character created by a fiction writer: a handsome, dashing, risk-taking member of a wealthy Philadelphia family who became an exceptional hockey player and a World War I flying ace. But that's exactly what Baker was, the first homegrown star of U.S. hockey, and exactly why the annual award for the top player in U.S. college hockey carries his name.

HOBEY KNOWS HOCKEY

From 1910 to 1914, Baker used his formidable athletic ability to captain both the football and hockey teams at Princeton. He was an excellent running back and, newspaper reports from that time claim, even better at hockey as a rover with dazzling speed and agility and splendid stickhandling. When he led Princeton to an undefeated season in his sophomore year and scored 92 points, Baker drew big crowds everywhere the team played.

HOME OF THE BRAVE

When Baker graduated, the pros were eager to sign him. But he didn't want to leave the east to join the Portland Rosebuds, and not even a salary of $3,500 could lure him to the Montreal Wanderers. Because money was no problem, he joined the amateur St. Nick's team in New York, a good club that beat a few top Canadian sides in exhibitions. When WW I started, Baker trained as a fighter pilot and was among the first members of the fabled Lafayette Escadrille Squadron that was shipped to France in 1917. He painted his one-seat Spad fighter orange and black Princeton colors and was as natural at airborne dog fights as he was at hockey. Bakey is credited with shooting down three German planes.

ONE LAST FLIGHT

When the war ended Baker was at loose ends without flying or sports. A month after the armistice, he drove to the airfield and said he was going "on one last flight." He reached 2,000 feet when the engine went dead and his efforts to glide back to base failed. The plane crashed and Baker died at age 26. But the memories of him are preserved in an impressive trophy.

* * * * *

"I just don't know what to think. I play in Colorado, they tell me they like me, and I get traded. I play in Calgary, and at the end of the season the GM tells me he likes me, and I get traded. I just hope my fiancée doesn't tell me she likes me."

—Chris Drury, forward,
Colorado Avalanche, Calgary Flames

"We have to get families back in the game, get back where Saturday night, everything stops. A case of beer comes out and a bottle of rye and anyone who comes to the house, they better want to watch hockey."

—Bobby Hull

* * * * *

THE UPSIDE OF CONCUSSIONS

"One good thing is that when I forget something, maybe I could tell my wife that it's brain damage."

—Murray Eaves, the Minnesota North Stars forward
after a second concussion in 3 months

* * * * *

"Listen fellas. I've got to tell you this. I'm not the greatest coach in the world. But if you look around this room you'll see that I don't have the greatest players either."

—Bernie Geoffrion, former coach,
New York Rangers and Atlanta Flames

HOW TO MAKE ICE

Uncle John goes to Florida to find out how they manage to keep the ice frozen in that heat.

If a city is granted an NHL franchise, it naturally must have an arena to host said club. How much would a city have to shell out to build, from scratch, an NHL arena? According to 2005 economics, the price tag would range from 200 to 250 million American dollars.

FREEZING IN FLORIDA

A good chunk of that money would go to the building and maintenance of the ice surface and its necessary parts. Mandatory NHL ice arena building figures, for all rinks, are that they be 200 feet long, 85 feet wide, and that each "corner" (though technically there are no corners) have a 28-foot radius. International hockey arenas are the same length, but are 100 feet wide. But how is an NHL ice surface built? How does the ice stay frozen? To answer these and other questions, Uncle John caught up with Ken Friedenberger, Director of Facility Operations (that is, ice maintenance) for the St. Petersburg Times Forum, home of the 2004 Stanley Cup champions Tampa Bay Lightning.

TRY TO AVOID THE SPAGHETTI

Friedenberger explains: First comes a sand and gravel base; then comes another sand and gravel base to prevent permafrost (perpetually frozen subsoil). "Permafrost," said Ken, "will eventually crack the piping and turn it into a big mess, which would look like spaghetti."

A WHOLE LOTTA ANTIFREEZE

"The piping" that Friedenberger refers to is perhaps the most important part of the building. A massive chilled concrete slab, with five to ten miles of antifreeze-filled piping in it, keeps the ice frozen. In Tampa the pipe is made of steel, though it can be made of other materials (a common one is high-density plastic). "Our concrete is 60,000 pounds per square inch, which is very dense," said Friedenberger. In Tampa the antifreeze is chilled by two massive air-conditioning units, generating approximately 200 tons of refrigeration. Some NHL rinks have as much as 300 to 400 tons of coolant.

HOCKEY'S LIFEBLOOD

Just as blood must continually flow through a person's veins, an NHL arena must have this antifreeze (or other forms of coolant; brine water was commonly used until it was discovered that the salt corroded piping) constantly flowing through its pipes so that the ice does not melt. The water is processed through the piping so that the surface of the concrete is below 32°F—the temperature at which water freezes to ice.

TWENTY-FOUR LAYERS OF GOODNESS

Players skate on ice, not concrete, so now comes the long process of putting layers of ice atop the concrete. "Here in Tampa we have 24 layers of ice. Each NHL arena will be different, according to what temperature each arena is kept at, as well as other factors," explained Ken. The first layers of ice in Tampa atop the concrete are "50 percent city water and 50 percent de-ionized water," stated Friedenberger. "This seems to cause very little 'snow' [from skate blades] and the ice holds up well. Some cities use well-water, others different forms of water. Each NHL arena has its own mixture."

KEEP IT COOL

The first layer of ice is given time to freeze on the concrete. Then the other layers of ice can be produced. At the home rink of the Lightning, six to eight new layers of ice are put down before the lines are painted. Each layer of ice varies in depth. When all of this is finished, the ice surface temperature runs between 22°F and 26°F. "We like to keep the temperature in the Forum anywhere from 60°F to 63°F with about 40 percent relative humidity. That's about what everybody in the NHL does," Ken said.

AND FINALLY, THE ZAMBONI

Zamboni machines resurface the ice before practices and between periods. Once the entire ice surface system is built, the chief duty of NHL ice maintenance folks is to keep the system operational. It is an unfortunate twist of fate that NHL ice maintenance chiefs' work—like that of referees—only gets noticed when a mistake or problem occurs.

DON'T BOTHER TO KNOCK

How a hockey coach was intimidated by Gordie Howe even when Ol' Elbows was wearing his pajamas.

Harry Neale spins the story with a smile and respect in his voice for the man many feel is hockey's greatest, Gordie Howe. Neale, who had a solid career as a college, junior, WHA and NHL coach and manager, was 40 when he coached Howe with the WHA New England Whalers in 1977–78.

STILL A FORCE AT FIFTY

Howe realized his longtime dream of playing with his sons Marty and Mark when he ended a two-year retirement from the Detroit Red Wings and joined the WHA Houston Aeros. The Aeros won the WHA playoff title in 1974 and 1975 with the Howe family in a prominent role. After two more seasons the Houston club, losing money despite on-ice success, allowed the Howe gang to shift to the Whalers, based in Hartford, Connecticut. "Coaching Gordie—a hockey legend and a wonderful man, a force on the ice at 50—was a great experience," Neale said. "He intimidated people, including me, even when I couldn't see him."

DEPRIVING AN OLD MAN OF SLEEP

The Whalers had a veteran club, players with considerable hockey mileage, who, occasionally, enjoyed life's pleasures well into the evening. Late in the season when the team had a shot at catching the leading Winnipeg Jets, Neale wanted his club at its best in an important game.

"I had no bed checks that season but a few guys stretched the late-night thing a bit and we needed the two points, so I told them I would drop in at 10:30 the night before the game," Neale said. "I checked some rooms—everyone was in—then I found myself at the door of Gordie's room. Cripes, I was like a grade three teacher on a field trip and I was checking a kid ten years older than me. I stood there a minute or two, raised my hand to knock but couldn't make my knuckles hit the door. I must have put my hand up a half dozen times but I just couldn't do it. So I left and went to bed.

"The next morning at breakfast, Gordie said to me, 'Where the hell were you last night? I thought there was a bed check so I stayed up to answer the door. If I knew you weren't coming, I'd have been in bed at nine.'"

* * * * *

BLOOD SPORT

"This is the most excited you can be as a hockey player. As much as you hate a team like Colorado, you love to play 'em. The juices will be boiling, and the blood will be flowing. Let's clarify that; flowing through your body. Not on the ice."

—Kris Draper, 2004 Selke Trophy winner (Best Defensive Forward)

"It's going to be good to be on his side for a change. I'll save a lot of energy since I don't have to concentrate on whacking him. I'm pretty excited about that."

—Doug Gilmour on playing with Blackhawks teammate Chris Chelios

"The hockey lockout of 1994–1995 has been settled. They have stopped bickering...and can now get down to some serious bloodshed!"

—Conan O'Brien, host, "Late Night with Conan O'Brien"

"The people who yell and scream about hockey violence are a handful of intellectuals and newspapermen who never pay to get in to see a game. The fans, who shell out the money, have always liked good, rough hockey."

—Don Cherry

"If I get run into again, I'm taking someone with me. I lost one knee. I'll take a head if it happens again."

—Grant Fuhr, goaltender, Edmonton Oilers and Calgary Flames

STAY-AT-HOME CZECHS AND RUSSIANS

During the Cold War, many of the greatest hockey players in the world were hidden (from North Americans) behind the Iron Curtain.

The Cold War lasted from the end of World War II to 1989. It was at its frostiest in the 1950s, when the political powers of America and the former Soviet Union were continuously bickering. The 1950s were also the decade when North America would first hear rumblings of the "superpower" of Soviet hockey.

THAT'S RUSSIAN FOR "USSR"

The Soviet teams, with their familiar red and white "CCCP" uniforms and their *helmets* (the Soviets caught onto their usefulness a little earlier than we did), were led in the 1950s by superstar left-winger Vsevolod Bobrov. In 130 Soviet league games from 1946 to 1957, Bobrov somehow managed to pick up 254 goals! He was 6'1", weighed 185 pounds and had precise control of both his slap and wrist shots. Like 1990s Russian sniper Pavel Bure, Bobrov could stickhandle at top speed, which happened to be rocket speed, and he always wanted to have the puck. After he retired, Bobrov became a hockey coach, for decades, in Moscow.

IN THE FOOTSTEPS OF VSEVOLOD...

Of the numerous great Soviet players of the 1970s, three names are most prominent: Valeri Kharlamov, Alexander Maltsev and Valeri Vasiliev. That these three men logged a lot of ice time in their different positions—Kharlamov at left wing, Maltsev at center or right wing, and defenceman extraordinaire Vasiliev—made the Soviet teams tough to beat during this time. And add a guy named Vladislav Tretiak as starting goaltender and you get the spectre of the famed "Big Red Machine." In the three Winter Olympiads of the 1970s, they tallied two gold medals and one silver. Most North Americans were first exposed to the Big Red Machine at the memorable 1972 Summit Series.

KHARLAMOV HEROICS

If the Soviet teams had one true leader on the ice, it was probably Kharlamov. Gifted with lightning speed, he seemed to have unlimited moves in getting past opposing defencemen when he had the puck. He was shifty at only 5' 8" and 155 pounds, and very difficult to get a piece of. Yet Kharlamov wasn't afraid to be hit; he would frequently skate full-blast into the corners to fight for possession. From game one of the Summit Series, Canada knew that they'd their hands full in trying to stop Kharlamov. He scored two goals in the second period of the USSR's 7–3 win, and played relentlessly until Bobby Clarke cut him down with a cheap two-hander in game six, breaking his ankle and knocking him out of the series.

Sadly, Kharlamov's sterling career was cut short when he was killed in an automobile accident in 1981 at the age of 32.

MALTSEV THE MAGICIAN

When the talented line of Kharlamov, Boris Mikhailov and Vladimir Petrov wasn't on the ice, Alexander Maltsev led the charge. Purported to be the greatest stickhandler in Soviet history, Maltsev highlighted his playmaking abilities at the Summit Series by leading the team with five assists. He wasn't a fan of physical play, but was fast enough to avoid it more times than not.

VALERI THE IMPALER

Defenceman Valeri Vasiliev abruptly ended North American delusions that Russians couldn't handle physical hockey. Born in Bor, USSR (a town so small it's not even listed in the *Rand McNally*), Vasiliev was one of those defencemen who found great satisfaction in completely vanquishing opposing forwards. Overall he played for 17 years, most of them as captain of the national team. Vasiliev also had a tremendous slapshot, but generally played a rock-solid defensive game where he rarely ventured deep into the offensive zone.

GLORY DAYS BEHIND THE CURTAIN

Two players who had their "glory days" (to borrow a title from Bruce Springsteen) while playing in their native Czechoslovakia need to be mentioned. They are Vaclav Nedomansky—who *did* make it to the NHL but only at the age most players retire—and Jiri Holecek.

A big man at 6' 2" and 205 pounds, the supremely conditioned Nodomansky rarely suffered an injury over 19 years of top hockey. His trademark play was to floor the opposing goalie with a cannon-like slapshot while barrelling into the offensive zone. More than any other Czech player of the 1960s and 1970s, Nedomansky was the reason why Czechoslovakia won an Olympic silver medal in 1968 and a bronze medal in 1972. He defected to Canada in 1974 and played three years for the Toronto Toros of the World Hockey Association. In 1977 he jumped to the Red Wings, and after his "rookie" year as a 34-year old, he exploded for seasons of 38 and 35 goals. All while adjusting to a new style of hockey—pretty good for an old man. Nedomansky was almost 40 when he decided to quit.

HOLOCEK BEGAT HASEK

Goaltender Jiri Holecek has largely been forgotten, especially after the emergence of his countryman "The Dominator" Dominik Hasek in the 1990s, but from 1963 to 1981 only the USSR's Tretiak could match Holecek's feats in international hockey. Holecek was a fan favorite capable of electrifying audiences with his acrobatic saves. He was so ambidextrous that he'd be just as quick to fire his blocker hand out to stop a puck as he would his glove. He had a stellar 2.21 goals-against average in World Championship and Olympic hockey, and in the ten World Championships he played in, was named top goalie five times. Of course Vladislav Tretiak, whom Uncle John considers to be "the founding father of modern-day goaltending" also never played in the NHL, but we devoted an article to him alone. You can look for it next time you're in here...

HE SHOOTS! HE SCORES!

Foster Hewitt's call of Maple Leafs games made hockey Canada's biggest Saturday night recreation for decades.

On a hockey night, walk past the television networks' trucks, parked both inside and outside any NHL arena, step over what seems a mile of cables wired to dozens of cameras and microphones, count the scores of technicians and broadcasters required to show a game on television, and it's difficult to remember that it all started with the equivalent of a telephone call.

IT SEEMED THE THING TO SAY

On March 14, 1923, a simple phone line carried the first radio broadcast of a hockey game in Regina, Saskatchewan, a Western Canada League game between Regina and Edmonton on a medium in its infancy, the broadcaster, Pete Parker. Eight days later, it happened again. This time the station was CFCA, owned by the *Toronto Star*, and high interest in a junior playoff series between Toronto Parkdale and Kitchener inspired a request to sports editor W. A. Hewitt to broadcast the game. A *Star* reporter, Hewitt's son Foster, who had no on-air experience, was told to describe the game into a telephone from a rail seat near the penalty box at the musty old Mutual Street Arena. He announced the first goal with "He shoots! He scores!" and the trademark for a fabled career was established, the phrase used to this day by most hockey voices. "I said it that way because it just seemed the thing to say," Hewitt said. "I just described what I was seeing on the ice. I didn't make many changes in that approach over the next 50 or so years."

HEWITT FOR PRIME MINISTER

That junior-game phone call launched an electronic love affair between a man and his audience that has few equals anywhere. Foster Hewitt played a major role in the evolution of the Maple

Leafs and Maple Leaf Gardens into national institutions via his Saturday night radio, and later, television broadcasts of Leafs games on *Hockey Night in Canada*. It's not hyperbole to say that Hewitt achieved fame that exceeded the eminence of politicians, entertainers and sports stars in Canada.

CARRIED ACROSS THE COUNTRY

When Conn Smythe purchased the NHL Toronto St. Patricks and changed the name to the Maple Leafs in 1926, he had the games broadcast by Hewitt on CFCA from a spot in the rafters of the Mutual Street building. From the first national broadcast of a Leafs' Saturday night game on January 1, 1933—starting with another Hewitt signature, "Hello Canada and hockey fans in the United States and Newfoundland"—Hewitt's sharp, somewhat nasally voice, the quality of it for calling play-by-play probably never equalled, was a fixture in a high percentage of Canadian homes.

A postseason barnstorming tour of western Canada by the Maple Leaf players in the mid-1930s demonstrated the popularity ladder of the team. "Every place the train stopped and we stepped off, a crowd of people would make a little fuss over myself, Busher Jackson, King Clancy, Joe Primeau and Red Horner," said Charlie Conacher, the team's star right-winger. "But soon they were asking: 'Where's Foster?' The most attention went to a skinny little guy who never scored a goal."

FOSTERING GREATNESS

Conn Smythe wanted a majestic structure for his hockey team, a huge task during the Great Depression. But Smythe and his canny assistant Frank Selke shrewdly raised the money, and Smythe always claimed that the popularity of Hewitt's broadcasts was critical to the project. "I don't think we could have built the Gardens at that time if it hadn't been for the clout of Foster's broadcasts," Smythe said.

PROGRAM PUSH PAYS

Hewitt remembers: "Response to the broadcasts told us how popular the team was and that helped convince investors to back the project when anyone with money was sitting tight. Program sales at the games were weak and I suggested we try to peddle some to the radio audience for 25 cents. I mentioned it briefly once on the air and we sold more than 3,000 programs." Smythe knew then that radio could do more than make the team popular, that it had money-making possibilities.

"The next season [1930–31], Frank Selke, editor of the program, produced a special edition that boosted the new building and had preliminary drawings. I mentioned it one Saturday night and on Monday, three bags of mail came in for the new book at a dime each. The plan was to sell 32,000 programs that season but we had to print 91,000. That convinced backers to put their money into the project."

THE FAMOUS GONDOLA

Smythe and Hewitt had reached a deal that gave the team's broadcast rights to Foster Hewitt Productions. When the Gardens was set for construction in 1932, Smythe told Hewitt to select his broadcast location and the architects included "the gondola" in their plans. It was approximately four feet wide, suspended from the rafters and reached by a narrow, latticework catwalk across the girders. Even Hewitt admitted that he was always nervous walking to his workstation, being careful not to look down.

MASTERS OF MARKETING

Hewitt joined forces with the McLaren Agency to sell advertising on the broadcasts, the rights purchased by General Motors for $500 a game. When the Leaf broadcast went coast-to-coast on the CBC starting in January 1933 it quickly became the most popular radio program in Canada and the advertising costs increased rapidly. Hewitt's company was paid what he called "a solid percentage" of revenue and the rest went to Smythe. "Hewitt was the best 'free' talent scout any hockey club ever owned," Smythe claimed. "Foster made every boy in English Canada want to be a Maple Leaf."

AS SEEN ON TV

During World War II, Hewitt produced a half-hour condensed version of the game to be sent to Canadian troops for rebroadcast, leading an army officer to say, "The boys overseas wanted three things in this order: the hockey broadcasts, cigarettes and parcels from home." By the 1950s, Hewitt had his own Toronto radio station, CKFH, and moved to another electronic phenomenon—television—eventually turning over the radio broadcasts to his son Bill. The telecasts took the same course as radio had in its early days, as the number of homes with screens increased almost daily.

HENDERSON SCORES FOR CANADA!

Hewitt slowed his schedule in the late 1960s, calling a few games on radio in his inimitable style, while Bill Hewitt did the television play-by-play. One of his last major broadcasting assignments, appropriately, was the 1972 Summit Series between Team Canada and the national team of the old Soviet Union. "Henderson scores for Canada!" to describe Paul Henderson's series-winning goal 34 seconds from the end of game eight is another oft-heard Hewitt milestone.

* * * * *

"You have to know what pro hockey is all about. You have to live and breathe and sleep it. You have to lose a few teeth and take some shots to the face. It's not a pretty thing."

—Ted Nolan, center, coach and First Nations advocate

"We know that hockey is where we live, where we can best meet and overcome pain and wrong and death. Life is just a place where we spend time between games."

—Fred Shero, former Flyers coach

HOCKEY GOES TO HOLLYWOOD

The two greatest stories ever told.

In the long history of hockey movies, two distinct plots appear time and again, "the ragtag team achieves unlikely victory" and "the star forward vs. the gangsters." Some films diverge from these well-worn paths, though, and sometimes farther than you'd expect—opera characters in drag? But keep your eyes peeled for real-life stars in these fictional fantasies, and remember not to fall in love with the coach's daughter.

The King of Hockey (1936)
Gabby Dugan is under pressure from a gambling syndicate to stop scoring a dozen goals a game. His goalie wrongly suspects him of giving in to temptation and cracks Gabby over the head with his goal-stick, blinding him. Gabby recovers in time to win the big game, then he and the goalie are friends again, no questions asked.

The Game That Kills (1937)
After the star forward of the Indians is "accidentally" killed during a game, his brother Alec joins the team under a false name in order to uncover the truth—he suspects a gambling syndicate. He falls in love with the coach's daughter (Rita Hayworth), but the Indians' evil owner kidnaps her in order to force Alec to throw the big game.

Idol of the Crowds (1937)
Star forward Johnny Hansen (John Wayne) comes out of retirement, not to win any championship but simply to make enough cash to expand his chicken farm. A gambling syndicate pressures him to throw the big game, but he refuses, and they make an attempt on his life that injures his brother Bobby, the team mascot.

Face-Off (1971)
A hockey player falls in love with a folksinger, and their relationship is complicated by their contrasting careers. Features speaking

roles for Jim Dorey, Paul Henderson, Mike Pelyk, Rick Ley, George Armstrong and Derek Sanderson, and based on the novel by Scott Young (musician Neil's dad.)

Slap Shot (1977)
Reggie Dunlop (Paul Newman), the player-coach of the Charlestown Chiefs, must deal with a bullheaded owner, angry crowds and on-ice thuggery in this legendary comedy, which displays a level of violence and profanity entirely appropriate to the minor league game of the mid-70s. Notable Chiefs include the brawling Hanson Brothers (remember *Idol of the Crowds*?).

The Hounds of Notre Dame (1980)
During the Great Depression, rough-talking, whisky-drinking Pere Athol Murray crafts an incredibly successful hockey program at Notre Dame College in Wilcox, Saskatchewan. More than 100 former Hounds have played in the NHL, including Rod Brind'Amour, Wendel Clark, Curtis Joseph, Vincent Lecavalier and Brad Richards.

Hockey Night (1984)
Cathy Yarrow (Megan Follows) meets with resistance when she wants to tend goal for her high school's team, but she also finds unexpected support from the team's star forward, Spear Kozak. Sparks subsequently fly between Spear and Kathy, who shines in the big game.

Youngblood (1985)
Dean Youngblood (Rob Lowe), gentlemanly forward for the Hamilton Mustangs, is told to fight if he wants to attract NHL scouts. He falls in love with the coach's daughter. Former Black Hawk Eric Nesterenko stars as Lowe's father, and Peter Zezel and Steve Thomas appear in speaking parts. A local goaltender named Keanu Reeves scored a bit part in the film due to his hockey skills; he was so excited by his big-screen debut that he (surely naively) packed and left for Hollywood to try for a new career in acting.

Perfectly Normal (1990)
Renzo Parachi is an inspector at a Toronto beer-bottling plant, goalie on the company team, and part-time cab driver. One of his fares plans on using Renzo's late mother's estate to finance a

restaurant at which the waiters will be opera characters in drag. A bloodthirsty on-ice rivalry with another factory's team continues.

The Cutting Edge (1992)
NHL prospect Doug Dorsey is injured in a game against West Germany at the 1988 Calgary Olympics. Unable to play professionally, he becomes pairs partner to ill-tempered figure skater Kate Moseley, and after torturous weeks of training they take both their budding romance and groundbreaking routine into international competition.

The Mighty Ducks, I-III (1992–1996)
I: Gordon Bombay (Emilio Estevez), a hotshot Minnesota lawyer, is ordered by the courts to coach the worst peewee hockey team in the league. A ragtag bunch, he eventually gains their respect and teaches them how to win, but in the big game they must face a team led by Gordon's old coach, witness to his greatest childhood failure.

II: Gordon becomes coach of Team USA for the Junior Goodwill Games in California. He whips the Ducks and a few new players into a crack squad, but becomes distracted by Hollywood hype and the threat of facing the hockey powerhouse of Iceland in the big game.

III: Back in Minnesota, the Ducks receive scholarships to prestigious Eden Hall Academy, but must labor under an uptight new coach as they prepare to face the favored Varsity team. Before the big game, Gordon must intervene to steer Duck captain Charlie away from his path of self-destruction.

Sudden Death (1995)
Fireman Darren McCord (Jean-Claude Van Damme) takes his kids to see the Blackhawks play the Penguins in the Stanley Cup final, but when his daughter is kidnapped by a mascot he learns that terrorists are also holding the vice-president of the United States. Before the game ends McCord must find and defuse ten bombs hidden in the crowded arena. Luc Robitaille can be seen scoring a pivotal goal.

Les Boys, I–III (1997–2001)
I: Made-in-Quebec film (where it's incredibly popular) starring Marc (as opposed to Mark) Messier. In a Monday-night league,

beloved coach Stan leads a ragtag bunch of guys—lawyers, police officers and mechanics—"with pucks tattooed on their hearts."
II: Champions at home, the boys travel to France for an international tournament, but their enthusiasm is quickly doused by nightmarish living conditions and the unexpected tenacity of the rival teams.
III: Back in Quebec, the team prepares for a new season, but, as Stan sadly discovers, his once-light-hearted players have been corrupted by big money.

Mystery, Alaska (1998)
Mystery, Alaska's amateur team agrees to play the New York Rangers in an exhibition game, and town sheriff John Biebe (Russell Crowe) offers his coaching position to the legendary Judge Burns (Burt Reynolds). Phil Esposito and Jim Fox appear as TV announcers, while Mike (*Austin Powers*) Myers does his best Don Cherry impersonation.

MVP: Most Valuable Primate (1999)
Jack, a chimpanzee with a genius IQ, sleeps through his stop for the El Simian primate reserve and winds up in a small Canadian town. Befriended by deaf Tara Westover, Jack joins her brother Steven's ragtag hockey team and tries to change their losing ways before he's whisked back to the research lab.

The Rhino Brothers (2001)
Widow Ellen Kanachowski has devoted her life to the hockey dreams of her three sons. The eldest, his professional career hampered by bad knees, is now unemployed; the youngest is the first player from their prairie town to make the NHL; while the middle son, lacking their talent, coaches the local team, the Rhinos.

Miracle (2004)
Minnesota coach Herb Brooks (Kurt Russell) is given the reins of Team USA and whips a ragtag bunch of college kids into a crack squad before they face the Soviets at the 1980 Lake Placid Olympics. Al Michaels asks the millions at home, "Do you believe in miracles?" As this retells one of the best-known hockey stories ever, you likely do.

JET-PROPELLED OILERS

How the WHA Winnipeg Jets, built on European talent, inspired the Edmonton Oilers' record-setting offence.

Glen Sather was a defensive pest during his ten-season NHL career with six teams, producing a grand total of only 80 goals and 193 points in 660 games. But placed in charge of the Edmonton Oilers, he built the highest scoring team in NHL history: They became the only club to score more than 400 goals in a season and did it five times over for good measure. While Sather learned a little about the speed-and-attack approach to the game in a season with the mid-1970s Montreal Canadiens, the organization that invented the "firewagon hockey" inspiration for the Oilers' style was the Winnipeg Jets of the World Hockey Association.

JETSETTERS

"I played and coached against that good Jets team and saw first-hand the way they played the game," Sather said. "I said if I ever was in charge of a team, the Jets style would be the way my team played." The "Jets style" was to build a roster around players with offensive skill, employing flair and creativity in the manner of top European teams. The value of the approach was particularly established by the USSR national team when it extended Team Canada's star-studded 1972 Summit Series lineup to a tightly fought eight-game series.

STAR SEARCH

The Jets were a charter member of the WHA when it was organized as a rival to the NHL in 1972. NHL superstar Bobby Hull was drawn to the Jets and the new league by a huge, league-shared signing bonus and the top salary in the sport, giving the new circuit instantaneous credibility. Hull did the expected, topping the 50-goal mark in his first two WHA seasons, even while toiling with competent but below-star-level linemates.

The escalation of big-league teams from six to 28 in five years had diluted the player pool, a factor that combined with the positive exposure of the 1972 series to force pro teams to consider Europe as a potential source of players. While NHL recruitment of Scandinavians started slowly due to the old notion that Europeans couldn't handle physical play, the WHA—led by Winnipeg—moved quickly to acquire Swedish and Finnish players.

ORTHOPEDIC SURGEON DISCOVERS THE SHOE

Dr. Gerry Wilson, a member of the Jets' executive, was a first-rate Montreal Canadiens prospect in the 1950s until chronic knee problems at the junior level led him to a new career as an orthopedic surgeon. During studies abroad, he watched the Swedish Elite Division and was impressed by the high caliber of players. Wilson became friends with young forward Anders Hedberg and suggested to the Jets that they consider recruiting Swedish players. In 1974, the Jets signed goalie Curt Larsson, defenceman Lars-Erik Sjoberg—known universally as "The Shoe"—forwards Hedberg and Ulf Nilsson from Sweden; and defenceman Hexi Riihiranta and center Veli-Pekka Ketola from Finland. When the 1974–75 season opened, one of pro hockey's most exciting teams hit the ice.

SCANDINAVIAN INVASION

"At the 1974 World Championship in Finland, the Shoe, Anders Hedberg and I talked about moving to Canada or the U.S. to play hockey," Ulf Nilsson said. "We all had contract offers from NHL clubs: Shoe from Minnesota, Anders with the Maple Leafs and me with Buffalo. But Shoe suggested that if we all went to one team, maybe we could influence that team to play our style of hockey. Winnipeg was the place and although signing with the Jets cost us some money over the long haul, it was the right move."

Because Hull was the Jet "franchise," the team would use the style he suggested. But when he played his first training camp shift with Hedberg and Nilsson, the Golden Jet knew the way to go. "When I saw the skill and intelligence they had on the ice, I volunteered to play their style and forget about mine," Hull said. "With Anders and Ulfie up front and the Shoe on the back end—their skill plus Lars-Erik's great mind about the game and his ability to quarterback the attack—we had a high old time for four seasons."

DON CHERRY JUST CALLS IT "THE ICE CAPADES"

The Jets played in circles, not in pro hockey's traditional straight lines, marking the first serious North American use of the "flow-and-motion" style. The three forwards, with 573 goals and 1,377 points in four seasons, were a joy to behold. Harry Neale coached against the Jets with two WHA teams, and after a stint in the NHL became a TV analyst for *Hockey Night in Canada*.

"In our big-league hockey, the neutral zone between the blue lines was just an area you had skate though to get to your attacking zone," Neale said. "But the Europeans used it to set up their attack. The Jets with Hull and the Swedes were the first North American team to adopt that style. They'd come into the neutral zone three abreast but by the time they hit your blue line, they'd be in different lanes than where they started. Their crossovers produced all sorts of offensive chances because the defences had problems figuring out who was covering which Jet."

OR, JUST CALL ON NO. 99...

Sather joined the WHA Oilers as a player in 1976–77 and was named playing coach halfway through the season. When the Oilers entered the NHL for 1979–80, Sather had accumulated the roles of club president, GM and head coach, making it pretty darn easy to strive for whatever kind of team he wanted. "I modelled our team after the WHA Jets, especially the way they had that little Sjoberg as a big part of their attack," Sather said. "He would move behind the play by the Hull line and somewhere on the rush, the puck often would go back to him and he would move it to an open man. He was the first defenceman to truly play the same role as the great midfielders in soccer, the guys who choreographed the attack."

Of course, the Oilers entered the NHL with a head start because they brought Wayne Gretzky with them...and all he did was become the highest scorer in NHL history. But Sather also drafted forwards Mark Messier, Glenn Anderson and Jari Kurri and fleet defenceman Paul Coffey, and quickly the gifted youngsters matured into the finest offensive team ever. Maybe the team names should have been reversed: The Oilers' speed made them the "jets" of hockey while the Jets' offshore work found them high-grade hockey "oil."

BRIEF TOUR OF DUTY

Mikko Jokela's first trip to the NHL lasted a little more than 12 hours, but it left him with a story he'll be able to tell for a lifetime, not to mention a pair of someone else's underwear.

The Vancouver Canucks called up Finnish defenceman Mikko Jokela from their American Hockey League affiliate midway through the 2002–03 season after a late injury to fellow Finn Sami Salo. Jokela, then 22, learned of his first trip to "the show" midway through morning practice in Winnipeg and was on a flight to Detroit by 1 P.M.

HOCKEY BAGS AND HAND-ME-DOWNS

His plane arrived at 6:30 P.M.—just as the Canucks were taking the ice to warm up for a game against the Red Wings—only to be told that his equipment bag had been misplaced. Despite the setback, Jokela got to Detroit's Joe Louis Arena just as the national anthems were being sung and managed to make his way to the Canucks bench midway through the first period—with Trent Klatt's extra skates on his feet and a Brent Sopel stick clutched inside Salo's gloves. Underneath all of the borrowed equipment, Jokela was wearing new teammate Darren Langdon's underwear.

WHO ARE YOU? WHY ARE YOU WEARING MY SOCKS?

Making his debut even more awkward was the fact that Jokela had been acquired in a trade with the New Jersey Devils less than a month earlier, meaning he didn't get to meet any of his Canucks teammates during training camp. After a lot of stunned looks and a couple of "Who are you?" queries on the bench, Jokela hopped over the boards, took a drop pass off a faceoff, and wired a shot through traffic at veteran Red Wings goaltender Curtis Joseph. He was only on the ice for five minutes and nine seconds, but Jokela recorded two more shots and even spent time on the power play as the Canucks rallied with a late tying goal before winning in overtime. Jokela didn't get to savor the victory—or his NHL debut—for long. The Canucks sent him back to the airport and back to the minor leagues the next morning.

1987: PURE HEAVEN

What was the greatest year in hockey? You may disagree, but we at Uncle John would like to suggest that both NHL and international hockey peaked in this memorable year.

THE BEST OF TIMES

All hockey fans have their favorite decades. For instance, many Montreal Canadiens supporters tout the 1950s, the golden age of the Flying Frenchmen, featuring such stars as Jean Béliveau, Maurice "Rocket" Richard, Henri Richard and Jacques Plante. Fans of hockey fights gravitate toward the 1970s, when the Big Bad Bruins of Boston and the Broad Street Bullies of Philadelphia made their mark with tough guys such as Terry O'Reilly, Stan Jonathan, Dave "The Hammer" Schultz, and Bob "Mad Dog" Kelly. But few would dispute the fact that the 1980s were the ultimate time for freewheeling, high-scoring hockey with end-to-end rushes and defencemen joining the attack. Granted, things went a little bit nuts in 1981–82, when the average total goals-per-game hit an all-time high of 8:03. Still, as the decade wore on, a balance between offence and defence emerged, which all added up to pure entertainment for hockey fans in 1987.

FLYING HIGH WITH THE OIL

In the 1987 NHL playoffs, the Edmonton Oilers were willing to do anything to put the humiliating memory of 1986 behind them. The previous year, they'd lost a heartbreaking seven-game series to the Calgary Flames, as Oilers defenceman Steve Smith put the winning goal in his own net by accidentally banking the puck off goalie Grant Fuhr's skate. The loss killed Edmonton's hopes of winning a third straight Stanley Cup. A May 1986 *Sports Illustrated* story then accused several unnamed Oilers of cocaine abuse, further tarnishing the team's image. But the 1987 postseason marked a turnaround. Superstars such as Wayne Gretzky, Jari Kurri and Mark Messier remained at the team's core, but GM Glen Sather also added fresh European talents such as Kent Nilsson and Reijo Ruotsalainen. The Oilers lost only two games en route to the finals, hammering Los Angeles, Winnipeg and Detroit along the way.

THE NICE VS. NASTY

Facing Philadelphia for Lord Stanley's mug produced the best finals since Montreal's 1971 triumph over Chicago, and one that even rivals the New York Rangers-Vancouver Canucks classic of 1994. Nasty and nice highlights abounded, from Philly netminder Ron Hextall's vicious slash on Nilsson to Kurri's overtime winner in game two. The Flyers rallied from a 3–1 series deficit to force a seventh and deciding game, and even though they lost on another big Kurri goal, Hextall was named playoff MVP for his brilliance. Gretzky, meanwhile, was at his playmaking best, leading the way with 29 assists and 34 points. In the first round, he got his 177th career playoff point, passing Jean Béliveau for tops on the all-time list.

INTERNATIONAL INSPIRATION

Rendez-Vous '87: Hockey fans around the world had reason to celebrate in 1987. In February, the NHL ditched its usual no-intensity All-Star Game format in favor of a two-game series versus the powerful Soviet national team. Hosted by Quebec City during the annual Winter Carnival, the series was called Rendez-Vous '87. The NHL side was Canadian-dominated but also featured Swedes such as Tomas Sandstrom, Finns such as Jari Kurri, and Americans such as Chris Chelios. The marquee Soviet offensive unit was the KLM Line of Vladimir Krutov, Igor Larionov and Sergei Makarov, but the second line of Andrei Khomutov, Slava Bykov and a young Valeri Kamensky was just as dangerous here. Dave Poulin's late tally gave the NHL a 4–3 victory in the Rendez-Vous opener, but Kamensky's dazzling three-point effort earned the USSR a 5–3 revenge in game two. "There is no winner except hockey itself, for these were excellent matches," said Soviet coach Viktor Tikhonov. Wayne Gretzky led the scoring parade with four assists.

World Championship: Canadian and Russian fans would prefer to forget what happened at the 1987 World Championship in Vienna, Austria. But Swedish fans still relish two highlights. First, Tre Kronor secured a 2–2 tie with the heavily favored Soviets thanks to a tic-tac-toe passing play involving Anders Eldebrink, Bengt Gustafsson, Tommy Albelin, Hakan Loob and goal-scorer

Tomas Sandstrom. The International Ice Hockey Federation calls this "the best goal ever scored" at the World Championship. The Swedes then hammered Canada by a stunning 9–0 margin and won the gold medal on goal differential.

Canada Cup: The year's best international hockey took place at the Canada Cup. The favored Canadians and Soviets both started out slowly, but they'd hit their stride by the time they met in a three-game final that's never been surpassed for hockey quality or excitement. Each game finished 6–5. The first encounter in Montreal went to the Soviets on Alexander Semak's overtime goal. But Canada came roaring back in the last two games in Hamilton. Game two saw Lemieux bang home the winner in double overtime, and Gretzky, who was so exhausted that he actually wet his pants, had a five-point night. Game three came down to an odd-man rush with Gretzky and Lemieux, and the Great One dropped the puck to Lemieux, who wired it over the glove of Soviet goalie Sergei Mylnikov with 1:26 remaining. Even in a losing cause, Krutov and Makarov were nearly as dangerous for the Soviets as Gretzky and Lemieux were for Canada.

FROM THE GREAT GRETZKY TO SUPER MARIO

Nobody knew it in 1987, but this was the last year that Wayne Gretzky was the unquestioned number-one player in hockey. He scored 62 goals and 121 assists that season, marking the last time he would lead the NHL in both categories. He also won the Hart Trophy as NHL MVP and was named to the First All-Star team. But Mario Lemieux took the experience of playing with Gretzky in the 1987 Canada Cup and parlayed it into his best hockey to date. In 1987–88, the Pittsburgh Penguins superstar would break Gretzky's string of eight straight scoring titles by racking up 168 points. And while Gretzky won only one more Cup, in 1988, Lemieux captained the Penguins to two championships in 1991 and 1992. Having two such offensive geniuses starring in the NHL simultaneously was a treat that hockey fans may never experience again.

THE MASKED MARVEL

How a painful shot to the face changed the course of hockey history.

Jacques Plante was not the first professional hockey goalie to wear a mask. That distinction belongs to the Montreal Maroons' Clint Benedict, who donned an awkward leather face protector in 1930. However, unlike Benedict's, Plante's mask was well-engineered for visibility and the rest, as they say, is hockey history.

HAVE A NICE TRIP

On November 1, 1959, the New York Rangers battled the four-time defending Stanley Cup champion Montreal Canadiens in an early season clash. Early in the game, Plante stuck his stick out and tripped all-star winger Andy Bathgate, who went head first into the boards. Not wearing a helmet, Bathgate could have been seriously injured, but luckily he was not. However, Bathgate vowed revenge. He left the ice almost right away and used the bottom of the dressing room door to put a wicked curve on his stick blade.

HEAD'S UP!

A few shifts later, Bathgate took a shot that Plante never saw. It nailed Plante right in the face, and he went down in a heap. In the dressing room, Plante, who had always wanted to wear a mask much to Canadiens' head coach Toe Blake's dismay, finally had the perfect opportunity. Plante told Blake that either he would be allowed to wear the mask, or he wouldn't go back out. Blake had no choice but to acquiesce as there was not another quality goaltender that the Habs could use (in those days, teams often only dressed one goaltender).

WHO WAS THAT MASKED MAN?

Plante came back out on the ice wearing something that looked like it was from a horror movie. Bathgate said years later that he told Plante he looked better with the mask on. The hockey media and fans thought Plante wouldn't see the puck, and the mask would only be a temporary measure. A headline even ran in French translating to "Halloween is over, Jacques." However, while Halloween was over, the masked Plante extended the win over the Rangers into an unbeaten streak of 11 games. He would lead the Habs to yet another Stanley Cup title in 1960, and the mask was here to stay.

* * * * *

THE PUCK STOPS HERE

"If you jump out of a plane without a parachute, does that make you brave? No, I think that makes you stupid. I will never play without the mask again."

—Jacques Plante

"Our first priority was staying alive. Our second was stopping the puck."

—Glenn Hall,
former Chicago Blackhawks goaltender

"I remember playing junior in Seattle and I almost got hit by a salmon. I don't know if it had to do with my style of play or what. It landed about two feet from my crease and splattered. I had fish guts on my pads for the next couple of days. Other than that, I've been pretty fortunate."

—Byron Dafoe,
former Boston Bruins goaltender

"There is no such thing as painless goaltending. If they could get enough padding to assure against every type of bruise, you'd have to be swung into position with a small derrick."

—Don Cherry

"Every time a puck gets past me and I look back in my net, I say 'Oh, oh.'"

—goaltender Bernie Parent,
when asked why he wore No. 00 in the WHA

A TALE OF TWO BLOCKERS

How injury forced a young goaltending prospect to tinker with his equipment.

As soon as goaltender Dan Blackburn hits the ice it jumps out at you like a Janet Jackson breast during a Super Bowl halftime show. You can't help but notice he is wearing a blocker on each hand, one to hold his stick like every other goaltender you've ever seen and another where his glove should be. The former Kootenay Ice junior standout uses it to steer pucks into the corner during warm-up—pucks he would normally catch.

THE PROBLEM

For Blackburn, the extra blocker has become a necessary distraction, his last hope to jump-start a promising career stalled for two years by a damaged nerve in his left shoulder. Despite finally undergoing surgery after more than a year of misdiagnosis, Blackburn's nerve is dead. It's caused a muscle behind his shoulder to waste away, leaving him with a softball-sized crater on his back and an even bigger hole in his game. Unable to lift his glove with his palm facing the shooter, Blackburn, who exploded into hockey's conscience as an 18-year-old rookie with the New York Rangers in 2001–02, was forced to get creative.

THE SOLUTION

Born in an off-the-cuff comment during a meeting with Rangers president and general manager Glen Sather, Blackburn began building his extra blocker, through trial and error, with the help of New York's equipment staff. With the new blocker, which has a small glove underneath to smother loose pucks and catch high dump-ins, Blackburn can square up with the top of his hand facing shooters. Because he's using a different muscle to move his arm, he isn't hindered by the nerve damage. After getting medical clearance from the Rangers and approval for the second blocker from the NHL, Blackburn was ready to start his comeback early in 2005 at age 21.

HAVE BLOCKERS, WILL TRAVEL

The only problem: the ongoing NHL lockout left him without a place to play. Undaunted, he signed with the expansion Victoria Salmon Kings in the East Coast Hockey League, forgoing $850,000 U.S. he was collecting on the NHL disabled list to play for $750 a week. Two levels removed from the NHL and on the other side of the continent from New York, Blackburn's double-blocker return almost attracted as much media attention as his remarkable rookie season with the Rangers. It was the first thing fans noticed and the only thing reporters asked about, leaving the young goaltender feeling like he was back at Madison Square Garden—when Barnum and Bailey's comes to town. "It's like a circus-freak appeal," he said after four games with the Salmon Kings. "Come see the goalie with two blockers!"

EQUIPMENT OF THE FUTURE?

Even as he was preparing to play games again in Victoria, Blackburn was tweaking the blocker, a process he expects to continue for as long as a year. But he feels it's getting closer to a finished product, one he plans to patent just in case the idea—and his career—takes off. After all, necessity has always been the mother of invention. "If I have a lot of success with it maybe it will catch on," Blackburn said, failing to note whether the pun was intended. "It will all hinge on how successful I am with it. Who knows, if things go really well, maybe kids will start using it instead of a regular glove."

LAST-MINUTE UPDATE

In September 2005, Dan Blackburn retired from professional hockey. Sadly, for Dan and for hockey fans everywhere, his injuries would not allow him to compete at the NHL level. He'd been invited back to Rangers training camp on a tryout basis and arrived with his two blockers. But it was not going to work.

Blackburn explained, "A glove was never an option because of my permanent disability. I've really had no significant improvement in my shoulder for two years and I tried everything in my power. I mean, I tried playing with two blockers [but] I couldn't do it…That's why I have to retire. I just can't compete at a high enough level."

NHL players take out insurance policies on themselves in the event of a career-ending injury. Blackburn is entitled to a financial settlement but says, "It still doesn't replace what I really wanted to do."

OWNERS OF THE GAME

Uncle John tells the story of five businessmen who have played pivotal roles in the development of their respective teams.

William Davidson: For an 80-year-old-plus man to be the first owner of two teams that won championships in their respective sports in the same season (the NBA's Detroit Pistons and NHL's Tampa Bay Lightning) is some feat—but Bill Davidson is one unique owner. He is quiet and respectful of his employees, willing to wait months or years for his teams to solidify into winners. A generous philanthropist, Davidson made his money with a company in the Detroit area that specializes in making automobile windshield glass and other flat glass products. As owner of the Pistons since 1974, he saw the team win consecutive championships in 1989 and 1990. He took over the Lightning in 1999 and oversaw the hiring of general manager Jay Feaster and head coach John Tortorella, an unheralded hockey duo if there ever was one. But Davidson's confidence translated into a Stanley Cup in 2004, the same year his Pistons won him a third NBA title.

Tom Hicks: This quiet but firm billionaire investment entrepreneur took control of what could have been a legal and economic nightmare—the selling of a hapless franchise that retreated from Minnesota under owner Norm Green—and managed to set a winning course. This was some accomplishment, considering Dallas had a brutal 26-42-14 record in 1995–96, Hicks' first season as owner. Key additions of head coach Ken Hitchcock and proven leaders Guy Carbonneau, Joe Nieuwendyk, Mike Keane and Brian Skrudland improved the team's record over the next two seasons and eventually led to a tightly focused organization that won two Stanley Cups.

Mike Ilitch: The owners of the Detroit Red Wings are very much a husband-and-wife team: Mike is owner and Marian is owner/secretary-treasurer/advisor. When Mike was 30, in 1959, Mike and Marian opened a pizza parlor in Garden City, Michigan, named "Little Caesar's" based on Marian's nickname for Mike. The pizza parlour gradually turned into a pizza chain, and eventually into one of North America's foremost take-out enterprises. In 1968, the Ilitchs started the Little Caesar's Minor Hockey program, the lifeblood of many youth hockey leagues throughout North America. The Ilitchs bought the Detroit Red Wings in 1982 for what now seems a bargain—$8 million U.S.—and the Detroit Tigers baseball team two years later. For the first few years the Wings were terrible, but patience paid off, particularly in the form of 1983 draft pick Steve Yzerman. The Detroit Red Wings have won three Stanley Cups and nine division championships in the Ilitch Era up to the 2004 lockout. In 2003, Mike was elected to the Hockey Hall of Fame in the Builders Category.

E. Stanley Kronke: When the NHL cancelled the 2004–2005 season, thousands of season ticket holders for various teams wondered what would become of their money. Colorado Avalanche owner Stanley Kronke moved quickly to comfort his team's fans with a two-option plan that was widely regarded as fair. And refreshingly, he expressed genuine remorse for the owners' role in the lockout of NHL hockey. This attitude seems to be consistent with his Kronke Group's approach to real estate investment and development: Despite being one of North America's leading developers in shopping centers and apartment buildings, it has aimed to build a reputation based on community improvements over environmental degradation. Kronke's purchase of the Avalanche bolstered a dramatic and successful run to the Stanley Cup in 2001.

Ed Snider: Like Mike Ilitch, Snider had a life-changing event happen to him around the age of 30. He sold his successful record company Edge Ltd. and then teamed up with two other investors to purchase the NFL's Philadelphia Eagles. Snider got involved with hockey by accident. While attending a Boston Celtics game, he noticed a crowd of Bruins fans lining up to buy the remaining 1,000 tickets for a last-place team. Soon thereafter, he learned that the NHL was planning to expand, and successfully lobbied in 1966 for a new team in Philadelphia. Under Snider, the brash-and-bash Flyers became the most hated new team in the NHL. They also were the most successful, winning consecutive Stanley Cups in 1974 and 1975. The Broad Street Bully heyday is long past, but the Flyers have remained contenders and on a daily basis the strong-willed Snider continues to take on the responsibility for team success. In 1988, he was elected as a Builder to the Hockey Hall of Fame.

* * * * *

PLAYING THE PERCENTAGES

"If everyone elevates their game by 2 percent with Mats gone, that equals 40 percent."

—Curtis Joseph, on how his Toronto Maple Leafs should respond to losing captain Mats Sundin to injury

"I know that he often gives only 60 percent of his capacity, but it's hard to punish him because at 60 percent he's better than our other defencemen at 100 percent."

—Montreal Canadiens executive Réjean Houle, on defenceman Vladimir Malakhov

"You miss 100 percent of the shots you never take."

—Wayne Gretzky

"Our team can't afford to have 5 percent of the guys not playing 100 percent. But when we've got 95 percent not giving 100 percent, we're in real trouble."

—Bob Berry, head coach of the Los Angeles Kings, 1980

THE FOUNDING FATHER OF MODERN-DAY GOALTENDING

Vladislav Tretiak's commitment to being a high-octane, world-class athlete left easygoing NHL models like Turk "the Fabulous Fatman" Broda in the annals of history.

George Washington was the Founding Father (or one of the Founding Fathers) of America. Simon Bolivar of Venezuela had the great dream of someday linking North, Central and South Americas into one massive country with one government (which, by the way, he would rule). It didn't happen, but at the very least he managed to garner the title of Founding Father in the southern continent. But who is the Founding Father of Modern-Day Goaltending, you ask? Well, Vladislav Tretiak, of course.

BORN TO LEAD

In retrospect, more than any other goaltender of his era Tretiak seemed to have all known aspects of the position figured out. Equipment; nutrition; physical fitness (including exercises to quicken his reflexes); positioning...Tretiak had thoroughly considered and studied all of these important aspects of netminding.

Washington and Bolivar were born to lead; Tretiak was born to play goalie. Interestingly, as compared to most Russian hockey players—who learn to skate and play hockey by the ages of five or six—Tretiak came to the sport at the greybeard age of 11. But his natural talents were so immediately obvious that by the time he was 15 he was regularly practising with the Central Red Army Team based in Moscow.

A BIRD CAGE WITH BUTTERFLY WINGS

Equipment: Tretiak was the first goaltender of international importance to have success while wearing the so-called "bird cage" goalie helmet. He was well-known for taking meticulous care of his catching glove, blocker and his leg pads. Tretiak also popularized the plastic toe guard for goalie skates.

Nutrition and Physical Fitness: The man ate and drank foods and liquids that were healthy for him; no excess pizza and beer for this Russian. Tretiak kept himself in prime physical condition all year long.

Positioning: Primarily a reflex goalie, he was unique in that he could play both the butterfly and stand-up forms of netminding, or even a combination of both (like Martin Brodeur of the New Jersey Devils would do later). Especially noteworthy for a man who was 6' 2" inches tall and weighed 202 pounds, he would adopt any style of goaltending that the situation called for.

Mental Outlook: Tretiak had considerable mental toughness and played at his best in important games. With a man like this holding up the back end, Tretiak's teammates felt they could win any game. And they usually did.

AN UNCLE JOHN LONG LIST OF ACCOMPLISHMENTS

When he was 17, Tretiak became a member of the Central Red Army Team and one year later he was the team's starting goaltender. This was about 1970. What he did in the sport for the next 14 years is almost beyond belief:

- Three Olympic gold medals in 1972, 1976 and 1984. In 1980, he was awarded a silver medal when the Soviet Union lost to the U.S. squad in Lake Placid, New York.
- Thirteen Soviet League Championships.
- Ten World Championship titles.
- Voted best goaltender in the World and European Championships in 1974, 1979, 1981 and 1983.
- Winner of the Tournament Most Valuable Player Award in the 1981 Canada Cup Series, which the Soviet Union won.
- In both Olympic Games and World Championship play, Tretiak's goals-against average was under 2.00 (1.74, Olympics; 1.92, World Championships).

Considering that he was playing against the best players in the world, these are incredible statistics.

FOUNDING FATHER IN THE GREATEST GAME

North American hockey fans first learned of Tretiak when he sparkled as the starting goaltender in the eight-game 1972 Summit Series between the Soviet Union and Team Canada. Canada won, but it was clear that Tretiak was perhaps the best player in the world. Three years later, on New Year's Eve, 1975, he played probably the greatest game of his illustrious career. Playing the Montreal Canadiens, Tretiak held Les Habs in check for a 3–3 tie—despite the fact his Red Army team was outshot 38–13. This matchup between two great teams, and two great goalies in Tretiak and Ken Dryden, is called by some hockey historians "the greatest game ever played."

FOUNDING FATHER IN THE HALL OF FAME

Tretiak—who never played an NHL game despite being drafted by the Canadiens—retired after the 1983–84 season. He was only 32, but not completely done with hockey. In the 1990–91 season, Tretiak became a goalie coach for the Chicago Blackhawks and tutored, among others, Dominik Hasek and Ed Belfour. In 1989, he became the first European and Russian player to be elected to the Hockey Hall of Fame. And in a poll, Tretiak was voted the greatest Russian athlete of the 20th century.

Washington and Bolivar have been remembered by historians long after their deaths. Likewise, Uncle John assures you that the legacy of Vladislav Tretiak will continue to be passed onto bathroom readers for decades and centuries to come.

* * * * *

THE RITUAL OF REDEMPTION

"If I play badly I'll pick a fight in the third, just to get into a fight. I'll break a guy's leg to win, I don't care. Afterward I say, 'Yeah all right I played badly, but I won the fight so who gives a damn.'"

—Derek Sanderson, former Boston Bruins center

SKIRTS AND SLAPSHOTS

The development of women's hockey was a slow, uphill battle—a parallel to progress of equality in many areas.

The contrast in style in the photographs taken approximately a century apart is startling, much more than the pictures of two men's sports teams over that much time...The Ottawa Canadian Banknote women's hockey team of 1905 shows six ladies in long skirts, turtleneck sweaters and toques with tassels. One player stands out because, barely discernible in the ancient photo, she is wearing what appears to be hockey skates while the others are in vintage figure skates. No protective gear, even the primitive padding of the time, is worn by any of the women.

Compare that to the team picture of the 2005 U.S. women's team, the world champions. They're wearing modern hockey gear made from space-age materials, their equipment identical to that worn by the 2004 Stanley Cup champion Tampa Bay Lightning—except that much of it is even custom-made for female players.

WOMEN TO HOCKEY LIKE BLADES TO BOOTS

For women, hockey has offered many more opportunities than other games. Soccer has been a game women have widely played in the postwar years, resulting in a competitive world championship and U.S. women's college program. While softball was played by girls for years, few if any women played baseball. And of course the mention of ladies playing North American football was scorned—even though a few teams were formed in the mid-1990s. But from the time steel blades were attached to boots by clamps, females have participated in skating, and when males first used a stick to knock a ball around the ice, women tried the same thing. Almost as soon as men formed the early versions of hockey, women did, too.

LORD STANLEY'S DAUGHTER

Hockey's most famous trophy, the Stanley Cup, was donated in 1893 by the Governor General of Canada, Lord Stanley of

Preston. Four years earlier, Stanley and his family had arrived in Ottawa from England and enjoyed watching the game with sticks and a wooden puck played on the Rideau Canal, the longest skating rink in the world, during the Ottawa Winter Carnival. A few weeks later the GG's daughter Isobel was playing for the Government House team against the Rideau Ladies Club. When Stanley's term ended in 1894 and the family returned to England, Isobel said that what she missed most from her term in Canada was skating on the canal and "playing a game of hockey."

A LONG HISTORY, IN BRIEF

Complete records of early women's hockey are rare, but a few newspaper reports list early forays into the game. Annie McIntyre was among the fastest speed skaters in Saskatchewan in 1896 and was behind the organization of a women's team. The paper in Medicine Hat, Alberta, had a report of an 1897 game between women's teams. Teams popped up in various cities across the country and by 1900, three teams from Montreal and one from Trois-Rivières formed the Quebec Women's League. In the era following World War I, women's hockey in Canada grew in popularity with many cities and towns having clubs. While interest was not as widespread in the U.S., a few areas had teams. Through the 1930s, the Preston Rivulettes from Ontario ruled the women's game, winning the championship every year for a decade, losing only twice in more than 350 games.

SCOURING FOR COMPETITION

Conservative views of women following WW II slowed the development of hockey for women but by the late 1960s, the feminist movement had changed attitudes and women were moving into areas considered inaccessible previously. In the Vancouver area, women's leagues were established by the mid-1960s with age limits similar to men's hockey. Soon leagues were organized in British Columbia and women's teams were traveling to eastern Canada and even Europe to find competition. There were several challenges in courts for girls wanting to play in boys' leagues because it was the only hockey available.

HOCKEY HUGE

By 1982, 12,000 females were registered for hockey in Ontario and the women's division of USA hockey had 116 teams registered. Canadian women's college hockey grew quickly with a national championship in the 1980s and, in 1984, the Eastern Collegiate Athletic Association in the U.S. created a league. In the next decade, close to 100 colleges had women's hockey programs and by the end of 1990s, close to 25,000 women were registered for hockey programs in the U.S. In 1993, the NCAA passed rules that produced a national championship by 2001 and in the hockey hotbed of Minnesota, where boys' high school hockey is huge, the number of girls' high school hockey clubs topped the 100 mark by 1998.

NEXT WE TAKE THE WORLD

The first women's world invitational tournament was held in Canada in 1987 and the first World Championship sanctioned by the International Ice Hockey Federation was held in 1990. Women's hockey made its Olympic Games debut in 1998 at Nagano, Japan, as a demonstration sport and was a full Olympic sport in 2002 at Salt Lake, Utah. While the U.S. and Canada remain the dominant world powers, several other countries are making strides to increase the depth of competition, notably Sweden, Finland, Russia and China.

* * * * *

"I tried to talk my daughter out of going with a hockey player but he's a good kid. He asked me if he could marry Carrie before he asked her. I said: 'You want to what?' I thought he was just going to ask for more ice time."

—Phil Esposito, on his daughter Carrie getting engaged to right-winger Alexander Selivanov

IT'S ALL ABOUT THE GAME...OR IS IT?

The business of hockey can be distracting...and confusing.

"When you ask for the house, car, cat, dog and all the fish when you're dealing with a player who's got questions about his health, no GM in his right mind is going to say 'yes' and offer to clean the aquarium, too."

—Eric Lindros, on Flyers GM Bob Clarke's inability to trade him

"It's beyond money at this point. They're not even treating him as a member of their family, unless it's a dysfunctional family."

—Brendan Morrison's agent Kurt Overhardt on contract negotiations with the Devils

"We're looking forward to building the type of team the Rangers are able to buy."

—Phoenix GM Bobby Smith

"The three important elements of hockey are: forecheck, backcheck and paycheck."

—Gil Perreault, former Buffalo Sabres forward

"Listen guys, I only want to be paid what I'm worth. I'm not asking for millions. Uh, excuse me, I meant to say that..."

—Patrice Brisebois, former Montreal Canadiens defenceman

"Winning is always fun, but the car is more important."

—Teemu Selanne, on the importance of the All-Star game

"It's not about the money. It's about what I believe in."

—Sergei Fedorov, on holding out for $6.5 million from the Red Wings in 1998

LOSING WITH PIZZAZZ

Harold Ballard had profit, celebrity and controversy as Maple Leaf owner—doing everything but winning.

Few have had as many adjectives to describe them, both laudatory and pejorative, as Harold Ballard. The longtime owner of the Toronto Maple Leafs was called a promotional genius, funny and warm, a philanthropist. He also was called surly, nasty, small-minded, bigoted, coarse and crude, the ultimate chauvinist, a self-serving publicity seeker, a bully and, most often, a loser and a convicted felon.

MAPLE LAUGHS

Selling out Maple Leaf Gardens for every NHL game and generating fat television revenue during Ballard's approximately 20 years at the controls, equalled far more than enough money to build a winning team. But the Leafs—especially in the 1980s, the last half of Ballard's reign—were the league's laughingstock. The club's front office operation was a circus, due mainly to Ballard's endless meddling and his belief that he was a hockey genius. And the on-ice product reflected the management caliber...

WHICH IS WHY THEY HIRED MANAGERS

In Ballard's more-or-less 20 seasons (1971–1991), the team owned by the man who once said, "I've forgotten more about hockey than any of these owners will ever know," played 1672 games with a 629-817-226 win-loss tie record. It's frightening to think what that mark would have been if the man in charge didn't "know everything about hockey." But through that time, Ballard's outrageous statements, his often vicious pronouncements and ridiculous ideas on how the NHL Board of Governors should operate kept his name in the media consistently. To Ballard, the stupidity of something he said did not matter; that someone wrote about it in a newspaper did. When he'd exhausted his musings on hockey, he'd earn more notoriety and scorn by turning his attention to politics and feminism.

CAREER KILLER

Ballard's big mouth and his desire to call the shots prevented an assortment of top hockey executives from working for him. Jim Gregory spent 40 years in the Leaf organization as a manager and coach in junior hockey and minor-pro. He was then granted a front-row seat to see the fruits of his labor when he became team GM in the 1970s. The fine group of young talent that Gregory had collected and developed was ready for show time. That was when Ballard stubbornly refused to match any contract offers from the World Hockey Association, and all that talent was quickly lost. Gregory still managed to counter some of Harold's interference, coming up with a brilliant reconstruction effort leading to a solid Leafs team from 1973 to 1978.

A JOB WORTH TURNING DOWN

When Ballard sacked Gregory—he never told Gregory or coach Roger Neilson face-to-face that they were fired—he attempted to hire Scotty Bowman, who had just coached the Montreal Canadiens to four consecutive Stanley Cup championships. "The Leaf job had much appeal because of the finances available and I looked at it very closely," Bowman said. "Harold Ballard promised me complete control but I felt that he would not keep his nose out of the operation, that he would want to be the guy quoted in the press about the team. I just couldn't see working under those conditions." Bowman instead became GM-coach in that hockey hotbed of Buffalo.

PUNCH IN BALLARD'S FACE

To fill the hole, Ballard hired Punch Imlach, who was GM-coach of the Leafs in four Stanley Cup titles in the 1960s before being sacked by Ballard and ownership partner Stafford Smythe in 1969. Imlach had built the Sabres from 1970 expansion team to Cup finalist in 1975 but hadn't taken the team past the quarterfinals the three years since. Of course with Ballard involved, Imlach's hiring evolved into a fiasco. Punch signed a contract as Leafs GM one evening with a press conference to announce his return scheduled for noon the next day. Next morning, Ballard breezed into Imlach's office with some suggestions for strengthening the team. "Harold, let's get one thing straight: I call the shots for the team, I decide what might make them better and I make the statements to the media," Imlach said. "I'll tell you what I think you need to know about the operation and if you can't live with that, then I might as well leave right now."

YOU WANT TO *DO YOUR JOB*? YOU'RE FIRED!

Ballard immediately contacted his accountant and lawyer to try to find a contract loophole (and quick!) to get out of Punch's "ink-is-still-wet" contract. Imlach ended up as Leafs "boss," but apparently neither man was too happy about it. Imlach not only went to war with the owner but with every Leafs player, plummeting a competent team into the league's basement. Early in the 1980–81 season, Imlach arrived at Maple Leaf Gardens one morning to find his name deleted from his parking place. "I had no idea just how big a roadblock Ballard was in trying to run an NHL team, how his shooting off his mouth to his friends in the press, much of it dead wrong, made it impossible to do the job," Imlach said.

THE GLORIOUS SEA FLEAS

In his youth, Ballard was a speed skater and powerboat racer, moving into a business owned by his father that built sewing machines for the garment trade and also produced a high-selling ice skate. Ballard became actively involved in the operation of hockey teams as a young man, serving as GM-coach of the Toronto National Sea Fleas when they won the Allan Cup as Canadian senior champs in 1932 and a silver medal at the 1933 World Championship. He was GM of the West Toronto Nationals when that team won the Memorial Cup as Canadian junior champs in 1939.

SHOULDA STUCK TO THE JUNIORS

As president and financial backer of the Toronto Marlboros junior club and a chain of minor teams, Ballard made a strong mark in hockey. Working with his close friend Stafford Smythe, the son of Conn Smythe (who had built Maple Leaf Gardens and the NHL Leafs into one of the great sports franchises in existence), Ballard turned the Marlies into a top junior organization, winning the Memorial Cup six times under his ownership.

When Conn Smythe decided to sell the Leafs in 1961, Stafford and Ballard, with a large bank loan, headed the group of wealthy Toronto businessmen known as the Silver Seven that bought the franchise. With Imlach at the helm, the Leafs went on a great roll, winning four Stanley Cups in five seasons from 1962 to 1967, perhaps giving the owners a notion that they were above and beyond the normal call. They turned the Gardens into a money machine, adding a restaurant and private boxes with advertising in every available space.

TAKEOVER STRATEGY #1: BE A CROOK

In 1971, Ballard and Stafford Smythe were charged with theft and fraud, mostly for using money from Maple Leaf Gardens Ltd., a public company, for personal use, and for tax evasion. The other Gardens directors thought it might be a good time to cash in their assets (and run!), many of them selling the shares they owned in the building to Smythe and Ballard. Before he could go to trial, Stafford Smythe died of a bleeding ulcer and despite his family's efforts to retain control of the company, Ballard, with the help of a bank, money-whipped them into selling their shares to him.

JAIL NOT BAD COMPARED TO HIS MESS AT MLG

In 1972, after a long trial, Ballard was sentenced to three years in prison, serving a year before being granted parole for good behavior. During a three-day pass, he told reporters that prison was "like living in a good motel: steak for dinner and good service, too." Of course, when that was reported, Members of Parliament were bombarded with questions about "soft" conditions in Canada's prison. Ballard could create trouble from anywhere.

AT LEAST HE PUT UP A FIGHT...

When Ballard returned to the Gardens, he embarked on his two decades mediocrity for the Maple Leafs, once a proud NHL team. Accompanied by another old-timer, former Leaf player King Clancy, Ballard was on the scene for all Leaf games, always willing to give an opinion, especially on subjects about which he knew very little. For the rest of his life his energy was high, his mouth active—conditions that all too often did not apply to his hockey team. Right up to his death in 1991, he fought with his three children, his staff, his fellow NHL governors and any reporter who dared to say that he wasn't the finest hockey mind in existence.

WILD AT THE WORLD HOCKEY CHAMPIONSHIPS

Win or lose, there's always excitement for Team Canada at the annual international tournament.

BIG SCORES OF YESTERYEAR

Before other hockey nations started to assemble competitive teams, Canada routinely toyed with its opponents at the World Championship. The Finns, for instance, clearly needed more time on the ice and less in the sauna in the 1950s. They lost 20–1 to Canada in 1954 and 24–0 in 1958. Now, Switzerland has come a long way since dropping a 23–0 decision in 1959, while poor old Belgium may never have recovered from its 33–0 drubbing in 1950. But what was the biggest margin of victory ever for a Canadian squad? Try 47–0 over Denmark in 1949! The Danes would take more than 50 years to climb back up to the top division of the Worlds. But in their return engagement with Canada in 2003, they got a little revenge with a 2–2 tie.

"VEE" IS FOR VICTORY

On March 7, 1954, the Soviet Union shocked the hockey world by winning its first ever World Championship with a 7–2 shellacking of the East York Lyndhursts, a Senior B amateur team representing Canada. Who would defend the pride of the true north, strong and free against the recently rampant Red Machine? The answer came in the form of the Penticton Vees, the hard-nosed 1955 Allan Cup champions from British Columbia's Okanagan Valley. Led by the three Warwick brothers and goalie Ivan McLelland, the Vees blitzed through seven straight wins at the 1955 Worlds in West Germany before facing the Russians in the decisive match. Early in the first period, defenceman Hal Tarala set the tone with a huge open-ice hit on Russian star Vsevolod Bobrov. The Vees completely dominated in a 5–0 gold medal triumph and then took the World Championship trophy home to

Canada with them. Rumor has it that they kept the original, made a replica and sent that one over to Europe the following year.

THE MAGIC OF MARTIN

Terry Sawchuk. Glenn Hall. Jacques Plante. Seth Martin. Most Canadian NHL fans would say it's the latter name that doesn't fit in this group of all-time great goaltenders. But to European fans, who never saw NHL games in the 1960s, Martin was a certified legend. He backstopped the Trail Smoke Eaters to a World Championship in 1961, the very last time Canada won the tournament with an amateur squad. The International Ice Hockey Federation also named him the top goalie in each of the four World Championships he played. Martin said he performed well against the Soviets because he'd adapted to their complex passing style: "I had to play goal the wrong way, as far as I was concerned. They just would not shoot the puck from where they should have shot from." The Soviets were so impressed by his consistency that when they arrived in Canada to start the 1972 Summit Series versus NHL pros, they wanted to know if Canada's netminders, Ken Dryden and Tony Esposito, were as good as Martin.

SILENCE OF THE 1970s

Canada doesn't win the World Championship every year, but it didn't even come close to the podium from 1970 to 1976. The reason was politics, not puckmanship. For years, Canada had complained about not being able to use its top NHL players at the tournament, while so-called "amateurs" from the Soviet Union, Sweden, and Czechoslovakia regularly reaped medals for their countries. When the 1970 World Championship was awarded to Winnipeg, Hockey Canada believed it had a deal worked out with the Europeans that would permit Team Canada's use of nine non-NHL pros. But International Ice Hockey Federation president Bunny Ahearne reneged on the deal weeks before the tournament was slated to begin, claiming that competing against pros would compromise other players' Olympic eligibility. Winnipeg lost its chance to become the first Canadian host city ever for the Worlds. The tournament was reassigned to Stockholm after Canada pulled out amid angry recriminations. Only in 1977, when the rules changed to allow using NHL pros, did Canada return to participating.

TO HELMET WITH YOU!

Phil Esposito was a proudly bareheaded star of the 1970s, but when the legendary NHL center joined Team Canada in Vienna in 1977, he was shocked to discover he'd have to cover up his dark locks and sideburns with a helmet due to international rules. Canada's performance was as spotty as Esposito's, with the team suffering 11–1 and 8–1 losses to the Soviets and finishing fourth. When the tournament-closing buzzer sounded in an 8–2 Canadian win over the Czechs, Esposito could restrain himself no longer. He skated past the IIHF directors' box, ripped off his protective headgear, and hurled it at IIHF president Gunther Sabetzki, shouting: "You can keep your !$#!$!@ helmet!"

COURAGEOUS CAPTAIN CANADA

Ryan Smyth of the Edmonton Oilers is an honest, hard-working player on the ice and one of the NHL's nicest guys to deal with away from the rink. But the veteran winger must have gotten testy when he considered his poor fortune at the first four World Championships where he played from 1999 to 2002. Not only was Smyth getting bounced out of the NHL playoffs in April, but he was also being "rewarded" with fourth, fifth, and sixth-place finishes in international hockey. Finally, it all came together for "Captain Canada" in 2003. Smyth became Canada's all-time leader in Worlds games played, passing James Patrick (40), and claimed his first gold medal at the tournament thanks to Anson Carter's dramatic overtime winner against Sweden.

* * * * *

TIT FOR TAT

"When I came to the Rangers, I wanted to be a defenceman, but nobody would chip in for an operation to have half my brain removed!"

—former New York Rangers goaltender Bob Froese

"It takes brains. It's not like a forward, where you can get away with scoring and not play defence. On defence you have to be thinking."

—1989 winner of the Norris Trophy (Best Defenceman) Chris Chelios

LENGTHY STAYS ON THE THRONE

The Canadiens top the list of teams that won the Stanley Cup in streaks to earn the "dynasty" title.

Compared to the great ones of history, say, the Bourbon dynasty which ruled France for 200 years, the hockey teams that have earned that name have had rather short rules. Hockey's longest run at the top was the five consecutive Stanley Cup championships won by the Montreal Canadiens from 1956 to 1960—the icebound equivalent of the Bourbon run.

BUT WHO SHOT J. R.?

The number of teams earning the dynasty sobriquet is not long, partly because the Cup has been so dominated by the Canadiens' three lengthy stretches of success. In addition to the five in a row, the Montreal club won four consecutive crowns from 1976 to 1979, and four in five years within a string of six in nine from 1965 to 1973.

The New York Islanders had four Cup triumphs in a row from 1980 to 1982 while the Toronto Maple Leafs were the first to win three consecutive Cups—from 1946 to 1949—making it four in five in 1951, and earned another three in a row in the early 1960s. The Edmonton Oilers collected four titles in five seasons, five in seven from 1984 to 1990.

In the early years of Cup competition, two teams—the Ottawa Silver Seven and Montreal Victorias—had lengthy stays in the throne room.

RICHARD'S REIGN (HENRI, THAT IS)

A couple of goals in the right places and the Canadiens' Cup streak in the 1950s would have been eight in a row. They won in 1953, then lost two seven-game finals to the powerful Detroit Red Wings before launching their record run of five crowns. On that roll, the Canadiens won 40 games and lost only nine, and in only two of ten series did their opponents win two games.

The Canadiens had it all: size, speed, offensive power, defensive acumen, great motivation and spirit—plus tough taskmaster in coach Toe Blake, who kept the team's ambition at a high level. The best testimonial to the team's greatness is that 11 members are in the Hockey Hall of Fame: Blake and general manager Frank Selke, goalie Jacques Plante, defencemen Doug Harvey and Tom Johnson, forwards Maurice "Rocket" and Henri "Pocket Rocket" Richard, Jean Béliveau, Dickie Moore, Bernie Geoffrion and Bert Olmstead.

TWO BIG GUNS, TWO BIG RUNS

Béliveau and Henri Richard were holdovers into the 1960s when the Canadiens started another splendid stretch in the 1964–65 season with excellent young players developed in their farm system. They won the Cup in 1965 and 1966, were upset by the Leafs in 1967, then won back-to-back titles in 1968 and 1969. With fantastic young goalie Ken Dryden and a cast of solid veterans, they added victories in 1971 and 1973, the latter with Scotty Bowman as coach.

While the Philadelphia Flyers were bullying their way to two wins, the Canadiens were building an extraordinary team with Dryden, defencemen Larry Robinson, Guy Lapointe and Serge Savard, and forwards Guy Lafleur, Steve Shutt, Jacques Lemaire and Bob Gainey. They ended the Flyers' reign in 1976, then won three more times with a two-way approach of strong defensive work and an opportunistic offence guided by the brilliant Bowman.

ISLAND STRONGHOLD

Born as a 1972 expansion team, the Islanders built a splendid roster through the amateur draft, under the wise guidance of GM Bill Torrey and coach Al Arbour. After crushing late-1970s playoff losses, the Isles filled the weak spots in their lineup with smart trades and beat the Flyers in the 1980 final on Bob Nystrom's overtime goal in the deciding game. That launched a four consecutive Cup victory streak in which the Islanders won an astonishing 19 consecutive playoff series before losing the 1984 final to the Oilers.

The Isles were led by goalie Billy Smith, defencemen Denis Potvin, Stefan Persson and Ken Morrow, the forward line of Bryan Trottier, Mike Bossy and Clark Gillies plus Butch Goring, John Tonelli, Nystrom, and Duane and Brent Sutter.

ALBERTA GOLD

The Oilers entered the NHL in 1979 as one of four refugees from the defunct World Hockey Association and brought with them a large advantage. One of the four players they were allowed to protect was Wayne Gretzky, starting his illustrious career as the highest scorer in NHL history. GM-coach Glen Sather and his staff drafted brilliantly over the next four years, adding goalie Grant Fuhr, defencemen Kevin Lowe and Paul Coffey, and forwards Mark Messier, Glenn Anderson and Jari Kurri to form the core of the highest scoring team in NHL history.

The young Oilers lost in the 1983 playoffs to the Islanders but in a year the team had matured into a powerhouse "run 'n gun' offensive team. Led by Gretzky, the Oilers won the Cup in 1984 and 1985, suffered a playoff loss to the Calgary Flames in 1986 when defenceman Steve Smith banked the puck off Fuhr into the Oiler net for the deciding goal, then won in 1987 and 1988. Gretzky was traded to the Los Angeles Kings, who eliminated the Oilers in the 1989 playoffs. However, with Messier taking the leading role, the Edmonton club rebounded to win the 1990 Stanley Cup.

LEAFS DON'T FALL

When World War II ended, the Maple Leafs had a splendid roster of young players with some dandy veterans in key roles. Centers Ted Kennedy and Syl Apps and goalie Turk Broda were cornerstones of the team that won the crown in 1947 and 1948. When Apps retired, owner Conn Smythe landed front-liner Max Bentley as a replacement in a major trade and the Leafs added wins in 1949 and 1951.

END OF A DYNASTY…ALL OF THEM?

Detroit flirted with a dynasty destiny at the turn of the century, but had started their run with an already-aged lineup and never could secure a goaltender reliable as a Dryden, Smith or Fuhr. Under the new salary-cap NHL, it seems unlikely any team could fit the talent of the 1980s Oilers or 1970s Canadiens into one payroll, let alone hold onto that talent for a sustained period. Even the Tampa Bay Lightning, after winning the 2004 Cup, could not keep all its key players after the imposition of the salary cap. The New Jersey model, good for three Cups in nine years with one spectacular goalie, a couple top defencemen and a revolving but consistently solid supporting cast, could be the only route left…if it weren't for the fact the league is simultaneously trying to stifle defensive hockey! Have dynasties gone the way of dinosaurs?

A NOVEL GAME

Nothing on TV in the offseason? Then try cracking these—and remember, wise fans keeps their bookshelves stocked for the next NHL labor dispute.

Amazons by Cleo Birdwell
The subtitle "An Intimate Memoir by the First Women to Play in the National Hockey League" explains most of the plot, though it's in fact a novel by acclaimed American writer Don DeLillo. As a New York Ranger, Cleo Birdwell is bashed, bruised and scores lots of goals over the course of her rookie season, but she also finds time to nursemaid her neurotic roommate, play strip Monopoly and sword-fight.

The Divine Ryans by Wayne Johnston
Draper Doyle Ryan grows up in a Newfoundland family whose members inevitably take the cloth, but he's more interested in unravelling the mystery of his father's death and following the ever-changing fortunes of the Montreal Canadiens. A priest, meanwhile, shows him how to throw a punch, while his tomboy-ish sister Mary teaches him a thing or two about stickhandling.

Finnie Walsh by Steven Galloway
Working-class Paul Woodward spends his childhood taking shots on wealthy Finnie Walsh, leading, strangely enough, to near-fatal injuries to both Paul's father and kid sister. After carrying the hometown Portsmouth Jaguars to the provincial championship, both boys are drafted into the NHL, where Finnie's overdeveloped sense of loyalty determines that only Paul will skate into the Stanley Cup finals.

The Good Body by Bill Gaston
Bobby "Loose" Bonaduce retires from minor hockey in the U.S. and lies his way into graduate school at the University of New Brunswick, just so that he can play on a collegiate squad with the son he hasn't seen in ten years and possibly reconnect with the boy's mother. Along with English classes, Bobby must also

come to grips with the multiple sclerosis slowly betraying his once-reliable body.

Hockey Night in the Dominion of Canada by Eric Zweig
A work of fiction cast with real-life players, following each from backyard pond to the big leagues. In the end the Renfrew Millionaires lose the 1910 Stanley Cup finals to the Ottawa Senators, but, on a lighter note, manage to thwart an assassination attempt on Canadian Prime Minister Wilfrid Laurier.

King Leary by Paul Quarrington
Percival Leary once executed a perfect "St. Louis Whirlygig" to score the winning goal in the 1919 Stanley Cup finals. Now living in a nursing home with Blue Hermann, the alcoholic reporter who chronicled his exploits, Leary looks back on his career, from hockey-playing monks teaching him the game to his glory days with the Canadiens, but his attention returns to the present when he's invited to star in a ginger ale commercial.

The Last Season by Roy MacGregor
Felix Batterinski grows up playing hockey in the backwoods Ontario town of Pomerania and comes to prominence as a "Broad Street Bully" on the mid-1970s Philadelphia Flyers. After his NHL career crumbles he becomes a player-coach in Finland, where he shakily attempts to put his own personal stamp on the European game.

Logan in Overtime by Paul Quarrington
The eponymous Logan is an alcoholic, semi-professional goalie, playing in a league where overtime is not broken into periods but just goes on and on and on. In the last game of the playoffs, broken and exhausted, his problems are compounded by his conviction that aliens are out to get him.

Salvage King, Ya! by Mark Anthony Jarman
Drinkwater is a tough-talking junkyard owner and semi-professional hockey player. Realizing that at 33 he'll never make the NHL, he looks for his life's true direction while attempting to salvage his relationships with his ex-wife, fiancée and mistress.

BOBBY ORR OF HOCKEY LORE

Bobby Orr, rated by many as the finest pure talent in hockey history, is also a classic on-the-pond development yarn.

The Seguin River is a wide, slow-moving stream through the town of Parry Sound in what is considered the southern portion of northern Ontario. In the cold winters, it freezes over early and becomes a large hockey and skating rink, the perfect ice surface for developing hockey skills.

IT ALSO MEANS IT WAS DAMN LOUD!

Bobby Orr's home, a simple white stucco house, had the railroad tracks on one side, the river on the other. That meant little distance for him to travel to learn the game at which some feel he was the best ever, the finest pure talent ever seen. Gordie Howe certainly was more durable, Wayne Gretzky perhaps had stronger instinct, Yvan Cournoyer might have been faster and John Ferguson was probably tougher...But no player had all those qualities in higher quantities than Orr.

NUMBER FOUR, BOBBY ORR

How that skill was developed in a very young lad is not a story unique to "Number Four," as Orr was simply known through his majestic career with the Boston Bruins. The Seguin River was to Orr as Walter Gretzky's backyard rink was to Wayne, the Bay of Quinte to Bobby Hull and the farm sloughs and empty hay mows to the six Sutter brothers. But Orr's total devotion to hockey from an early age—his father figures his son decided at nine or ten the game would be his life—was the key to his brilliance.

"If it got really cold when we were on the river and my face was a little numb, I could sneak home, walking across the road on the toes of my skates, and thaw out some by the stove," Orr said. "But I never stayed there too long. I might miss something in the game. The only thing that got me home was the dark and then only because it got colder."

LEARN HOW TO BE A PUCK HOG

The big game on the river was what Bobby's father Doug called "Parry Sound Keep-away." Others called it simply "hog." A player got the puck on his stick and kept it until another player checked it away from him. From an early age, it seemed the little blond-haired kid had the puck most of the time through a combination of his quick hands and even quicker feet.

AND LOUDER STILL...

Because the Orr family sometimes did not own a car, the garage was often empty. Bobby turned it into his shooting gallery in all seasons, winding up his day there with at least a half-hour of shots. They had cut a piece of plywood the size of a net, six feet by four, and nailed it to the back wall of the garage. "The garage was only 20 feet long," Doug Orr said. "He would open the garage doors and shoot from the drive and even from the street. I made special pucks by hollowing out pucks a little and putting some lead filament in them. They were about twice as heavy as a regular puck and helped him develop his shot and strength. Every night, even in the heat of summer, in the house, we would hear the thud of the shots, one sound if he was hitting his plywood net, another if he was missing. If the misses were a higher number, he would be grumpy when he finally stopped."

COACH BUCKO, MP

In a small town, the kid with talent gets to play a great deal on the local teams, often moving up a notch with the older boys. Bobby started in organized hockey at five and often played on two all-star teams, the "traveling" clubs that went into the Ontario play-downs. The Parry Sound all-star teams were coached by Bucko McDonald, the barrel-chested old belter who had an NHL career with the Detroit Red Wings and Toronto Maple Leafs, played for and coached the fabled Sundridge Beavers intermediate team, and served several terms as a Member of Parliament.

MITE ON THE DEFENCE

Defencemen usually were the bigger, rougher kids while the smaller lads were forwards. Orr always was smaller than the other kids; at 12 years of age, he was 5-foot-2 and 110 pounds. He was a winger for part of a season, then McDonald shifted him to defence. "Bobby tried the wing for a time, then I moved him back to defence," Bucko said. "Doug Orr once asked me if I didn't think he should be a forward and I told him that Bobby was born to play defence. I'd never thought much about it but he just had all the equipment to be a defenceman, except size at the time. He was the best young player in town and that's why I asked him to play for the bantams."

ALL HE HAS TO DO IS GROW INTO THAT SWEATER

Playing with boys two years older led to Orr's "discovery." The Parry Sound team met the team from Gananoque on the St. Lawrence River in eastern Ontario in the provincial final. Gananoque is just east of Kingston, where the Bruins' farm team in the short-lived Eastern Pro League was located. An executive from the Bruins, a team struggling in the NHL, was in town and attended the bantam game to check on two highly regarded 14-year-olds on the Gananoque team. The rest is history, a fine part of hockey folklore. The kid who grabbed the attention was the little squirt in baggy pants and too-big sweater on the Parry Sound defence. Orr played 58 of the 60 minutes in that game, his only rest coming during a penalty.

"It was incredible that this little kid, who looked like he shouldn't be playing with the big guys, ran the show for the entire game," said Lynn Patrick, the Bruins' general manager at the time, years later when he held the same job with the St. Louis Blues. "There were few players in the NHL who could feather a pass the way he could at 12."

SHOOTING LOW

Orr became the most scouted player in hockey because, at that time, NHL teams could tie up young players at 14. Representatives of all six NHL clubs were regular visitors to Parry Sound games and the Orr home. The most persistent was Wren Blair, a Bruin scout who would be GM of the Oshawa Generals when that team returned to top level junior hockey. Years later, Doug Orr revealed that it was Bobby himself who decided the Bruins were his club. "He saw that they were well down in the NHL standings and one day he said that he could probably get to the NHL quicker than with one of the teams at the top of the league with a lot of talent," he said.

SERVING IN THE 'SHWA

At 14, Orr joined the Generals in the Toronto Metro Junior A League, playing against boys as old as 20. But his skill, smarts and anticipation allowed him to survive. His ability to read and react to the opposition's plays stood out at that age. He would start heading for a spot on the ice long before there was an indication to anyone else that the puck would end up there and, sure enough, most times the puck would end up on his stick. He scored 29 goals in his second junior season and dominated the Ontario Hockey League. In his third season, a Toronto columnist had this lead on a yarn on the prodigy: "If Bobby Orr turns out to be merely human, strong men in Boston will weep."

A BOY AGAINST MEN

A game in Orr's pre-NHL days that sealed the deal on his surefire stardom came in his final junior season when he neared his 18th birthday. The Toronto Marlboros juniors were scheduled to meet the great national team of the old Soviet Union and added several other top junior players including Orr, Serge Savard and Derek Sanderson. Orr was exceptional in a 4–3 loss, the first time he had been on display against men.

BUT ALAN, HE'S NOT EVEN OF AGE

Orr was represented by lawyer Alan Eagleson in negotiations on the prodigy's first contract with the Bruins, whose business was handled by the stern Hap Emms, a longtime coach of Bruins junior development teams in Barrie and Niagara Falls. The contract was signed on Emms' yacht in Ontario's Lake Simcoe, the biggest deal ever for an NHL player. When the signatures were on the paper, Eagleson suggested that it was an occasion that demanded a cork out of champagne bottle. A noted tightwad who ran his junior teams on a strict low budget, Emms opened the boat's fridge, took out a can and the signing of "Number Four," maybe the greatest ever, was celebrated with a sip of Fresca.

BEST BEHIND THE BENCH

Scotty Bowman had a long and honorable coaching career.

Larry Robinson, the standout Montreal Canadien defenceman during the team's exceptional success in the 1970s, offered perhaps the best summation of head coach Scotty Bowman: "There were times when I didn't think I could stand him any longer but I didn't want to marry him. I did know that if I did what he told me and the team did, too, we would all be successful. You might not like his approach but, most of the time, the end results were the thing you loved—winning!"

AND WIN HE DID...

Bowman stands alone among NHL coaches. In 30 seasons at the helm of four teams, Bowman won the Stanley Cup a record nine times: five with the Canadiens, one with the Pittsburgh Penguins and three with the Detroit Red Wings. One of his mentors and coaching heroes, Toe Blake, guided the Canadiens to eight Cup championships from 1955 to 1968. Only one other man, Hap Day, coached teams to more than four championships—five with his Toronto Maple Leafs. In 2,141 schedule games, Bowman's teams won 1,244 and tied 313 for a winning percentage of .654. Only one other coach, Al Arbour, has more than 700 wins. In the playoffs, Bowman has 223 wins in 353 games, 100 more wins than second-place Arbour.

VIEWS AT VARIANCE

Survey the dozens of players on his teams over those 30 years, and it would be rare to find two with the same impression of the man. Some saw him as a whip-cracking disciplinarian who was cold and aloof personally, unable to express emotion, true feelings or sincere encouragement. Others felt he was a genius—much smarter and more knowledgeable than the men behind the other benches—and the best praise they could receive from him was when he said nothing about their play.

A SIMPLE GAME

In discussing the game, Bowman always made his outlook on hockey sound simple. Asked once what the most important part of coaching, his reply was terse: "Having the right players on the ice." Pressed to expand on that, Bowman said, "If the other team is using, say, a right-winger and he will overpower the left-winger we have opposite him, then we have to make a quick change and get a guy out there who can handle him. If we leave out an over-matched player and the opposition scores a goal, then we have to score two to get a lead. That's much more difficult to do than making the change of players to keep the other team from scoring. If they don't score, then we only need one to get the lead."

DEFENCE, WHO NEEDS IT?

While Bowman's championship teams with the Canadiens, Penguins and Red Wings all had high-scoring attacks, their strongest asset was always defence. But even on the subject of goal prevention, he had a unique approach. "Often teams that can score never get enough credit for their defensive play," Bowman said. "With, say, the Canadiens, puck control was a big part of our defence. The so-called thinkers in the game figured a great defensive team was one that turned the puck over to the opposition, then checked them strongly. I always figure that if we had the puck ourselves and it was under control, the other team wasn't going to score much. That seemed like pretty good defence to me, anyway."

WHAT A RISE!

A Montreal native, Bowman played top level junior hockey in the Canadiens system, then suffered a serious head injury. Contrary to popular belief, the injury did not end his career; he played 90 junior games afterwards. When his junior days were over, he moved into coaching youngsters and scouting for the Canadiens, rising through the ranks to be coach of major junior clubs in Peterborough and Montreal. He logged time with the Canadiens minor-pro farm teams, working as assistant manager and coach to Sam Pollock, who became hockey's top executive with the NHL Canadiens. When the NHL expanded by six teams in 1967, Bowman was hired by the new St. Louis Blues as GM and head coach. Assembling a team of veterans and overlooked youngsters, Bowman remarkably took the

Blues to the Stanley Cup final in each of the team's first three seasons in the league. He returned to the Canadiens organization as head coach in 1972 and over the next seven seasons with them he recorded five Stanley Cup wins—four consecutive from 1976–1979.

FOUR MORE

When Pollock left the GM's job to go into private business, Bowman felt snubbed when not named as replacement and resigned from the team. He was hired as GM and coach of the Buffalo Sabres, where he encountered the only weak stretch in his career. The Sabres were only a .500 playoff team in his six years at the helm, after which he did television analysis for a season. He joined the Penguins as personnel director but when head coach "Badger" Bob Johnson—who had guided the Pens to the Cup the previous season—died suddenly just before the 1992–93 schedule, Bowman was named coach and he led them to the 1993 crown. He moved to the Red Wings as head coach for the 1993–94 season, a stay that lasted for nine seasons, winning the Cup in 1997, 1998 and 2002. With all the coaching records strongly in his book, Bowman announced his retirement from coaching during the 2002 on-ice victory celebrations.

* * * * *

"Ice hockey is a form of disorderly conduct in which the score is kept."

—Doug Larson

"A puck is a hard rubber disc that hockey players strike when they can't hit one another."

—sports columnist Jimmy Cannon

"Hockey is murder on ice."

—defenceman Jim Murray

"We take the shortest route to the puck and arrive in ill humour."

—Bobby Clarke,
captain of the Philadelphia Flyers, 1972

THE GREAT UNCLE JOHN'S BATHROOM READER HOCKEY QUIZ

1) In 1971, the Montreal Canadiens traded to acquire the first-round draft position to select a young Guy Lafleur. With what team did they make the trade?
   a) Cleveland Barons
   b) Atlanta Flames
   c) California Golden Seals
   d) Minnesota North Stars
   e) Vancouver Canucks

2) Who is the only coach to lose 12 Stanley Cup Finals?
   a) Dick Irvin
   b) Scotty Bowman
   c) Al Arbour
   d) Jack Adams
   e) Don Cherry

3) The floundering Vancouver Canucks of the 1970s once employed an outside consultant to help winger Rosaire Paiement out of a scoring slump. Who did they hire?
   a) Reveen the Impossiblist
   b) Dr. Joyce Brothers
   c) Maurice Richard
   d) A Las Vegas stripper
   e) A priest

4) Match the following players to the appropriate nationality:

a) Sergei Priakin	1) Slovakian
b) Ivan Hlinka	2) Yugoslavian
c) Ivan Boldirev	3) Ukrainian
d) Alexei Zhitnik	4) Czech
e) Marian Gaborik	5) Russian

5) Who said, "I don't like hockey. I'm just good at it."
   a) Eric Lindros
   b) Pavel Bure
   c) Brett Hull
   d) Mike Bossy
   e) Jacques Plante

6) In the early 1950s, a young Maple Leaf named Les Costello abandoned a promising NHL career to become a priest. But Father Costello was far from finished with hockey. He formed a barnstorming hockey team of priests from all parts of Ontario. What was the name of this righteous squad?
   a) The Holy Terrors
   b) The Flying Fathers
   c) The Sacred Order of Skaters
   d) The 12 Disciples
   e) The Fishers of Men

7) Joe Nieuwendyk, three-time winner of the Stanley Cup as a member of the Calgary Flames, Dallas Stars and New Jersey Devils, once used the Cup itself as a rather unconventional receptacle. What did he put in it?
   a) French fries and gravy
   b) Geraniums
   c) A tropical fish
   d) Potpourri
   e) Bridge mixture

8) Who is the only player to score twice in a 10-second span in an All-Star game?
   a) Dennis Maruk, Washington Capitals
   b) Dennis Hextall, Minnesota North Stars
   c) Denis Savard, Chicago Blackhawks
   d) Dennis Ververgaert, Vancouver Canucks
   e) Dennis Hull, Chicago Black Hawks

9) Which **TWO** of the following teams were **NOT** in the World Hockey Association (1972–1979)?
   a) Calgary Cowboys
   b) Colorado Rockies
   c) Denver Spurs
   d) Houston Aeros
   e) Kentucky Colonels
   f) Quebec Nordiques
   g) San Francisco SeaHawks
   h) San Diego Mariners

10) Which of the following players **NEVER** won the Conn Smythe Trophy (awarded to the most valuable player of the Stanley Cup playoffs)?
   a) Butch Goring
   b) Jean-Sebastien Giguere
   c) Stan Mikita
   d) Jean Béliveau
   e) Mark Messier
   f) Roger Crozier

* * * * *

"Most people have friends, but no money. I have the opposite. I don't have a chance to talk to my real friends, the ones I've had since I was five years old. Sometimes I wish I could bring Czechoslovakia to America. Then I would be the happiest guy in the world."

—Jaromir Jagr

THE GREAT UNCLE JOHN'S BATHROOM READER HOCKEY QUIZ — ANSWER KEY

1. c) California Golden Seals; 2. a) Dick Irvin; 3. a) Reveen the Hypnotist; 4. a) Sergei Priakin is Russian; b) Ivan Hlinka is Czech; c) Ivan Boldirev is Yugoslavian; d) Alexei Zhitnik is Ukrainian; e) Marion Gaborik is Slovakian; 5. c) Brett Hull 6. b) The Flying Fathers; 7. a) French fries and gravy; 8. d) Dennis Ververgaert, Vancouver Canucks; 9. b) Colorado Rockies & e) Kentucky Colonels; 10. c) Stan Mikita.

TIGER TALK

Random thoughts from former NHL tough guy Tiger Williams, who was as quick with a quote as he was to drop the gloves.

On the problem with some NHL tough guys of today: "As they mature as players and get used to the pro lifestyle, they kind of want to look like their bankbook. They want to be a little more dignified, but there's no job for them in that area. They forget what got them there and they're not around very long."

On being a team enforcer: "Does anybody want that job? Anybody who says yes, you know the guy's an idiot. You just do what you do. And then again, you get in that lane and you better stay in that lane or you won't be in any lane."

On the Todd Bertuzzi-Steve Moore incident: "What I find interesting is that 200 people died in (terrorist) bombings in Spain and the biggest news story across Canada was Todd Bertuzzi. I think we need to get our priorities set straight as to what's really important in life."

On the way hockey players can get pigeonholed: "With a lot of great players, you'll always hear the knock: 'Well, defensively, he's not any good.' Do you know why? Because he doesn't want it to be known that he's any good at it. It's by design. But for other guys, that's not the way they are. If they're asked to do something, they just do it. But unfortunately, they get pigeonholed and they stay there forever."

On the penalty box at old Maple Leaf Gardens: "The box was kind of a gross place to go. The guys in there are bleeding and have bloody noses. They have greenies and yellows and drip all over the boards, and no one's cleaned the place since 1938."

On leading a personal charge against bylaws banning road hockey games in some Canadian cities: "We have to put a stop to this. We have to find out who these aliens are who dropped in on us with these bylaws and step on them. Squash them like a bug."

EDDIE SHORE'S WILD RIDE

One road trip to Montreal was a nightmare for Boston's great Eddie Shore when he was late for the train.

COULD I BORROW YOUR LIMOUSINE?

Tales of Eddie Shore's toughness and persistence fill hockey history books but topping the list of stories on the mighty defenceman is the yarn of one extraordinary trip from Beantown to Montreal. On January 2, 1929, a severe snowstorm had blanketed the eastern part of the continent and traffic problems in Boston caused Shore to miss the train taking the Bruins to Montreal for a game against the Maroons the next night. But Shore would not be stymied by the weather. At the railway station, he met a wealthy Bruins fan, who loaned his limousine and chauffeur to Shore for the trip.

THROUGH SLEET AND SNOW

The storm worsened with every mile when they managed to reach Vermont. But the driver abandoned the wheel when Shore refused to stop and hockey's big star drove himself with the chauffeur as passenger. When the wipers stopped, Shore drove with his hand on the outside of the windshield, melting a spot to allow at least a small view of the road. The duo was forced to push the car back on the road several times when it skidded off. Just across the border in Quebec, when the limo went deep into a ditch in the dark night, Shore walked through waist-deep snow to a farmhouse and convinced the farmer to bring his team of horses to haul it out.

BUT HOW'D THE CAR LOOK?

At 6 P.M. on January 3, the car reached the hotel where the Bruins were just leaving for the arena to play the game. Shore's hands were frost-bitten hooks from driving with the window open and his eyes were bloodshot because he had not slept. Bruins boss Art Ross told Shore to go to bed and show up the next morning for the train home but Shore insisted on playing. He ate a snack and caught a catnap in the trainers' room, then played his usual 40 minutes against the tough, physical Maroons. The Bruins won the game, 1–0. Of course, Shore scored the only goal.

HEY KID, SUIT UP!

A geography test almost cost a university student his 15 minutes of NHL fame.

While Chris Levesque, a third-year student and third-string goaltender at the University of British Columbia, was studying in the library for his exam the following morning, the Vancouver Canucks were searching frantically for him to be an emergency fill-in between the pipes.

With the Pittsburgh Penguins in town to play on December 9, 2003, the Canucks were caught with their pants down after their number one goaltender Dan Cloutier injured his groin during the morning skate. Their minor league goaltenders were all traveling with their respective teams back east and couldn't make it to Vancouver in time for the 7:08 P.M. start, leaving the Canucks with egg on their faces and no one to back up second stringer Johan Hedberg that night.

TO THE LIBRARY!

The Canucks first call was to the nearby UBC campus, but the team's top two goalies were both ineligible under the NHL's amateur emergency call-up rules, one because he was an undrafted European and the other, ironically, because he once played pro as a prospect in the Vancouver organization before giving up on his career and returning to school. That left the unlikely Levesque. The only problem was no one could find him.

Levesque had been given the day off from practice to cram for the geography exam at 8 A.M. the next morning and his roommates hadn't seen or heard from him since he announced he was heading to the library to study. The UBC campus has more than a half-dozen libraries. "We had guys all over campus trying to find him," UBC coach Milan Drajicevic said.

THIS IS A JOKE, RIGHT?

When teammates finally tracked down Levesque at 4:30 P.M., they had a hard time convincing the 23-year-old they weren't playing a prank. Considering he hadn't even started a university game—about five levels below the NHL—in almost three months and was sporting an unimpressive 0-4-1 record, 4.77 goals-against average and .855 save percentage with the Thunderbirds, it was hard to blame Levesque for his skepticism. "Actually, I thought the guy that found me was yanking my leg because we were talking about playing a prank like this on another guy about a week ago," Levesque said.

After finally convincing him the surreal NHL call-up was for real, Levesque rushed to GM Place and, after getting the university sport governing body to sign off on a one-time release, signed a one-day amateur agreement with the Canucks. A couple of hours later he was on the ice wearing a No. 40 Vancouver jersey, taking warm-up shots from superstars Markus Naslund and Todd Bertuzzi, then settling into a spot at the end of the bench for what he assumed would be nothing more than a chance to get closer to the action than any of the other 18,622 spectators at GM Place that night. Instead, he almost got into the action.

PHEW! THAT WAS CLOSE

A violent collision with Penguins' forward Konstantin Koltsov sent Hedberg's mask flying down the ice and left the Canucks goaltender lying motionless while team medical staff rushed to his side. Cameras quickly zoomed in on a horrified Levesque on the bench, chewing his gum so hard it looked like he too might soon need medical attention. To ease the tension, veteran Mike Keane yelled down the bench: "Don't worry! He'll get up."

"I was a little frightened at first," Levesque admitted after the game. "I tried to play it cool on the bench, just kept chewing my gum and looking up at the scoreboard with a camera right in my face. But luckily Hedberg wasn't hurt seriously and he shook it off."

REMEMBER, IT'S A SCHOOL NIGHT

Hedberg continued despite suffering a wrist injury in the collision and a relieved Levesque watched his new team come from behind to win the game 4–3 in overtime. Before he could escape back to campus to resume studying, Levesque had to face a media scrum bigger than the one in front of Naslund, the Canucks captain who scored all four of his team's goals. "It's a little different than after a UBC game where we just have one guy from the paper," said

Levesque, who grew up playing minor hockey in the nearby suburb of Port Coquitlam and spent some time in Manitoba's junior-A league. "There's like 40 people here."

Levesque kept his No. 40 jersey and later received a "highlight film" of his gum-chewing exploits on the bench and massive post-game media scrum. As for the geography exam, Levesque, still wired from his six-hour study break in the NHL, hit the books into the wee hours of the morning and scored 88 percent.

* * * * *

"We start out with goalies wearing masks. Every club has a defenceman or two who goes down to smother shots. Soon, they'll want masks. All forwards will wear helmets. The teams will become faceless, headless robots all of whom look alike to the spectators. We can't afford to take that fan appeal away from hockey."

—Muzz Patrick, former New York Rangers defenceman

"I've always felt we weren't physical enough on the back line. Now there's a no-parking sign in front of our net."

—San Jose Sharks GM Dean Lombardi on the addition of Marty McSorley

"Sometimes you think they must have come out of the chimp cages at the Bronx zoo."

—former Boston Bruins goaltender Gerry Cheevers on New York hockey fans

"He had better get married soon, because he's getting uglier every day!"

—Mark Recchi on Flyers teammate Stewart Malgunas

"They were checking us so closely, I could tell what brand of deodorant they were using."

—Flyer Gary Dornhoefer, after playing Montreal

"The only difference between the Coyotes and *Days of Our Lives* is that nobody has been shot on our team yet."

—Jeremy Roenick on the trade rumors around Phoenix captain Keith Tkachuk

MIRACLE ON ICE

The 1980 U.S. Olympic team: Legends of American hockey history.

In the long history of ice hockey in the United States, one team stands out as the high point in American hockey—the 1980 U.S. Olympic hockey squad, winners of the gold medal on its home turf (or ice) in Lake Placid, New York.

POLITICS OF HOCKEY

There were numerous reasons why the focus of the world press was not on the Olympics and these reasons made what happened in Lake Placid all the more meaningful for many Americans. On November 4, 1979, Muslim college students raided and overtook the U.S. Embassy in Tehran, Iran. In the process, the students took 51 hostages and held them captive for the next 444 days.

One month later, Soviet tanks and soldiers invaded Afghanistan. As a result, U.S. President Jimmy Carter announced that if the Soviets did not pull out of Afghanistan by February of 1980 the Americans would boycott the 1980 Summer Olympiad in Moscow. The Soviets, if anything, increased their military actions in Afghanistan and, as promised, the American athletes did not participate in the Summer Games. Some thought the Russians would boycott the 1980 Winter Olympics, but Soviet Premier Leonid Breshnev approved participation.

ENTER COACH BROOKS

U.S. Olympic Head Coach Herb Brooks had his own battles to fight. The charismatic Brooks was the most successful collegiate hockey coach in America, winning numerous NCAA hockey titles as leader of the University of Minnesota squad. Out of the 20 players who comprised the 1980 U.S. Olympic squad team, nine (almost half) were from Brooks' home base of the University of Minnesota. Mike Eruzione was named team captain. Other notable players were Mark Johnson of the University of Wisconsin and defencemen Ken Morrow of Bowling Green (Ohio).

Brooks had a personal, inner fire motivating him to do well in the Olympics. As a player, Brooks was the last man cut from the 1960 U.S. Olympic team, which went on to win the gold medal by beating Czechoslovakia in Squaw Valley, California. As they watched the win on television, Brooks' father turned to Herb and said, "Well, it looks like the coach made the right decision."

THE HERB BROOKS EXPERIENCE

A 60-game exhibition was arranged for the 1980 U.S. team to build up experience together. Their final record was 42 wins, 15 losses, and three ties. The game that really set the tone was a disappointing 3–3 tie against the Norway national team. Furious with the team's lackadaisical effort, Brooks made his players do line-to-line skating sprints for an hour after the game. The arena's maintenance man actually turned out the lights, but Brooks made his players keep skating. This act cemented his players together for two common causes: to work a lot harder as a team, and to demonize Herb Brooks. The coach's hard-line but colorful approach to discipline led to his "Brooksisms," imaginative dressing-downs of players slacking off at practice; two of the most popular were "You look like a monkey screwing a football" and, "Your playing gets worse and worse every day and now you're playing like it's next week." The team was clearly getting better, but in February 1980, three days before the start of the Olympics, the team was wiped out in an exhibition with the Soviets 10–3.

DURING THE OLYMPICS

On February 12, 1980, the Olympic cauldron torch was lit and the Winter Olympics officially began. The Americans' first opponent was Sweden and the U.S. was losing in the third period. With 29 seconds left, they scored to salvage a 2–2 tie. Two days later they played Czechoslovakia, and in what was probably the team's biggest win of the tournament, they upset them by a score of 7–3. Momentum was building...The U.S. then beat, in order, Norway, Romania and Germany. They struggled in the last game, but rallied to come out on top. All of this set up a mighty match-up versus the Soviet Union.

U.S. VS. USSR

The Soviets were in a separate bracket than the American team and defeated all their competition, including Canada and Finland. So on Friday, February 22, 1980, at 5 P.M. Eastern Standard Time, the hockey game pitting the Soviet Union against the U.S. began. Before the game, Brooks gave an inspired pep talk to his players, telling them "You were meant to be here...This moment is yours...It's our time." His amateur collegiate players were about to play the professional Soviets in the most important hockey game of their lives.

UNCLE JOHNSON SHOOTS AND SCORES

The U.S. came out to an inspired start, yet the Soviets scored the first goal and had a 2–1 lead as the final seconds of the first period were ticking down. Many of the players on both teams began to slow down and skate towards their respective team benches, but not the U.S.'s Mark Johnson. Breaking into the Soviet zone with the puck with only five seconds left, Johnson slipped past a Soviet defencemen, deked Soviet goaltender Vladislav Tretiak out of position, and tied the game just as the first period ended.

SOVIET MIND GAMES

Then came a move by Soviet head coach Viktor Tikhonov that surprised everybody, even Brooks. Between periods, Tikhonov decided to bench Tretiak and replace him with backup netminder Vladimir Myshkin. The manoeuvre seemed to spark the Soviet team, as the second period was their best of the game. When it ended they were winning, 3–2, and had outshot the U.S. 30–10 after two periods of play.

COUNTDOWN TO GOLD

The U.S. Olympic team was not to be denied. Johnson scored to tie the game in the third period. ABC-TV commentator Ken Dryden had just finished telling play-by-play announcer Al Michaels that "The Americans are relying too much on [goaltender] Jim Craig" when captain Eruzione scored, giving a 4–3 lead to the U.S. with exactly ten minutes left in regulation. The crowd chanted "USA! USA!" as the minutes and seconds wound down. With three seconds left, Michaels asked the eternal question "Do you believe in miracles?" and answered it by yelling "Yes!"

Two days later, the U.S. played Finland for the gold medal. Before the game, Brooks told his players "If you lose this game, you'll take it to your f—-in' grave." After two periods, Finland was winning by a score of 2–1. The Americans exploded for three goals in the final period, winning the game 4–2 and also the gold medal.

WHERE ARE THEY NOW?

Out of the 20 U.S. Olympic players, only Ken Morrow won the Stanley Cup in the NHL, four times with the New York Islanders. Jim Craig became a salesman and Eruzione works an inspirational speaker. Craig Patrick went on to work for the Pittsburgh Penguins, helping create the template for a team that would win back-to-back Stanley Cups in the early 1990s. Mark Johnson had a strong NHL career with the New Jersey Devils and later became an assistant coach for the University of Wisconsin women's hockey team. Mike Ramsey, Neal Broten, Mark Pavelich, Dave Christian, Jack O'Callahan, Steve Christoff, Rob McClanahan, Dave Silk and Bill Baker also all went on to play in the NHL.

After the Lake Placid Games, Brooks coached the New York Rangers (1981–1985), where he reached the 100-victory mark faster than any other coach in franchise history. He coached the Minnesota North Stars (1987–1988), the New Jersey Devils (1992–1993) and the Pittsburgh Penguins (1999–2000). He also led the French Olympic team at the 1998 Nagano Games. Brooks returned to the U.S. Olympic hockey team in 2002 to lead them to a silver medal. Tragically, Herb Brooks passed away the next year in a car accident.

* * * * *

"He's a gutless puke, that's what Travis Green is. That's why he doesn't wear an Islander uniform any more."

—Islander Mike Milbury, on former Islander Travis Green's hit on Kenny Jonsson

"Luc Robitaille is a great kid and a good player but ask anybody on the street and they'd probably think Luc Robitaille is a type of salad dressing."

—L.A. Kings Bruce McNall

BATTLE OF ALBERTA

From tiddlywinks to three-down football, Edmonton and Calgary enjoy quite a rivalry. It is most heated when served on ice.

Those who hail from outside the borders of the Wild Rose province may never fully understand it. If you're from Edmonton, you are genetically predisposed to hate Calgary. Or at least all of its sports teams. If you come from Calgary, you automatically dislike...well you get the picture.

THIS WILD ROSE HAS THORNS

Any professional athlete who has plied his trade in either of the two cities certainly doesn't need it explained to him. The Battle of Alberta is old hat to the Canadian Football League as well, where the Stampeders and Eskimos wage a three-down holy war each and every Labor Day. But it is on the ice where the intense rivalry of these two cities is borne out. It is through hockey that a generation of young Calgarians learned to loathe Edmontonians and their precocious 1980s Oiler lineups dotted by Wayne Gretzky, Mark Messier, Paul Coffey and Grant Fuhr. It is through hockey that Edmonton fans looked enviously at their southern cousins while Lanny McDonald, Doug Gilmour, Al MacInnis and Mike Vernon sipped from the Cup in 1989 and while Edmonton-native Jarome Iginla (*horrors*) led a gutsy band of Flames into the 2004 finals.

CITY OF CHAMPIONS

The ultimate scoreboard—the one that registers Stanley Cup championships—reads Edmonton 6, Calgary 1. This qualification alone likely justifies the pretentious "City of Champions" nickname the Alberta capital awarded itself during the Oilers' salad days. That nickname rubbed Calgarians the wrong way. It was bad enough they had to watch the Oilers win six Stanley Cups and the Eskimos dominate the Grey Cup during the 1980s. They didn't want to be reminded of it whenever they landed at Edmonton International, too.

"I always say to Edmonton people, it's grand to boast about all the championship teams you've had," Calgary sportscaster Russ Peake once told the *Calgary Herald*. "But the fact is you still have to live in Edmonton." Every time these two hockey teams play, no matter if they are battling for first place in their division or simply to stay afloat in today's billion-dollar hockey industry, there is something a little extra on the line. They're called provincial bragging rights and, make no mistake, they do matter. To the players, to the fans, to the politicians, even.

WHOSE SIDE ARE YOU ON, ANYWAY?

"Part of the learning curve in the city of Edmonton is learning to hate the city of Calgary," former Oilers defenceman Steve Smith once said. He should know. He was a central figure in one of the most memorable single battles in the War of Alberta. During game seven of the 1986 Smythe Division finals with the dynasty Oilers seemingly poised for another Stanley Cup run, Smith put an attempted pass from behind the net off the leg of his own goaltender, Grant Fuhr. The wayward puck ricocheted into the goal and gave Calgary a 3–2 third-period lead and ultimately the series victory. In subsequent visits to the Saddledome, Calgary fans would taunt Smith with chants of "Shoot! Shoot!" whenever he got the puck behind the net. And who could blame them? They were simply doing their part in the battle.

Later Smith would join the Flames as a player and assistant coach, giving him a unique perspective of one of hockey's greatest rivalries from both sides. He once told the *Calgary Herald* that what he remembered most about playing the Flames was "that I was going to come into Calgary and shed some blood. Every time you touched the puck you were going to get hit or whacked across the back of the legs."

LONG LIVE THE ETERNAL GRUDGE

More recent versions of the battle may not have been quite as heated. Still, in 2003 Oilers coach Craig MacTavish took the rivalry to unprecedented heights when he ripped the tongue out of the mouth of Flames' mascot Harvey the Hound. The now-classic showdowns of the 1980s are still the ones that resonate the most, however. "As vicious, fast, competitive, hard-hitting and volatile as those games were, I'm shocked no one was seriously hurt," former Flame Jim Peplinski told the *Calgary Sun*.

Former Flames general manager Cliff Fletcher, who guided Calgary to its only Stanley Cup win in 1989, has fond memories about those rough-and-tumble affairs. "To me, the rivalry between Calgary and Edmonton is what sport is all about. It wasn't phony. There was competition between the two cities in everything, whether it be a tiddlywinks tournament or whatever. They can't stand each other. And I think that's a good thing."

* * * * *

A Kindergarten teacher in Calgary tells her class she's a BIG Flames fan.

She's really excited about it and asks the kids if they're Flames fans too.

Everyone wants to impress the teacher and says they're Flames fans too, except ONE kid named Wayne.

The teacher looks at Wayne and says, "Wayne, you're not a Flames fan?"

He says, "Nope, I'm a Oilers fan!" She says, "Well, why are you a Oilers fan and not a Flames fan?"

Wayne says, "Well, my mom is an Oilers fan, and my dad is an Oilers fan, so I'm an Oilers fan."

The teacher's not happy. She's a little hot under the collar. She says, "Well, if your mom's an idiot, and your dad's a moron, then what would you be?!"

"Well," Wayne says, "then I'd be a Flames fan!"

* * * * *

"I am not afraid to stop the puck with my head. I try to do it sometimes even in practice; not everyday but once in a while, I say to my teammates, shoot me in my head and I'll try to stop the puck. I am not afraid at all of the puck, so sometimes, if the shot comes at my head, it's an easier save to make with your head. Maybe the people think a different way, but for me, I do it with my head."

—Dominik Hasek, goaltender, Ottawa Senators

DON'T MENTION THAT TRADE

More than a few NHL trades turned out big for one team, and an embarrassment for the other.

Not long after the famous "Espo Deal" between the Chicago Black Hawks and the Boston Bruins in May 1967, Hawks general manager Tommy Ivan encountered the GM of another NHL team. "Tommy, the whole league wants to say thanks to you," the man said, "for creating a monster in Boston." In that trade, Ivan had sent forwards Phil Esposito, Ken Hodge and Fred Stanfield to the Bruins in exchange for center Pit Martin, defenceman Gilles Marotte and goalie Jack Norris.

THE MONSTER MASH

Seldom has a trade involving front-line players turned out to be such a boost for one team. Over the next nine seasons, the three big forwards produced 860 goals and 2,089 points, key men with defenceman Bobby Orr in the glamor team of the early 1970s, winners of two Stanley Cup championships. The Bruins set most scoring records that the Edmonton Oilers fractured in the next decade. Martin was a good center for the Black Hawks with 243 goals and 627 points in 740 games but Marotte's development stalled and the Hawks traded him after three seasons. Norris never made it as an NHL goalie, playing only 58 big-league games with three teams.

PHIL SCREWS IT UP

"I had fun playing the game and the Black Hawks brass thought I should be more serious about it," Esposito said. "We finished first for the first time in the team's history in the 1966–67 season and had a little party to celebrate. I drank too much champagne and got brave. I told Tommy Ivan, 'We have a dynasty here. Don't screw it up!' After we lost the first round of the playoffs to Toronto and I didn't have a point in six games, I was gone."

TAKES ON TRADES

The Hawks-Bruins trade is on a long list of NHL deals that turned out to be one-sided. One theory on trades is that the team that lands the best player, even in a multi-player deal, is the winner of the swap. Often the benefits of a deal are much more subtle than that. A team overloaded with star players can deal one of them to strengthen its "foot soldiers"—checkers, penalty killers and grinders—improving its depth enough to be an immediate challenger while the traded front-liner gives the other club strength over the long haul.

MAYBE YOU SHOULD SLEEP ON IT, JACK...

When Red Kelly, a Norris Trophy defenceman who was an anchor on four Stanley Cup winners with the Detroit Red Wings in the 1950s, was traded to the Toronto Maple Leafs for defenceman Marc Reaume in 1960, the deal was made in anger by Wings boss Jack Adams. Kelly told a Canadian magazine writer that Adams once had ordered him to play despite a cracked bone in his ankle and when Kelly refused and discussed it publicly, Adams saw it as disloyalty to the organization. While Reaume played only 47 games as a Wing, Kelly switched to center in Toronto and played a large role in four Cup wins in the 1960s.

SMYTHE SWIPES LEAF FOR LIFE

Over the decades, the Leafs were a team that made several shrewd deals in which they appeared to have swindled their trading partners. In 1930, Leafs owner Conn Smythe felt his club needed a leader/sparkplug to give the franchise a lift both on the ice and off, where Smythe was trying to assemble a money package to build Maple Leaf Gardens. The Ottawa Senators were struggling to survive financially and when Smythe offered $35,000 in cash plus two fringe players for defenceman King Clancy, the offer was snapped up. Clancy filled the role perfectly, a Leaf for life—on the ice, behind the bench and in the executive suite.

CONN RARELY WRONG

When Smythe sent $5,000 to the Red Wings in 1935 for goalie Turk Broda, it appeared that the Leafs had picked up a minor leaguer. But Broda became one of the great goalies in NHL history, the backbone of five Stanley Cup champions. When star center Syl Apps told Smythe he would retire after the 1947–48 season, the Leaf owner swung one of the game's biggest deals, landing center Max Bentley from the Chicago Black Hawks in exchange for five competent NHL players. Bentley played a large role in three Leaf Cup titles. In 1943, the Leafs traded fringe defenceman Frank Eddols to the Montreal Canadiens in exchange for the NHL rights to young forward Ted "Teeder" Kennedy, perhaps the greatest Leaf ever.

Other deals that fall in the one-sided category:

The Montreal Canadiens traded their fading star Newsy Lalonde to the Saskatoon Sheiks in 1922 in exchange for young, 145-pound amateur winger Aurel Joliat, who became an exceptional scorer on a line with the great Howie Morenz.

In 1967, the expansion St. Louis Blues traded veteran forwards Ron Stewart and Ron Atwell to the New York Rangers for center Red Berenson and defenceman Barclay Plager, who became mainstays of the Blues' three trips to the Cup final.

In 1970, the Canadiens traded forward Ernie Hicke and their first-round pick in that year's draft (center Chris Oddleifson) to the Seals for defenceman Francois Lacombe and that team's first-round pick in the 1971 draft. The Canadiens used that pick to select winger Guy Lafleur, the dominant player of the 1970s.

In 1974, the Philadelphia Flyers landed winger Reggie Leach from the California Seals in exchange for two players and a draft pick. Leach was a valued sniper for the Flyers with seasons of 61 and 50 goals.

The Bruins acquired big winger Cam Neely from the Vancouver Canucks in 1986 in exchange for center Barry Pederson. While Pederson's career declined, Neely became a Hall of Famer who scored 344 goals in 525 games for the Bruins.

Halfway through the 1991–92 season, the Leafs landed center Doug Gilmour from the Calgary Flames in the largest ever NHL deal (ten players) and Gilmour led the Toronto team back to contender status after a decade of futility. Three seasons earlier, Gilmour helped lead the Flames to their only Stanley Cup win after being acquired from St. Louis with two other regulars for a package of players that went on to accumulate only 23 points total for the Blues.

In 1996, the Vancouver Canucks traded failed first-rounder Alek Stojanov to the Pittsburgh Penguins for winger Markus Naslund. Naslund took a couple seasons to find his game, but became the Canucks captain and one of the game's best scorers of the early 21st century.

A BOY AND HIS DOG

Don Cherry's dog Blue became as much a part of the Boston Bruins' 1970s success as the players on the ice.

The material was complete for a television series that might have endured longer than Lassie. There was a dog, albeit not an especially pretty or loveable mutt, and a boy, well, at least a male human being who was young at heart. The human claimed that he talked often to the dog, obviously basing his selection of clothing on the pup's suggestions. While the boy gained considerable fame, he always said that the dog was better known than his master.

BLUE COME HOME

It's too late for the series pilot to be shot, at least not with the original cast. Blue passed away, undoubtedly her spirit elevated to a canine Valhalla, where a Bobby Orr look-a-like is the host and a Terry O'Reilly clone is the valet. Blue, a bull terrier, belonged to Don "Grapes" Cherry, hockey coach (Boston Bruins, Colorado Rockies), raconteur, broadcasteur (*Hockey Night In Canada*), and premier provocateur at stirring the hockey pot…or any other pot that's handy.

BEAUTY, EH?

Because it's not kindly to make nasty remarks about any departed's lack of beauty, nothing will be said about the time Blue walked down a street backwards and no one detected that she wasn't going frontward. Besides, beauty is in the eye of the beholder and in Grapes' beholder eyes, Blue was Miss Canada, Miss Universe, Miss Congeniality and the golden age of good looks in one package.

BULLDOG STAN

Blue first became a personality when Cherry coached the Bruins in the 1970s. Grapes' preference would have been to place the leash on general manager Harry Sinden—or at least have Harry sit up and beg occasionally—and when that didn't happen, Cherry turned to Blue. During a losing streak, Cherry mentioned that when he returned home after a defeat, his dog Blue tried to hide.

A Boston writer asked about the dog and a star was born. Soon, pictures of Blue appeared in the papers—today she would have her own website—plus film clips on the early news.

At every press palaver with Cherry, someone would ask about Blue and Grapes would be off and winging on the embroidery of a folktale about his dog's latest feat. He always compared Bruins enforcers John Wensink and Stan Jonathan to Blue, qualifying it as the highest compliment he could imagine.

LUNCH-PAIL LOGIC

When the Cherry-coached Bruins excelled in the late 1970s, meeting the Montreal Canadiens in two Stanley Cup finals and a memorable seven-game 1979 semifinal in three springs, the reporters covering the series had a high time. The ingredients were ideal—Boston and Montreal in May; the powerhouse Canadiens against the underdog "lunch-pail" Bruins; coaches Grapes and Scotty Bowman waging brilliant psychological verbal warfare; Grapes, with his tongue-in-cheek, working his *poor-us, powerful-them* needle in an effort to rankle the serious Bowman.

LOST IN THE WOODS

During the 1979 series, Cherry wove a splendid yarn about he and Blue going back to nature to clear their minds before a key game. They took a walk in a large conservation area near the Boston suburb where the Cherry family lived, and stopped for a snooze in the warm mid-spring sunshine beside a stream. When Grapes awoke, he and Blue proceeded in the wrong direction and became lost. "Okay, I used a little—what do the thinkers call it, poetic licence?—in a few of my Blue stories but the one about us getting lost is 100 percent true," Cherry said. "We wandered through that big park until we came to a highway and started walking along it. Both of us were getting pretty tired when a guy stopped his car and offered us a ride. Now, this is the absolute truth: He didn't recognize me until he stopped but he had recognized Blue."

BLUE TOO HIGH, TEAM TOO LOW

After the 1979 seventh-game overtime loss to the Canadiens after a too-many-men penalty against the Bruins late in the third period allowed Montreal to tie the score, Grapes' stormy relationship with Sinden saw him sacked from the Bruins job. His relationship with Blue was strained seriously when he moved to Denver in 1979 to coach the lowly Colorado Rockies. "That was when Blue stopped talking to me altogether," Cherry said. "She was getting up in years and moving to Denver in mile-high country was tough on her. In that altitude, she lost her energy and couldn't walk ten feet without needing a rest." Cherry tried hard to sell hockey in Denver but the struggling Rockies never really caught the fans' fancy. He was whipping a horse on its way to the glue factory and after one season, the Rockies released him.

TIRES, TRIUMPHS AND TEARS

Cherry's high-buck, long-term contract gave him a chance to sniff the roses and look at all alternatives. A few guest appearances on hockey telecasts, with frequent mentions of Blue, gave him something to do while he waited for a call to come with the offer of another coaching job. But the phone never rang and Cherry became a regular on the *Hockey Night in Canada* telecasts with his controversial "Coach's Corner." Blue was offered a commercial for a tire company and included her master in the deal. His *Grapevine* TV show, a national radio show and a chain of restaurants meant he couldn't afford to return to coaching hockey.

Blue died in the mid-1980s at the "old" breed age of 15 and Cherry found a new pet, named—what else?—Baby Blue. "Baby Blue was a gamer but she was like a good rookie defenceman trying to replace Bobby Orr," Cherry said. "We had a good time with Baby but there really only could be one Blue."

* * * * *

LISTEN UP!

"I've got nothing to say and I'm only gonna say it once!"

—Maple Leafs coach Floyd Smith
after a disturbing loss

THE FIRST GREAT DRAFT

Two great junior stars, Guy Lafleur and Marcel Dionne, created much speculation in the first big NHL entry draft.

The Flower and Little Beaver! Guy Lafleur and Marcel Dionne were the first two high-level junior hockey stars to be publicized heavily as candidates for the first overall pick in the NHL draft. Through the 1970–71 junior season, the two spectacular French-Canadian forwards were analyzed and compared endlessly the way U.S. college football and basketball stars were touted for the top draft role in their sports. And when the two junior aces led their teams into a controversial playoff series that still is debated today, it supplied a rare chance to examine them under the same microscope. Of course, the view then that the two players were remarkable prospects for NHL stardom, the kinds of forward around which a big-league attack could be built, was verified by their distinguished NHL careers.

PERRAULT'S PARADE OF NEWFOUND SCRUTINY

The draft had generated considerable excitement the previous season, 1969–70, when Gilbert Perreault, the magnificent, free-wheeling center of the Montreal Junior Canadiens, and Dale Tallon, a talented rushing defenceman of the Toronto Marlboros, were touted for the first-pick role. The Buffalo Sabres had first selection and took Perreault, who had a Hall of Fame career while Tallon went to the Vancouver Canucks and enjoyed ten solid but unspectacular seasons with the Canucks, Chicago Black Hawks and Pittsburgh Penguins. But the media attention earned by the two junior stars showed the NHL how valuable the draft could be as a publicity tool.

CANADIENS FIRST

Adding a unique twist to the season-long draft debate was the Montreal Canadiens' ownership of the first selection through a trade with the California Golden Seals in 1970. Canadiens general manager Sam Pollock traded winger Ernie Hicke and their top pick in the 1970 draft (center Chris Oddleifson) to the Seals in exchange for defenceman Francois Lacombe, cash and the Seals' first pick in the 1971 draft. The Seals obliged by finishing last in the 1970–71 schedule, handing the Canadiens a dream situation—the surety of obtaining one of two great young players, both Francophones.

DON'T LOOK BACK

The Dionne-Lafleur run for number one had an assortment of unique twists to it. Lafleur was born in Thurso, Quebec, and achieved junior stardom with the Quebec City Remparts. Dionne, too, was Quebecois, born in Drummondville, but at 17 his entire family moved to St. Catharines, Ontario, the only way a player could shift from province-to-province. In the heated French-English political climate of the time, Dionne was viewed as a "traitor" for "selling out" to Ontario interests. In three seasons in St. Catharines, long one of the country's best junior hockey towns, Dionne went from 37 to 55 to 62 goals, 100 to 132 to 143 points, winning the Ontario league scoring title in his last two seasons. He was a chunky lad but with extraordinary quickness, toughness around the net, and a dandy playmaking sense.

130 GOALS!

Lafleur spent four full seasons with the Remparts, producing 103 and an astonishing 130 goals in his last two terms. He was slender and intense, quick off the mark, and able to absorb much punishment without retaliation, especially on his way to the net to unload his deadly shot.

SERIES OF DREAMS

When the Remparts won the Quebec League playoffs and the Black Hawks were Ontario champs, the stage was set for a ferocious junior match-up in the Eastern Canada final of the Memorial Cup playoffs. Adding to the many factors of intensity was that Remparts coach Maurice Filion had been Dionne's coach in Drummondville at the junior-B level and was bitter when Dionne departed to Ontario. When the Remparts arrived in St. Catharines to open the series, Filion stated, "Guy Lafleur is the best junior player in the country, no doubt about it." The feeling among hockey scouts seemed to be that the player who led his team to the series win would be the Canadiens' pick.

SERIES OF NIGHTMARES

But the series that started with great interest ended with bitterness and recriminations from both teams. Lafleur scored twice as the Remparts won the opener 4–2, his winning goal on a shot that broke the stick of goalie George Hulme on its way into the net. The second game belonged to Dionne, who scored four goals in an 8–3 win while Lafleur did not produce a single point. When the series shifted to Quebec City, the mood changed completely. Not long after the FLQ crisis, Prime Minister Pierre Trudeau's use of the War Measures Act and the loud backers of an independent Quebec, perhaps any Ontario team would have encountered loud reaction. But one with a lad from Drummondville as its star seemed certain to draw a harsh reaction.

WHERE'D THAT WAR MEASURES ACT GO?

In game three, Lafleur scored twice, Dionne had a single assist as the Remparts won 3–1, though the Hawks had 47 shots at goalie Michel DeGuise. Lafleur then scored three goals when the Remparts won game four 6–1 for a stranglehold on the series. The Hawks played tough in the late stages, earning six game misconduct penalties and leading to incidents involving players and fans. The tires on the Hawks' bus were slashed and a police escort was required for the team to reach its hotel.

ACCUSATIONS GALORE

The Remparts, of course, blamed the Black Hawks for the violence and St. Catharines supporters pointed to the Quebec fans who had directed every imaginable obscenity at Dionne and the team's other Francophone, Pierre Guite, and threw loads of debris at the Hawks players. The fifth game was played at Maple Leaf Gardens in Toronto without incident before a crowd of 15,343, the Hawks winning, 6–3. Dionne had two assists, Lafleur a goal in the tame game. When hockey officials refused to post a bond guaranteeing adequate protection for the Black Hawks in Quebec City or to move the game to Montreal, the Black Hawks—led by the players' parents fearing for their sons' and their own safety—forfeited the series by refusing to play the sixth game. Lafleur had eight goals and an assist in the five games, Dionne, five goals and three assists, and at the draft the Canadiens made Lafleur the first pick; Dionne was second, claimed by the Detroit Red Wings.

ONTO BIGGER AND BETTER THINGS

The two players had extraordinary NHL careers. Lafleur needed a couple of NHL seasons to boost his play to a high level but he was the league's best player for seven or so seasons in the late 1970s. Dionne spent four years with the Wings—Gordie Howe gave him the nickname Little Beaver—then moved to the Los Angeles Kings as a free agent, a controversial move that was settled by a trade. In 19 seasons, Dionne had 731 goals and 1,040 assists for 1,771 points in 1,348 games. Lafleur played 17 seasons with a 560-793-1,353 point total in 1,126 games. Lafleur became a superhero to the Canadiens fans and led the team to five Stanley Cup crowns. Dionne, who never won a Cup, played magnificently in California but received little national attention.

* * * * *

It's Game 7 of the Stanley Cup Final, and Sam makes his way to his seat right at center ice. He sits down, noticing that the seat next to him is empty. He leans over and asks his neighbor if someone will be sitting there.

"No" says the neighbor. "The seat is empty."

"This is incredible," says Sam. "Who in their right mind would have a seat like this for the Stanley Cup and not use it?"

The neighbor says, "Well, actually, the seat belongs to me. I was supposed to come with my wife, but she passed away. This is the first Stanley Cup we haven't been to together since we got married."

"Oh, I'm sorry to hear that. That's terrible...But couldn't you find someone else, a friend or relative, or even a neighbor to take the seat?"

The man shakes his head "No. They're all at the funeral."

OTHER NHLS

Make sure you know which league you're signing up for.

We've all been there: After a 50-goal season with the Brandon Wheat Kings, you arrive at the big-city convention center for the NHL draft, Mom and Dad on either arm, visions of Bruins jerseys and million-dollar contracts dancing in your head. But things do not seem right. Where are the fluttering team banners and ESPN cameras? Why is everybody playing the harmonica or discussing gnostic codices? Mom and Dad start to panic. There can't possibly be more than one NHL, can there?

National Historic Landmarks: A subsidiary of the U.S. National Park Service, the NHL preserves, protects and promotes over 2,000 buildings and locales of historical significance. Landmarks of baseball, cricket, football, basketball, tennis, track and rowing appear on their register, but no sites relevant to hockey.

Nag Hammadi Library: In 1945, an Egyptian farmer outside the town of Nag Hammadi found 13 papyrus volumes sealed in an earthenware jar. Published in English in 1970 as *The Nag Hammadi Library*, the long-lost "Gnostic Gospels" of the NHL, hidden by heterodox Christian monks around 390 AD, have prompted a major re-evaluation of Christianity and its teachings.

Noordelijke Hogeschool Leeuwarden: A university with 9,000 students and 850 staff members, located in the capital of Friesland province in the Netherlands, NHL offers undergraduate and graduate courses for both full- and part-time students, as well as opportunities to participate in sports such as "Mixed Hockeyclub" and "Tafeltennis."

Norske Homeopaters Landsforbund: Founded in Oslo in 1930, the NHL is one of five different organizations representing Norwegian homeopaths. Its 400 members must fulfil the standards of medical and homeopathic education while practicing their profession according to the organisation's exacting ethical standards.

Non-Hodgkin's Lymphoma: Like Hodgkin's Disease, non-Hodgkin's lymphoma originates in the lymph nodes—oval, pea-sized organs that filter the blood of infection and disease—but, unlike Hodgkin's Disease, NHL often spreads to areas beyond the lymph. While the five-year survival rate for NHL is a less-than-reassuring 56%, 81% of patients survive HD, including Mario Lemieux, who received treatment for the disease in the winter of 1993.

National Harmonica League: Britain's national harmonica club is more globally minded than their name would indicate, as they send their quarterly publication, *Harmonica World*, to membership in more than 20 countries. According to their mission statement, "The NHL...caters for all people with an interest in the harmonica, ranging from non-players to virtuoso professionals, regardless of race, creed, or color, and regardless of tastes in music."

NCL-1, HT2A and LIN-41: NHL is a protein domain 30 to 40 amino acids long, and often repeated several times in a single protein. An ancient motif, it occurs in humans as well as in a wide range of other organisms, including the arabidopsis plant and the microscopic C. *elegans* worm, both widely used in genetic research. Very likely it predates the better-known NHL which was created in Montreal in 1917.

* * * * *

OUCH!

"I just tape four Tylenols to it."

—Rangers defencecman Boris Mironov, on playing with a sore ankle

"Getting cut in the face is a pain in the butt."

—former Calgary Flames defenceman Theoren Fleury

THE FLYING FEM FINN

Perhaps the world's best female player, Hayley Wickenheiser made hockey history by playing for a Finnish men's team.

Hayley Wickenheiser was not the first female to play for a men's professional hockey team. But she was the first to play as a regular for at least part of a season. Granted, the team for which Wickenheiser played 23 games in the 2002–03 season, Kirkkonummi Salamat, was in the Third Division of the Finnish Hockey League, hardly an indicator that an NHL career was a step away. But the longtime star of the Canadian national women's team, the most valuable player on the gold medal team in the 2002 Olympics and the woman often mentioned as the best female hockey player in the world proved that she could hold her own in the men's league—and on a team that played well enough to move up to the Second Division.

STATS AT SALAMAT

Wickenheiser initially talked with a team in Italy but the Italian Federation said it did not want female players. Salaat offered her a three-game tryout and when she showed well, she received a contract for the remainder of the season. In 23 games, she scored two goals and 13 assists. Wickenheiser, 25 at the time, returned to the team for a second season in 2004–05 but a lack of ice time and the desire to be with her family—her boyfriend and his son by a previous relationship—brought her back to Canada after a few weeks in Finland. "Overall, the experience of playing in Finland was a good one and it served the intended purpose of helping me to improve as a player because it challenged me," Wickenheiser said. "I was treated very fairly by the team and opponents did not play any different against me than they did against the guys on the team."

HOLDING HER OWN

Four female goalies—Manon Rheaume, Erin Whitten, Danielle Dube and Kelly Dyer—had played in North American minor-pro hockey. Rheaume had attracted considerable attention when the

Tampa Bay Lightning used her for a period in a preseason game against an NHL opponent. But goaltender is not a position where there's a chance of heavy contact, the big risk for female skaters who are outweighed by at least 50 pounds by many of the opposing players. A gifted athlete, Wickenheiser is among the bigger female players at 170 pounds and, always tremendously conditioned, she held her own in the corners and along the boards in the Finnish league.

"Hayley certainly had the skill, speed and strength to play in our league," said Parmalat coach Matti Hagman, who played 237 games in the NHL with the Boston Bruins and Edmonton Oilers. "She was the complete professional about everything and the men on our team liked her very much and trusted her on the ice. After a couple of weeks when the fuss died down, she was viewed as a hockey player, not a woman. She was especially good on faceoffs and passing plus working hard defensively."

IN A LEAGUE OF HER OWN

Wickenheiser does not see herself as a pioneer carrying the women's hockey torch for participation in men's leagues. She had attended the Philadelphia Flyers' rookie camp in 1998 and showed well, especially in the game's basic skills. She was offered tryouts by teams in the East Coast League but felt that the Finnish league on the large European ice surfaces suited her speed and skills. Her determination is legendary in women's sports. She had played softball as a recreation sport through her teen years before devoting more time to hockey. But she decided to try for the Canadian women's softball team at the 2000 Olympic Games and long, intense hours of training, hitting and fielding drills earned her a spot.

"The softball training helped my conditioning for hockey," Wickenheiser said. "I had been playing women's hockey a long time and felt that if I wanted to make myself a better player, I needed a change for at least part of a season, a step up to a better level."

ALWAYS A NAYSAYER

While there was little criticism of Wickenheiser's Finnish stint in men's hockey circles—the prevailing attitude seemed to be that if that's what she wanted and she earned the spot on merit, fine—one high-ranked official rankled many with his comments. Rene Fasel, president of the International Ice Hockey Federation, the world governing body of the sport, suggested that Wickenheiser should give up her try at hockey in a men's league for her own safety. Fasel opined she was at risk in contact hockey after playing in the women's game where deliberate bodychecking is not allowed. The IIHF president's outlook was that Wickenheiser and others would better serve hockey as champions and role models within the women's game.

"That's a better choice than as banged-up, and maybe hurt, pioneers in a provincial third-level men's league," Fasel said. Wickenheiser allowed such opinions to pass without comment from her. After all, she prefers to do her talking on the ice, helping the Canadian national team to a silver medal in the 2005 Women's World Championship.

* * * * *

KNUCKLES AND BOOM BOOM?

As in all sports, hockey players have some interesting, descriptive and just plain weird nicknames.

Aubrey Victor "Dit" Clapper
Bernie "Boom Boom" Geoffrion
Chris "Knuckles" Nilan
Curtis "CuJo" Joseph
Dave "The Hammer" Schultz
Dave "Tiger" Williams
Francis "King" Clancy
Frank "Mr. Zero" Brimsek
Fred "Cyclone" Taylor
Freddie "The Fog" Shero
George "Punch" Imlach
Hector "Toe" Blake
Larry "Big Bird" Robinson
Lorne "Gump" Worsley
Louie "The Leaper" Fontinato
Maurice "The Rocket" Richard
"Terrible" Ted Lindsay
Walter "Turk" Broda
Yvon "The Roadrunner" Cournoyer

EUROPE INVADES

Despite a short supply of talent in the rapid proliferation of teams during the 1970s, the NHL was slow to add European players.

ORIGINS OF THE BROAD STREET BULLIES

The climb from "chicken Swede" and "fearful Finn" to NHL team captaincies was a long ascent over three decades. Major league hockey expanded rapidly in the 1970s, the NHL growing from six teams in the 1966–67 season to 18 for 1976–77; and the World Hockey Association starting as a rival for 1972–73 with a dozen teams. The major source of talent, the Canadian junior hockey leagues, simply could not produce players fast enough to stock the NHL and WHA with front-line players. And even while growing rapidly, U.S. hockey supplied a few but not a big group of players. A large pool of players existed in Europe but the good ones in the Iron Curtain countries were not available. NHL thinking was that players in Sweden and Finland had the necessary skill, but would not function effectively in the physical pro style.

RUMBA ON THE TUMBA

European players had been tried by NHL teams. In the early 1960s, the Boston Bruins had invited forward Sven "Tumba" Johansson, high scorer for the Swedish national team, to training camp. The easygoing Johansson—he later changed his name to Sven Tumba—was a target for the Bruin players, some of whom were outspoken in their criticism of this "foreigner" trying to take a job. "In training camp, the Bruins did not attack each other the way they attacked me," Johansson said years later.

ULF THE FIRST

Swedish star Ulf Sterner spent the 1963–64 season in pro hockey, including four games with the New York Rangers. Although he scored 30 goals in the minor leagues, Sterner did not return for a second North American season but had a long career as a star in his home country. The first player from a Communist country to try the pros was forward Jaroslav Jirik, a strong player in the top

Czechoslovakian league and the national team. Jirik managed to escape from his country and join the St. Louis Blues organization for the 1969–70 season. He played three NHL games, spent the remainder of the season in the minors, but did not return for camp the next season.

JUST IGNORE INSULTS FROM OWNER'S BOX

Swedish defenceman Thommie Bergman was the first European to play a full season in the NHL with the Detroit Red Wings in 1972–73. He performed solidly, a plus player on a weak team. Their roster stripped bare by WHA raids, the Toronto Maple Leafs signed winger Inge Hammarstrom and defenceman Borje Salming from the Brynas team in the top Swedish league. While Hammarstrom played solidly, Salming quickly became a front-line star in a 17-season career. A marvelous athlete who absorbed much punishment and "chicken Swede" slurs, Salming was the first European to be an NHL all-star.

SCANDINAVIANS RUN RAMPANT IN WHA

Despite the strong play by the Leafs' Swedes, the NHL was still slow to recruit more Swedish players. The WHA was not. The Winnipeg Jets gave the WHA a big shot of credibility when they signed NHL star Bobby Hull in 1972 as the new league's major star. To build a strong supporting cast for the Golden Jet, the Jets signed Swedish forwards Anders Hedberg and Ulf Nilsson who joined Hull on one of hockey's most exciting and prolific forward lines. When the Jets won their first WHA championship in 1976, their roster contained seven Swedes and two Finns.

DISPLACED BY WHA DOWNFALL

Other WHA teams recruited strongly in Scandinavia while the NHL added only a few players from the Sweden and Finland. The Toronto Toros of the new league scored a major coup in 1974 when they convinced center Vaclav Nedomansky, long the top player in Czechoslovakia, and countryman winger Richard Farda to defect from their country. "I had accomplished everything I could in hockey at home," Big Ned said. "I asked to be allowed to move to North America to play but I was turned down. I wanted to test myself in pro hockey and was able to find a way out of the country."

The WHA folded in 1979, four of its teams joining the NHL as expansion clubs. Nedomansky moved to the Red Wings where he had some productive seasons; his success inspired others to seek ways to lure excellent Czechoslovakian players out of their country.

NORDIQUES ENGAGE IN ESPIONAGE

One of the WHA "refugees," the Quebec Nordiques turned their team into a contender by aiding in the defection of the three Stastny brothers, Peter and Anton in 1980, Marian in 1981, from Czechoslovakia. Center Peter was the NHL's second highest scorer in the 1980s behind only Wayne Gretzky and was voted into the Hockey Hall of Fame.

RUSSIANS NYET (NOT YET)

When the teams from the old USSR dominated world "amateur" hockey through the 1960s into the 1980s, NHL clubs longed for a shot at recruiting "the damned Russians," as they were called. Rumors surfaced occasionally of NHL teams close to luring Russian stars, especially after the first USSR-Canada hockey confrontation, the fabled 1972 Summit Series. Harold Ballard, the loudmouthed owner of the Maple Leafs, offered the Russians one million dollars for winger Valeri Kharlamov after the first game of the series.

TRETIAK TRIGGERS NUCLEAR HOLOCAUST

While Soviet artists such as ballet stars Rudolf Nureyev and Mikhail Barishnykov had defected to North America, Soviet hockey players were reluctant to bolt, fearing the punishment that could be inflicted on their families. A coveted Soviet was goalie Vladislav Tretiak, an international star for a dozen years and four-time Olympic gold medallist. Years later he admitted wanting to try the NHL, but because he was an army officer in addition to being a star athlete, his defection would have had Cold War ramifications he didn't want to risk. One comrade did make it: Forward Viktor Nechayev, from Siberia, appeared with the Los Angeles Kings for three games in 1982–83, scoring a goal. Details of his escape were never revealed; regardless, he lacked the ability to stick in the NHL.

THE REDS ARE COMING

Through the 1980s, signs that the Iron Curtain was disintegrating grew each year with the labor uprisings in Poland, the fall of the Berlin wall and the ascent of Mikhail Gorbachev to the top of the USSR government. In 1987, Soviet stars were permitted to talk to western journalists for the first time at international events and predicted they would be permitted to join NHL teams in "a short time." The first Soviet player to be allowed officially to move was winger Sergei Priakin, who played three games with the Calgary Flames in 1988–89. After the 1989 World Championship in Stockholm, brilliant young Soviet forward Alexander Mogilny did not return home with the Soviet team, defecting to the NHL's Buffalo Sabres.

THE GREENS ARE COMING

Through the 1980s, the Soviet domination of world hockey was led by the brilliant "Green Unit," forwards Sergei Makarov, Igor Larionov and Vladimir Krutov, and defencemen Slava Fetisov and Alexei Kasatonov. They were allowed to move to the NHL, Makarov with Calgary, Larionov and Krutov with the Vancouver Canucks, Kasatonov and Fetisov with the New Jersey Devils. All but Krutov played strongly in the NHL.

IT'S GLOBALIZATION, BABY

The Iron Curtain's fall opened up the world hockey market completely. From the early 1990s on, European players have flocked to North America, at both the pro and Canadian junior level. The NHL entry draft quickly became dotted with European names and, by 2000, 42 percent of 293 players selected were in the "international" category and in 2004, nine of the 30 first-round picks were in that classification. In the 2003–04 season, eight of 30 NHL team captains were from Europe and no one said, "And a chicken shall lead them!"

JOLLY JACK?

Jack Adams, who guided the Detroit Red Wings to great success for 35 years, was a tough tyrant both admired and detested.

To some, most of them away from the rink, he was viewed as "Jolly Jawn," the pink-cheeked, cherubic, chortling man who enthusiastically promoted hockey nonstop. But many who knew Jack Adams, hockey man, general manager and/or coach of the Detroit Red Wings for 35 years, viewed him as the antithesis of the public figure. Adams was a tough, bad-tempered, referee-baiting martinet who ruled his teams with an iron fist. Players who ventured outside of his strict rules were viewed as "traitors to the family."

RAPID RISE UP THE RANKS

That Adams was in the front ranks both as a player and GM-coach isn't debated. He played on two teams (the Toronto Arenas and Ottawa Senators) that won the Stanley Cup and was Red Wings coach for three Stanley Cups and GM for four. He took over the reins of the Detroit Cougars in 1927, who were called the Falcons for two seasons before becoming the Red Wings in 1932. By careful constructing a solid farm system and making shrewd deals, he filled houses at the Detroit Olympia and moved the team to the top of the NHL. The team won back-to-back Cups in 1936 and 1937, establishing Adams as strong both in the front office and behind the bench. The owners of the team, the Norris family, were impressed enough to give him full control of team operations.

CALLING DR. JEKYLL...

While Adams was regarded as a genial glad-hander in many areas, his hockey style was confrontational. He carried on an endless war with on-ice officials, berating referees as if they were deliberately sabotaging his team. He was twice suspended for physical contact with officials and fined several times by the league for statements undermining their credibility. Adams also frequently argued with newspapermen in other cities if they wrote with even mild criticism of his demeanor. He fought a never-ending war with other teams' owners, GMs and coaches, often knocking them in print or engaging in loud arguments in arena hallways. Some NHL folks, both with teams and in the media, felt that Adams was the ultimate "Jekyll and Hyde," the warm charmer away from the arena who turned into a madman when near an ice surface.

THE MOST IMPORTANT FEATURE IN HOCKEY

As a player, Adams took advantage of the loosely structured contract situation in hockey and over his career moved freely to five different teams for higher salaries. But in control of the Detroit organization, Adams led the NHL's tightening of the leash on players. He often said that the most important feature in hockey was the reserve clause in players' contracts that bound the player to the team from signature of the first contract until he was sold or traded. While purists argued that such control of players, even young, unsigned amateurs on reserve lists was unfair, Adams loudly claimed the system was simply a way for an owner to control his team's assets. Through the 1930s and 1940s, players simply went along with the rules, happy to have careers playing hockey that paid reasonably well.

GETTING GORDIE

Through much of his time at the helm of the Wings, the Norris family gave Adams a set figure to operate the team and what he didn't spend was his salary, the perfect situation to inspire a penny-pinching approach. After a Stanley Cup win, three regulars on the team received pay cuts the next season to allow Adams to give top stars a small raise and keep his own salary intact. When the Wings pulled a scouting coup in 1944 by signing a 15-year-old winger from Saskatchewan named Gordie Howe, the team's future—and Adams' job—was secured. Howe played 32 seasons of major league hockey.

MINI MOGULS OF THE AUTO INDUSTRY

But when the 1950s arrived and the players slowly became more sophisticated, the potential for a serious clash was established. The auto industry was booming in Detroit and some Red Wings players, notably star winger Ted Lindsay and Marty Pavelich, developed businesses in supplying the car makers with products. Adams often ranted about the players paying too much attention to non-hockey matters, but the Red Wings' success (four Cup wins in six years from 1950 to 1955, seven consecutive first-place finishes from 1949 to 1955) made his claims ludicrous.

PENSION? WHAT PENSION?

Adams had signed Lindsay from the grasp of archrivals Toronto Maple Leafs and the tough little left-winger was a perennial all-star. Lindsay and Doug Harvey, the splendid defenceman from the Montreal Canadiens, were named as the players' representatives on the NHL pension plan board. When Lindsay asked simple questions about the pension—the players made large donations, the owners very small ones—the league officials more or less told him to mind his business. That inspired Lindsay's 1957 efforts to form an NHL Players' Association, and inevitably led to bitter confrontations with Adams.

UNION-BUSTERS

Adams, with enthusiastic aid from Maple Leaf owner Conn Smythe, mounted a strong campaign to squelch the "union." Lindsay had representatives from all six teams on his executive and used his own money to hire a New York labor lawyer who had helped major league baseball players gain their first collective bargaining agreement. Adams called Lindsay, among the game's hardest workers, a "traitor" and a "communist" and even showed a false contract to a reporter listing Lindsay's salary as $25,000 when the all-star had really earned only $17,000. When such great Wings stars as Howe, Marcel Pronovost and Red Kelly failed to back Lindsay, it was a setback for the union cause. Adams then traded Lindsay and one of his supporters, outstanding goalie Glenn Hall, to the miserable Chicago Black Hawks. Other teams followed by trading their union reps (the notable exception being the Habs' Harvey), and the association was crushed.

A GOOD GUY?

Typically, Adams claimed he traded Lindsay because the quality of his play had declined. That was after Lindsay had the highest points total (85) of his excellent career. Just to show that loyalty could be a one-way street, two years later Kelly told a writer that Adams had ordered him to play with a cracked bone in his ankle and when he wouldn't, the stellar defenceman was immediately dealt to the Maple Leafs. In 1962, Adams, 66, was sacked by the Red Wings after 44 years in the NHL and decades later, controversy still exists in how he is viewed.

THE STYLISH SWEDE

Tough and talented Toronto Maple Leaf Borje Salming established himself as the first legitimate NHL "star" from Europe.

Kiruna, Swden, the hometown of Hockey Hall of Fame defencemen Borje (pronounced BOOR-YAY) Salming, is at one of the highest longitudes on Earth. Yet it was Salming's strange fate that, while he was at the top level of NHL defencemen during his playing days, he was never part of a team which reached the NHL's annual summit of honor. In other words, Salming was never a member of a team which won the Stanley Cup.

TOUGHING IT OUT IN TORONTO

With his invaluable combination of smooth-skating and aggressiveness, Salming proved himself as a formidable player right from his very first season (1973–1974) with the Toronto Maple Leafs. Playing in the media microscope of Toronto helped promote this reputation, but it also exacerbated the constant scrutiny from coaches, fans and opposing players who expected that Europeans couldn't handle the NHL's physical play. Borje Salming shattered this media-created stereotype. Blocking shots and not being afraid to deal out a check, and using his smarts to quickly pick up a puck and start a rush on the offence, Salming quickly developed into a fan favorite. Although he certainly had goal-scoring ability (tallying a career-high 19 for the Maple Leafs during the 1979–80 season), Salming's chief talent while on offence was as a pinpoint passer.

BUT FIRST IN OUR HEARTS

On the Maple Leaf teams of the 1970s, he had some talented players to pass the puck to—Lanny McDonald and Darryl Sittler being the most prominent. It also helped Salming that he played with the offensively talented defencemen Ian Turnbull. However, most of Salming's seasons with the Leafs—under the disastrous ownership of Harold Ballard—were disappointing. Whatever was missing from the team (and it was usually a lot), it wasn't hard work from the stylish Swede Salming. He finished second to Montreal's Larry Robinson for the Norris Trophy for the 1976–77 campaign and tied for the league lead in assists (66) that same season. Salming again came in second to Robinson for the Norris Trophy for the 1979–80 season. This problem of forever coming in second plagued Salming all of his career. He was named an NHL Second Team All-Star five times, only in 1977 making it First Team. But these were simply amazing accomplishments for an unheralded free agent who quietly signed with the Leafs on May 12, 1973, and then gratefully and persistently showed up to play every day for one of the league's most miserable teams.

PIONEER OF BIZARRE FACE INJURIES

On June 12, 1989, Salming was signed as a free agent by the Detroit Red Wings. Salming's most memorable association with Detroit was when Red Wing Gerard Gallant accidentally stepped on the Toronto defenceman's face in a game in 1986. Over 200 stitches were required to close the deep gash trailing from above Salming's right eye all the way down to his chin. This was his third facial injury in the same season, but this is the one that impelled Salming to become one the first NHLers to experiment playing with a shield visor on his helmet.

After the 1989–90 season, Salming retired from NHL play, but did play three years for AIK Solna Stockholm, a team in his native Sweden. He was also a member of the 1992 Swedish Olympic hockey team. In 1996, Salming was selected for the Hockey Hall of Fame.

* * * * *

THE GEOMETRY OF HOCKEY

"People talk about skating, puck handling and shooting, but the whole sport is angles and caroms, forgetting the straight direction the puck is going, calculating where it will be directed, factoring in all the interruptions. Basically, my whole game is angles."

—Wayne Gretzky

WINNER'S HEART IN A COMEDIAN'S BODY

Gump Worsley is primarily remembered for his odd name and quick wit, but he was also one of the best goaltenders of his generation.

Lorne "Gump" Worsley got his nickname when some hockey folks noticed that he had a facial resemblance to an animated movie character named Andy Gump. Something must have clicked in Lorne's mind, for he proceeded to act much like a cartoon character all the way through his career. Yet within this friendly, portly (5' 7" and 180 lbs.) man beat the heart of a winner and the fury of a fierce competitor.

THE SAME AS YOUR PRE-GAME MEAL?

Worsley will always be remembered as a comic. How could you not be if you happened to be the man who told a sportswriter that his favorite postgame dinner was a beer and a cigarette? But by the time he had retired at age 45 (for a 21-year NHL career), he had collected 335 wins but also had 352 losses. Worsley's glory years were with his hometown Montreal Canadiens, 1963–1969. Twice he shared the Vezina Trophy with other Canadiens netminders: in 1966 with Charlie Hodge and in 1968 with Rogie Vachon. "Les Habs" won four Stanley Cups in Gump's Great Goaltending Days.

WHISKY BELLY

Montreal was his mid-career. He had already spent ten unremarkable years with the New York Rangers—except for the season he played in a league-leading 70 games (winning 32, losing 28 and tying 10). But there were always the quips...Once when he was asked, "What team gives you the most trouble?" Worsley quickly replied, "The Rangers." And when Rangers coach Phil Watson called Worsley a "beer belly" in a newspaper interview, Gump was incensed: "As always, Watson doesn't have a clue what he's talking about. I never drink beer, only good Canadian whisky." This was true—despite his remark quoted earlier, no teammate ever saw Worsley drink beer.

THE GUMP TECHNIQUE

His method of stopping the puck was to flop all over the place, simply keeping—as the radio announcers like to say—"the biscuit out of the basket." Mercurial off the ice, he was a gladiator on it. When opposing players would get breakaways (this happened frequently during his tour of duty with the Rangers), Gump would often rush out of the net to meet the surprised would-be shooter, frequently knocking the puck away. After he got traded to the Canadiens, Worsley didn't have to act as a third defencemen as often as he had to while a New York Ranger. Worsley won 30 playoff games while a Canadiens goalie.

MINNESOTA MELLOW-OUT

Worsley was traded to the Minnesota North Stars during the 1968–69 campaign, and eased out of hockey over four years as a backup with the new expansion squad. He even played with a mask in his final season of 1973–74. Worsley ended up with a NHL regular-season total of 43 shutouts (a mind-bending fact when one considers all those years with the Rangers and North Stars) and a 2.88 goals-against average. Worsley shares the NHL mark with Terry Sawchuk, for most seasons played by a goalie, 21. He was elected to the Hockey Hall of Fame in 1980.

* * * * *

GRETZKY RULES!

"I don't like my hockey sticks touching other sticks, and I don't like them crossing one another, and I kind of have them hidden in the corner. I put baby powder on the ends. I think it's essentially a matter of taking care of what takes care of you."

—Wayne Gretzky

"You'll never catch me bragging about goals, but I'll talk all you want about my assists."

—Wayne Gretzky

THE GRETZKY CHRONICLES

"By far Gretzky is the most talented player ever. Every time he gets the puck something exciting happens."

—Islander GM Mike Milbury

"The only way you can check Gretzky is to hit him when he is standing still singing the national anthem."

—Boston GM Harry Sinden

"The NHL needs something to hang its hat on and Gretzky looks like a hat tree."

—Gordie Howe

"Wayne's like having your own Fantasy Island. It's so much fun to play with him. I had no goals and no assists before getting on his line and then I almost made the record book."

—former Oilers forward Dave Lumley

"We were just brain-dead in our own end. If you are brain-dead against Wayne Gretzky... I mean, he can set my four-year-old son up to score if you leave him alone."

—Leafs right wing Tom Fitzgerald

"There should be a league rule where he is passed around from team to team each year."

—Rangers coach Terry O'Reilly

"We would have won if we had Wayne Gretzky."

—Paul Reinhart of the Calgary Flames, after losing to the Oilers in the 1988 finals

"Some guys play hockey. Gretzky plays 40 mph chess."

—Lowell Cohn, journalist

"Gretzky would dominate in any era. It doesn't make any difference. He may well be the smartest hockey player who ever played the game."

—Phil Esposito

"Wayne is bigger than life. What better place than L.A. for a bigger-than-life person?"

—LA Kings' Owner Bruce McNall

"Edmonton with Wayne was a glittering city. Edmonton without Wayne is just another city with a hockey team."

—Dave Lumley

SINDEN'S THOUGHTS ON *GLASNOST*

North American hockey did not adopt wholesale the ideas to be learned from hockey in Europe, especially the USSR.

Long before the NHL discovered that money could be made from games against visiting teams from the old Soviet Union and other European countries, taking command of that segment of "international diplomacy" in the 1970s, Harry Sinden had tried to tame the Red Menace on ice as a $30-per-game amateur defenceman...He did, too, as an important player with the Whitby Dunlops when they beat the Soviets in the key game to regain the World Championship crown for Canada at Oslo, Norway, in 1957.

SINDEN & THE SOVIETS

Sinden was out of hockey in 1972 after coaching the Boston Bruins to the 1970 Stanley Cup title—their first in 30 years—when the NHL, under the Team Canada banner, decided to play the Soviet national team in the Summit Series. He was the ideal man to be manager and coach of the Canadian team, and led them to glory. Paul Henderson's goal 36 seconds from the end of game eight gave Team Canada a "victory" and created an occasion engraved in the memories of everyone in the country old enough to remember.

SECRETS OF THE COLD WAR

The widely held outlook was that the team of top NHL players would have an easy time handling the Russians, who had defeated the best Canadian amateur teams over the previous decade. But the Soviets, with skilled, superbly conditioned players and an approach to the game quite different from the NHL's, pushed Team Canada to the limit. This led many observers to jump to the conclusion that the Russians had many lessons on the sport to teach Canadians, who always had seen hockey as "our" game.

GLOBAL VILLAGE OF HOCKEY

Sinden went from the Moscow triumph to the GM's job with the Bruins, adding the team president's title along the way. From that perch he had a good chance to study the Russians and their influence on the game in Canada and the U.S. "The Summit Series not only produced some of the finest hockey the world had seen, it also encouraged a look at how the game is played across the globe," Sinden said. "The series and the fact that the Russians were a superb team opened up healthy discussions on the state of hockey. That hasn't stopped in the 30 or so years since 1972."

STUDY UP ON YOUR RUSSIAN

The Canadian knee-jerk reaction was that the Soviets had taken the development of the North American game and carried it to heights about which the stodgy, tradition-bound pros could only dream. Actually, hockey scholars went overboard in their instant devotion to hockey Russian-style. "Of course, we had become a little complacent about the game, the way we were playing it, coaching it and preparing it," Sinden said. "Perhaps we did need a stick in the back that the competitiveness of the 1972 series gave us. But the reactions to the Russians got out of hand by a very large amount. We read wrongly, very wrongly, how they played the game and their preparation for it, especially with the idea that they had created all these ideas about the game."

THE HABS ARE RED(S)!

As an example, not long after the 1972 series, another NHL GM suggested that the pros had used an unimaginative power play strategy by having one or two large players jamming the front of the opposition net and blasting away from the points, but he had learned a new approach from the Russians' slick passing outside the defensive box formation to create good scoring chances. "When he says that we learned the pass-pass style from the Russians, I guess he never saw the Montreal Canadiens' power play from the 1950s, the one that led to the rule change to end a minor penalty after one goal," Sinden said. "That unit (Doug Harvey and Boom-Boom Geoffrion on the points, Jean Béliveau, Rocket Richard and Bert Olmstead up front) passed the puck around as well as anyone from any country, communist or democratic."

CUP-WINNERS MUST'VE BEEN COMMUNISTS

Sinden expressed amazement at how many in North American hockey viewed the way the Russians played and practised hockey, suggesting that their game tactics were much superior and their workouts contained drills of a sophistication that lifted them far above the pros. "The Russians always have been superbly conditioned athletes, good skaters with solid fundamental skills, discipline in their play, stamina to sustain a fast pace for 60 minutes and an excellent transition game, going from defence to offence very quickly," Sinden said. "Funny, isn't it, but that's the description of many Stanley Cup winners?"

HOW CAN WE POSSIBLY MATCH *THIS*?

Sinden adds: "I've been watching Soviet teams practise for years, trying to find new drills for my own team, mystery tactics that could produce supermen. Know what their workouts are: some line rushes, goalie warm-up and a large number of scrimmages. One feature of their game that we don't have on our national teams: They're together for long stretches with no games, just workouts, and that produces their team play."

RUNNING INTERFERENCE, RUSSIAN-STYLE

Sinden still feels that the biggest influence the Soviets have had on NHL hockey is negative. "One thing we really learned from them is interference," Sinden said. "Until 1972, interference in the NHL was something the refs called closely and there was very little of it. The Soviets were masters of it in 1972 and it got under our players' skins when it wasn't called. Fred Shero [coach of the Philadelphia Flyers in the 1970s] was a big devotee of the Soviet style and he had the Flyers [setting] picks a great deal. Since then, interference, which many call obstruction, has been the NHL's biggest problem because not enough of it gets called."

THE SMELL OF BOILING RUBBER...

While hockey was separated into two camps, Europe and the NHL—even after the Summit—the end of the Iron Curtain in the late 1980s opened the door for Russian and Czechoslovakian players to migrate to the NHL, producing a puck-melting plot. While Russia still produces players with strong basic skills, their move to Canadian junior hockey and the NHL has made the style of play much closer in all countries.

THE MEN IN STRIPES

Hockey officials figure they have done their best work when no one notices them, but many stayed sane one laugh at a time.

NO DEATHS, NO STRESS

The Plager brothers, Barclay, Bob and Billy, were rough and ready guys who frequently stepped outside the rulebook in their playing careers. They should have been familiar with the legislation governing hockey because their father, Gus, was a longtime referee of the game at all amateur levels in northern Ontario—a miner who augmented his income wearing a striped sweater. After a Stanley Cup playoff game during his days with the St. Louis Blues when he and his mates had received a fat share of the penalties, Bob Plager said he wished his father had officiated the game. Asked to explain what his dad would have done differently than the NHL referee who handled the game, Plager placed his tongue in his cheek. "His approach in the playoffs, that's why," Plager said. "Gus always said he had a motto in the playoffs when the teams should decide the outcome, not the zebras. No autopsy, no penalty—that's how Gus said he decided the calls when a lot was on the line."

THREE CHEERS FOR THE REF?

Obviously, Gus Plager wanted to keep his nose out of the action if possible, giving the players plenty of leeway. Most men with the whistles in the NHL take that approach, especially in big games, by only calling the severe fouls. Others crack down from the start and when they feel they're in control of the game, allow the players to produce the final result. Many of the game's "characters" wore striped shirts and cracked funny lines when away from the rink. Often players on the ice would be seen smiling, even laughing, and the inspiration for the glee was a comedy routine from the referees or linesmen. One complaint many officials had was that they never played a home game. Their traveling schedule was hectic, either traveling alone or in company with the other officials. That's why the majority of men with whistles are easygoing, friendly guys—being laid-back a necessity in a stressful occupation.

THE HAROLD BALLARD OF REFEREEING

George Hayes was that way, a linesman with a zest for life that frequently landed him in trouble with his superiors who felt Big George should toe the line a little more than he did. Hayes was a large chap from Ingersoll, Ontario, who had a 19-season career, feuding almost nonstop with NHL president Clarence Campbell, himself a former referee. Hayes once ended a discipline session by threatening to heave the NHL referee-in-chief off a moving train. When the NHL launched an insurance program for officials, Hayes refused to contribute. When the league enrolled him anyway as part of his contract, an angry George made his dog Pete the beneficiary.

BUT THE FANS KEEP CALLING YOU BLIND

Hayes was ordered by Campbell to take an eye test but he refused, telling the president that his eyes were perfect because he could read the label on every bottle in the Montreal bar favored by the officials for a post-game libation. The NHL rules stated that officials were to travel first class on trains and sleep in a berth. Hayes preferred day coach and could sleep in a seat, pocketing the difference between coach and first class. Hayes always scoffed at the idea that he would be voted into the Hockey Hall of Fame. But soon after his death, 22 years after his 1965 firing by Campbell, Hayes was elected to the Hall.

CLANCY KING OF MARBLEHEADS

King Clancy spent close to 70 years in the NHL as an Ottawa Senators player, then as a player and executive with the Toronto Maple Leafs. He also was a top NHL referee, a job that he turned into as much fun as he did everything else in his life. One of the game's great storytellers, the King loved to spin yarns about his time as an official, especially his exchanges with fans. One man Clancy knew was a Toronto doctor who had rail (front) seats, and the absence of the glass on the sideboards made it easy for the man to berate the official. One night, the doc yelled at Clancy that he had never seen anyone be wrong so often. "You could be right, Doc, but at least I don't bury my mistakes," Clancy shot back. Anyone named Clancy had to be big in Boston, where the King was needled mercilessly by his fellow Irishmen. "There was one guy with a great set of Irish lungs who often let fly at me," Clancy said. "His favorite was: 'Clancy, we named a town in New England after you. We called it Marblehead.'"

BUTTRESSED BY EVIDENCE

Before the sideboard glass was installed in Chicago, referee Clancy scrambled up to sit on the boards out of the way of flying bodies. A lady in a rail seat stuck a hatpin into his backside and said, "How does that feel, smart guy?" Clancy went to the Black Hawks management and told them that if the lady wasn't tossed out of the Stadium, he would refuse to finish the game. "I had the proof—a hatpin in my butt—and the lady was ejected," Clancy said.

A BARB FOR BARBER

Don Koharski, a top NHL referee from 1977 through the next 1,500 or so games, could ease the tension in a tight game with his humor. That showed in one of Koharski's first NHL assignments in Philadelphia during the late days of the brawling Broad Street Bullies. Philly winger Bill Barber was rated as the best diver in the league, capable of turning an innocuous play into an elaborate pratfall. He decided to test the young official's judgement and a small hit became a large sprawl. Koharski skated over the prone Barber, looked down and said, "I hate to tell you this, son, but the pool is frozen over."

LAST CALL

The Flyers, who brawled their way to Stanley Cup titles in 1974 and 1975, were not big favorites of the officials. Their fights and brawls meant a lot of work for the linesmen breaking up the battles, and a challenge for the referees to control the game because of what seemed their deliberate starting of fights. Flyer games could run as long as four hours because of the scraps and their constant arguments about penalties.

John Ashley, an excellent referee at the time, was working a game in Vancouver in which the hometown Canucks and the Flyers had fought almost nonstop from the opening faceoff. The Flyers had a win locked up with a minute to play when Flyers coach Fred Shero sent out his number-one goon, Dave "The Hammer" Schultz, who was yapping at a Canuck as if trying to initiate fistic combat. Spying Schultz, Ashley skated to the Flyer bench and said to coach Fred Shero, "Freddie, what are you doing? If this one lasts much longer, we're going to miss last call at all the bars. Get that guy off the ice so we can get a cold one before everything is closed." A chap who enjoyed a post-game pop or two, Freddy the Fog replaced the Hammer before any game-extending trouble could start.

THE GREEN-MAKI STICK FIGHT

Wayne Maki's brutal stick attack on Ted Green heralded an era of senseless violence through the 1970s.

The 1969–70 NHL season had many highlights. Longtime goalie Terry Sawchuk played his final season (for the New York Rangers). Chicago Black Hawks rookie netminder Tony Esposito totalled 15 shutouts and 38 wins, both NHL highs. Boston Bruins defencemen Bobby Orr won the Hart, Norris, Art Ross and Conn Smythe trophies, the only time the feat has been accomplished in NHL history. But another more ominous incident happened during this particular season: St. Louis Blues left-winger Wayne Maki hit Bruins defenceman Ted Green in the head with his stick during a September 21, 1969 match in Ottawa. Green received a compound skull fracture that required a steel plate to be inserted in his head by surgeons.

TERRIBLE TED TAKEN DOWN

What happened to cause the Green-Maki stick fight? In the first period, Maki rushed Green during a scrum near the Boston net. Green was able to get one of his hockey-gloved hands free and pushed it in Maki's face. Before he fell, Maki speared Green in the stomach. "Terrible Ted," as Green was known, then swung his stick and nailed Maki on the shoulder. When Green turned to skate away, Maki cracked him over the head with his stick, sending the helmet-less Green down for the count. After the game, a number of Bruins went to visit Green at the hospital where he was taken for evaluation. Teammate Ed Westfall later remembered that "There was even a rumor that he was dead."

LIFE GOES ON...AND DOESN'T

Both Green and Maki were arrested and slapped with assault-with-attempt-to-injure charges. Both were eventually acquitted in separate trials, but NHL President Clarence Campbell suspended Green for 13 games and Maki for 30 days, both without pay.

Green took one year off to recuperate, then came back to play two more seasons for the Bruins before joining the WHA. He was later an assistant coach for the Edmonton Oilers during their Stanley Cup–winning dynasty years of the 1980s, and their head coach for a short time in the early 1990s. Maki played two years for the Vancouver Canucks before being diagnosed with brain cancer in 1972 and dying two years later at the tragically young age of 29.

THE SICK SEVENTIES

This attempted slaughter with sticks was just the beginning of the Sick Seventies, probably the most violent decade in the history of the NHL. Some of these nauseous events were:

- Boston's Dave Forbes hitting Minnesota North Star Henry Boucha in the eye with his stick during a 1975 match.
- Marc Tardif of the WHA's Quebec Nordiques being cross-checked by the Calgary Cowboys' Rick Jodzio for no apparent reason. As Tardif lay unconscious on the ice, Jodzio punched him in the face…with both fists…several times. Really.
- A 1976 playoff game at Maple Leaf Gardens between the Maple Leafs and Philadelphia Flyers that got so out of control that a Flyer would hit a female usher in the head with a stick and a total of four Flyers would be charged with assault.
- A playoff game in 1974 between the Flyers and the New York Rangers in which Flyer Dave Schultz beat up the Rangers' Dale Rolfe with such abandon that Rolfe's own teammates were afraid to come to his rescue.
- In hindsight, it seems inevitable that a physical and intense game like hockey could erupt into a period of such violence. The important thing is that the NHL made it through this tunnel; the sport was even better once it came out on the other side.

* * * * *

"Hockey is the only job I know where you get paid to have a nap on the day of the game."

—Chico Resch, former New York Islanders goaltender

BEST IN THE CRUNCH

The goalie is the hero of every successful Stanley Cup contender.

The subject was goaltenders and the late King Clancy, who had seen many of the great ones in his 60 years as a National Hockey League player, coach, referee and executive, summed up succinctly the matter of rating the men in the nets. "Talk to a half-dozen hockey men about who was the best goalie they had seen, especially in the playoffs, and if you got two answers the same, it was a miracle," Clancy said. "I've heard more arguments about which goalie was the best than any other subject in hockey." That's why attempting to rate the greatest goalies, schedule or playoffs, is a tricky business…

LORD STANLEY'S PRESSURE COOKER

The Stanley Cup tournament is a tremendous testing ground for goalies, the time when the pressure is squarely on their shoulders as the last line of defence. At various times in Cup history, winning goalies have had to play as few as four games, then the maximum was 14 over two series for many years, eventually stretching to a possible 28 games over four series in the modern 30-team league. As an example, the seven-game 2004 Stanley Cup between the Tampa Bay Lightning and Calgary Flames capped the postseason brilliance of two European goalies: Nikolai Khabibulin of the Lightning and the Flames' Mikka Kiprusoff. The Lightning won their first Cup by a score of 2–1 in game seven. In 23 playoff games, Khabibulin recorded the necessary 16 wins with a goals-against average of 1.71 per game, while Kiprusoff fell one win short and in 26 postseason contests, his average was a comparably stellar 1.85.

THE GREAT BOUSE

In attempting to rate playoff goalies, it would have helped if one had watched J. B. "Bouse" Hutton at work, if for nothing else but to find out about that nickname. Bouse was the goalie for the Ottawa Silver Seven, winners of the Stanley Cup in 1903, 1904 and 1905. Or how about Hugh Lehman, goalie for the Cup-champion Vancouver Millionaires in 1915 and a chap who participated in eight Cup challenges with a variety of teams? Or Georges Vezina, the "Chicoutimi Cucumber," keeper for two Montreal Canadien Cup winners, father of 22 children and the man for whom the NHL's top goalie trophy is named? Then there's Hap Holmes, who played on three Cup winners in five years from 1914–1918. But they are merely names from the far distant past, men remembered in the record books and those old Hall of Fame photos. Measuring their performances against the playoff marathons of modern goalies is a difficult task.

MARATHON CHAMPIONS

Two goalies in the modern era have carved huge niches for themselves near the top of the list of best playoff (or any other time) performers. In his 19-season career, Patrick Roy backed four Stanley Cup champions: the Montreal Canadiens in 1986 and 1993, and the Colorado Avalanche in 1996 and 2001. Roy owns two playoff records: most games played by a goalie, 247; and playoff wins, 151. In his Cup-winning springs, Roy had a 63–22 win-loss record and an average of 1.96. Martin Brodeur of the New Jersey Devils has three Cup wins, in 1995, 2000 and 2003, and in 67 playoff games in those springs, his goals-against average was a glittering 1.64. To add a little more luster to his reputation as an extraordinary "pressure" goalie, Brodeur also excelled for Team Canada in the gold medal victories at the 2002 Olympic Games in Salt Lake City and the 2004 World Cup of Hockey.

TURK WAS TOUGH

Although his name means little now to the new generations of fans, the goalie regarded by many longtime hockey watchers as perhaps the best in playoff history was Walter "Turk" Broda of the Toronto Maple Leafs, one of the game's great characters. The Turk was a member of five Leaf teams that won the Cup. Broda was no slouch during the season, sporting a goals-against average of 2.56 in 630 matches. But in the playoffs, Broda's mark was an exceptional 1.99 in 101 games. "When the playoff bucks are up for grabs," a Toronto sportswriter once enthused, "the Turk could catch lint in a hurricane."

MODEST BOBBY

From 1974 to 1983, three goalies dominated the playoffs. Bernie Parent was brilliant for the Philadelphia Flyers in their 1974 and 1975 championships. Ken Dryden won six Cups in nine seasons, including four in a row from 1976 to 1977. Battlin' Billy Smith had four in succession with the New York Islanders from 1980 to 1983. "How good was Bernie Parent in those two Cup wins?" said Flyers captain Bobby Clarke. "If you had given him to one of four or five teams in those playoffs, that team would have won the Cup."

PLANTE'S A BIG ONE

Ranking with Broda and all others on the playoff greats list is Jacques Plante, who is tied at six with Dryden for most Cup wins by a goalie. Plante owns a 2.16 playoff average in 112 games and when the Canadiens won a record five consecutive cups from 1956 to 1960, Plante had a 1.90 average.

A FEW OTHER PLAYOFF HIGHLIGHTS:

- Alex Connell had a 13-season NHL career with the Ottawa Senators, Detroit Red Wings and Montreal Maroons, played on two Cup-winners and owned a 1.24 average in 21 playoff games.
- Four goalies won the Conn Smythe Trophy as the most valuable player in the playoffs, despite being on teams that lost the finals: Roger Crozier with the Red Wings in 1966, Glenn Hall with the St. Louis Blues in 1968, Ron Hextall of the Flyers in 1987, and Jean-Sebastien Giguere with the Anaheim Mighty Ducks in 2003.
- The great Terry Sawchuk, the choice of many as best ever, had four shutouts and allowed only five goals in eight games as the Red Wings swept two series on their way to the 1950 Cup.
- Sawchuk, 37 at the time, and Johnny Bower, 42, combined to play agelessly in the 1967 playoffs, leading the Leafs to a surprise victory.

TWINKLE, TWINKLE, LITTLE PUCK

How Fox TV invented a puck that had a red tail to help hockey fans follow the bouncing disc in televised games.

A reason often listed for U.S. sports fans in non-hockey areas having little interest in the game is that the puck is too small and too difficult for casual fans to follow. Canadian hockey supporters, the majority of the population north of the 49th parallel, figure that's goofy. Consider the size of a golf ball in comparison to a hockey puck and the size of a golf course compared to a hockey rink and it's a wonder any Americans watch that game.

WHY NOT THE HISTORY OF MANKIND?

In 1996, the Fox Television Network, which was trying to interest more U.S. fans in hockey, decided to make the puck easier to see. The result was "Foxtrax," the puck with the bright red tail that Fox called "the greatest innovation in the history of sports." Most Canadian fans who had the Fox network on their cable program thought it was "the silliest backward step in sports history."

EXPENSIVE LITTLE DEVILS

The pucks Fox created cost $50,000 each, which meant network employees had to be quick to the scene when one went over the boards into a fan's grasp. There was a blue glow around the puck on the TV screen and when it traveled any distance, the "puck-man" in the control truck would hit a switch that saw the disc followed by a red tail. To create the more visible disc, a normal rubber puck was cut in half like a bagel and electronic transmitters plus tiny batteries inserted in it and the pieces glued back together. Sensors were placed around the rink to track the wonder puck. The puck's power lasted approximately ten minutes, then it was replaced, the used one recharged.

MAYBE IT WAS THE RISE IN THE PRICE OF GLUE

The glowing, flashing puck was introduced at the 1995–96 NHL All-Star Game and for a few weeks, Fox claimed the response to the gadget was positive. But when the next season rolled around, the puck was back to good old basic black rubber, always frozen to reduce the bounce before it is used. Fox claimed that it wasn't the cost of the electronic trinket or the adverse reaction among true hockey fans. In fact, the network didn't really give good reasons for junking the "greatest innovation in the history of sports."

* * * * *

"I think the game has gotten better. (The two-ref system) keeps players from taking cheap shots behind the play. I never thought I'd like it, considering the way I like to hack."

—center Brian Skrudland on the new two-referee system

"I don't know if Anna (Kournikova) told him to get tougher or what."

—Dallas captain Mike Modano, on Detroit's Sergei Fedorov breaking three sticks on Dallas players

"It felt like a golf swing and my head was on the tee."

—Blue Jacketes center Tyler Wright, on being clubbed by right wing Joe Murphy

"The Russians are the dirtiest players I've ever seen."

—Bobby Clarke, April 1976 (four years after breaking Valery Kharlamov's ankle with a slash)

"For the most part, with the possible exception of me, I don't think anybody goes out to try to hurt somebody."

—Jeremy Roenick, former Chicago Blackhawks forward

"All the other players had to test us. We were just chicken hockey players from Europe. For a couple of years, it was chicken Swede this, and chicken Swede that. I never hear it any more. A few elbows took care of that."

—Borje Salming, former Toronto Maple Leafs defenceman

MILLION DOLLAR "M"

The Black Hawks offered a million for Frank Mahovlich when a joke turned serious at an All-Star Game party.

The NHL All-Star Game matched the Stanley Cup champion Toronto Maple Leafs against the league's best players in Toronto in October 1962. After the glittering dinner the evening before the game, team owners and executives met in a hospitality suite for a drink or two. Chicago Black Hawks owner Jim Norris, an influential NHL governor, decided to test the new owners of the Toronto Maple Leafs. Leafs' founder Conn Smythe had sold the team to a group headed by his son Stafford, Harold Ballard and Toronto publisher John Bassett.

NORRIS' TRY FOR DYNASTY

After a long stretch as NHL doormats, the Hawks were among the elite teams—winners of the Stanley Cup in 1961—led by Bobby Hull, Stan Mikita, Pierre Pilote and Glenn Hall. The Leafs had climbed to the top, too, with a strong reconstruction and an assortment of young stars including Dave Keon, Carol Brewer and "The Big M," Frank Mahovlich. Much all-star weekend talk concerned Mahovlich's problems in reaching an agreement with the Leafs on a new contract. During their party talk, when Stafford Smythe and Ballard mentioned their bank loan to buy the Leafs, Norris suggested a method of reducing it. He offered one million dollars for winger Mahovlich, a 48-goal-scorer in 1960–61.

TRUST BALLARD...

Those within earshot regarded it as a joke when Norris and Ballard shook hands on the "deal" and the Black Hawks owner gave Ballard a $1,000 bill as a deposit. Gord Campbell, a sports writer for the *Toronto Star* who was at the party at Ballard's invitation, wrote the story as a serious offer by the Hawks and when the paper hit the streets the next morning, reaction was enormous.

NORRIS LEARNS ABOUT LEAFS

Norris met a hastily summoned banker and dispatched Hawks general manager Tommy Ivan to Maple Leaf Gardens with a certified

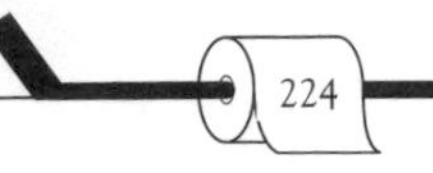

cheque for $1M. But by the time he reached the Leafs executive offices, the Leaf owners had changed their minds. Conn Smythe convinced his son that the deal was bad for hockey and would hurt the team's credibility. Stafford Smythe announced that the Big M was not for sale at any price. Norris claimed the Leafs had backed out of a legitimate deal.

* * * * *

MUSIC TO MY EARS

Hockey has been the inspiration for some very fine song writing. Here are some of the best.

"The Hockey Song" by Stompin' Tom Connors. No game would be complete without it: "Oh, the good old hockey game, is the best game you can name." Enough said.

"Hockey" by Jane Siberry. You can't beat this mellifluous ode to Sunday afternoon hockey on a "frozen river."

"Hit Somebody! (The Hockey Song)" by Warren Zevon—a heartfelt appreciation of hockey's goons and grinders.

"Slapshot Love" by The Zambonis, the ultimate hockey band sings the ultimate hockey love song ("skating on the blue line, that's when I saw your green light.")

"The Zamboni Song" by the Gear Daddies. "Now ever since I was young it's been my dream/That I might drive a Zamboni machine." Don't we all?

"Fifty Mission Cap" by the Tragically Hip tells the tragic story of Maple Leaf Bill Barilko, who died in a plane crash on a fishing trip in 1962.

THE LABOR FRONT

The 2004–05 season-killing lockout of the players by the NHL ended a relatively peaceful owner-player history.

The lockout of the players by the NHL teams after failure to reach a new collective bargaining agreement and cancellation of the 2004–05 season plus the Stanley Cup playoffs, a dispute involving billions of dollars, was a great distance in time and money from the league's first serious labor action. The initial tiff was the 1925 strike by the Hamilton Tigers when the NHL refused to pay 11 players a demanded $200 each when the schedule increased from 24 to 30 games and no bonuses were offered for lengthened playoffs.

STRIKES AND PAY HIKES

In the 80 years between those happenings, the league and its workers had a smooth relationship with only a few labor disputes, one involving the minor league Springfield Indians. The most serious was a 103-day lockout that reduced the schedule from 84 to 48 games in 1994–95, though the players also went on strike for ten days in April of 1992, delaying the start of the playoffs. The NHL officials staged a 16-day strike in the 1993–94 season, but use of replacement officials meant no games were cancelled.

Creation of the NHL Players' Association was an uphill task. The league owners crushed the first serious bid by the players to form a union in the late 1950s. A decade later, led by Toronto lawyer Alan Eagleson and with most players in a newly expanded league signing on, the NHLPA compelled the owners to reluctantly deal with them.

THE RED GREEN SHOW

The Quebec Bulldogs became the Hamilton Tigers in 1920, joining the Ottawa Senators, Montreal Canadiens and Toronto St. Patricks in the fledgling NHL. The club won only 28 of 96 games in four seasons in the league basement, often needing player aid from opponents. But good young players Alex McKinnon and brothers Red and Shorty Green with top scorer Billy Burch and goalie Jumpin' Jake Forbes lifted the Tigers to first place in the 1924–25 season.

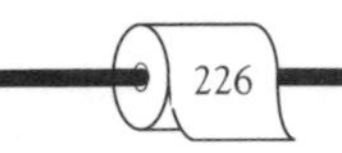

NHL'S PROBLEM-SELLING SKILLS

The schedule increased from 24 to 30 games and salaries—average pay was $1,100—were not boosted. Playoff participation was increased from two to three teams, the first-place Tigers receiving a bye to the final against the winner of a Toronto-Montreal series. NHL president Frank Calder suspended the Tiger players indefinitely and declared the Canadiens, 5–2 winners over the St. Pats in a two-game, total-goals series, as NHL champs. The Canadiens lost the Stanley Cup final to the Pacific Coast champs, the Victoria Cougars. The NHL solved the "problem" by selling the entire Tigers roster to Manhattan bootlegging king Bill Dwyer for $75,000, and the team became the New York Americans.

INDIAN REVOLT

In the late 1950s and 1960s, the AHL Springfield Indians were owned and operated on a shoestring budget by Eddie Shore, the former Boston Bruins great. Shore had such unorthodox ideas on how the game should be played that NHL teams used assignment to the Springfield club as a punishment threat to players. Shore ran a notoriously penny-pinching operation and his ruthless treatment of players is part of hockey folklore. Shore, not the club doctors, decided when injured players were ready to play. In the 1966–67 season with the NHL on the verge of expansion, the Indians had three good defencemen (Bill White, Dale Rolfe, Dave Amadio) who refused to play until Shore gave them pay raises. Suprisingly, he offered them small increases, then during an eight-day pre-Christmas gap in the schedule, he suspended the trio for "indifferent play," the pay loss equal to the paltry raise he had given them.

THE HUMANE SOCIETY HAS LANDED

The Springfield players called Toronto lawyer Eagleson, who had made hockey headlines earlier in 1966 when he negotiated a record first contract with the Boston Bruins for 18-year-old defenceman Bobby Orr. Eagleson described the Springfield situation succinctly: "If you ever treated dogs the way Shore treated these men, someone would call the humane society." Eagleson gained an agreement that Shore would reinstate the suspended players and step aside from the team's operation. Eagleson's "victory" over the hockey establishment gave much impetus to his forming the NHLPA that season.

MARATHON-WINNERS

A 14-hour bargaining session on April 10, 1992 ended a ten-day strike by the players that threatened the concluding week of the schedule and the Stanley Cup playoffs. The two-year agreement, retroactive to the start of the 1991–92 season, changed the rules on free agency, increased the award money for regular season finishes and playoff bonuses, improved the players' pension plan, installed a minimum salary of $100,000 and made adjustments to the salary arbitration process.

The NHL owners had extended the previous agreement by a year in 1991. Negotiations on a new deal through the summer of 1991 produced no agreement, even when owners abandoned binding arbitration to settle the dispute. The season opened with no negotiations between September 1991, and March 1992. Fruitless March meetings led to the players announcing on March 20 a strike deadline of March 30. The deadline was later extended by one day but when the players voted 560–4 in favor of strike, NHL president John Ziegler announced at 3 P.M. on April 1, the league would suspend operation "on a day-to-day basis." An April 10 deadline was set when the season and playoffs would be ruled out if no agreement was reached. Marathon bargaining prevented the cancellation, creating temporary peace in the NHL.

PRE-GAME WARMUP TO '05

The NHL conducted the 1993–94 season on an extension of the previous agreement, gaining a season of labor stability while a plan was devised to reduce costs, especially skyrocketing payrolls—the average player salary climbing from $232,000 in the 1989–90 season to $680,000 in 1994–95. The players balked at the move, and training camps opened in early September with threat of either a lockout or strike hanging heavily over the team preparations. The opening of the schedule was delayed by two weeks, then postponed indefinitely. On December 12, the owners decreed that January 16 was the last possible date for a 50-game schedule, the minimum number the owners would accept. Again, a two-day negotiation brought an agreement, a six-year contract, training camps opened quickly, and a 48-game schedule started on January 20. While nothing in the new deal slowed the escalation of payrolls, the players' big aim along with unrestricted free agency at 31 years of age, an assortment of small adjustments to arbitration and pensions produced a deal neither side really liked.

KILLING A SEASON

The victory by Team Canada on September 14, 1995, 3–2 over Finland to decide the World Cup of Hockey, was more than an uplifting triumph by the Canadians. At 12:01 P.M. on September 16, the NHL governors locked out the players to start a labor dispute resulting in the cancellation of the entire schedule and Stanley Cup playoffs. While an assortment of smaller issues were never discussed, one big issue produced the impasse. The owners, who claimed to have lost more than $200 million in each of the previous two seasons, insisted on a salary cap while the players did not believe the owners' financial claims and would not agree to a cap. After a frustrating lack of progress, the players finally relented on the salary cap at the last possible time to save the season, January 2005, but the two sides could not agree on the number. The first full season in professional sports history was cancelled due to a labor dispute.

A NEW GAME

In July, excitement in hockey was renewed, but it came at a cost to the players. Having moved away from NHLPA Director Bob Goodenow's hard-line stance on the salary cap in January, the association executive finally agreed to a 24 percent rollback on all current salaries and a hard cap of $39 million per team. Aspects of both revenue sharing by the teams, and a tying of salaries (the cap) to overall league revenue were also part of the deal. To the advantage of the players, the league minimum salary was brought up to $450,000 and qualifications for unrestricted free agency will be reduced to from age 31 to age 28, or after seven seasons in the league, by 2008. In an attempt to bring back fans, the league also embarked on initiatives to increase excitement in the game: primarily the elimination of the center red line rule against two-line passes; an enlargement of the offensive zones and reduction in the area behind the net; stricter limitations on the size of goaltenders' equipment; and shootouts to decide tie games. Goodenow, clearly defeated in his determination to prevent a salary cap, resigned shortly after the agreement was announced.

DEFINING MOMENT IN HOCKEY

When the Edmonton Oilers traded Wayne Gretzky to the Los Angeles Kings, it sent a shockwave through the NHL.

In the late summer of 1988, life could not have been much better for Wayne Gretzky. The Edmonton Oilers had won their fourth Stanley Cup championship in five seasons and with the hefty list of stars on their roster in the prime years of careers, they appeared likely to add to that achievement. Gretzky's wedding to actress Janet Jones was the highlight of the summer in Alberta and during the playoffs, she had informed No. 99 that he was going to be a father. The Gretzkys were looking for a home in Edmonton.

THE NAIVE ONE

"I figured the Oilers had three or four Cups still to win because we had started as a gang of teenagers in the very early 1980s, climbed to the top four times and everyone on the team was still hungry because we knew how much fun winning was," Gretzky said. "There had been a bit of guff around the NHL and a little in Edmonton that Janet didn't want to stay in Edmonton but that was absolutely not true. I was four years away from unrestricted free agency and I wanted to be an Oiler at least until then when I could make my own deal to change my career. Janet had agreed to all that. But I guess figuring I would have control over my life was pretty naive."

L-OIL-TY

The Oilers were a success on the ice and at the gate, playing to capacity crowds (16,239) every night in Northlands Coliseum in a city of 600,000. After four Cups and all the individual awards the team had won, the payroll was becoming a challenge for owner Peter Pocklington and GM-coach Glen Sather. Several of the team's stars knew there were greener pastures in bigger markets but there was a great deal of loyalty to the Oilers—the team that gave them a chance, the team where Gretzky, Mark Messier, Jari Kurri, Paul Coffey, Glenn Anderson, Grant Fuhr, Kevin Lowe and

Esa Tikkanen had become stars. The big money in other cities was inviting but the chance to add to their winning mark with the freewheeling fun-to-play hockey style was a big lure, at least until they knew the team had run its championship course.

THE WOES OF POOR PETER PUCK

But while the Oilers were doing good business, owner Pocklington's other businesses (oil, meat packing, land development, trust company, car dealerships) were encountering trouble and he needed an infusion of capital to keep his empire afloat. His expensive art collection had been sold and the Oilers were used as collateral for a loan. A year earlier, Gretzky had signed a personal services contract with Pocklington when the Oilers owner was thinking of turning the team into a public company as a way to raise cash for his other businesses. The plan was to make Gretzky part of the team. "It turned out that Janet, my father and my agent Mike Barnett had known all through the playoffs about Pocklington having discussions with several teams about a deal for me that would include a lot of cash. But they didn't tell me because they knew I was zeroed in on the playoffs and they knew I wanted no distractions."

HONEYMOON INTERRUPTED

Gretzky and Janet were on their honeymoon in Los Angeles when he received a call from Los Angeles Kings owner Bruce McNall, a flashy Californian who was regarded as a genius for amassing a fortune dealing in antique coins. McNall said that he had the Oilers' permission to talk to him about a contract that would follow a deal. "It was slap in the face not to have the Oilers tell me about the whole matter," Gretzky said. "But when I thought about it, I realized that if I was going to be traded, L.A. was good because it would mean Janet could pick up her acting career again."

GRETZ HELPS NEGOTIATE TRADE OF HIMSELF

McNall said he would pay $20 million plus three first-round draft picks and two players for Gretzky and two or three players. "I told him one of the other guys had to be Marty McSorley," Gretzky recalled. "The Kings had been a bad team, one without much grit, and McSorley was one of the toughest guys in the NHL. I actually was in McNall's office when Pocklington called him and Bruce said McSorley had to be one of the players. I told McNall to tell him if Marty wasn't in the deal, I wouldn't report to the Kings." The deal finally was hammered out. Gretzky, McSorley and forward Mike Krushelnyski would go to the Kings in exchange for three draft picks, young forwards Jimmy Carson and Martin Gelinas, and $15 million. The trade could not be announced for two weeks because the Oilers were staging their season ticket drive and word of No. 99's departure would hurt that.

WHAT HEART?

A reporter in Quebec where Gretzky had owned the Hull Olympiques junior team somehow grabbed the scoop on what most call the biggest deal in NHL history in a story on August 8. The next day, Gretzky flew to Edmonton where a press conference was held in which Pocklington wanted Gretzky to say the trade was his idea but Gretzky refused. On the nationally televised conference, Pockington talked of his "heavy heart" that he had when granting Gretzky's request to leave the Oilers. "What do you do when an outstanding, loyal employee approaches you and asks for an opportunity to move along?" Pocklington said. "You know you don't want to lose him but at the same time, you don't want to stop him from pursuing his dreams."

TEARS OF GRACE

When Gretzky tried to speak of his feelings, tears ran down his face. "The tears were real because I realized that I had nothing but great times, big wins, awards and the best of everything hockey can offer and now that was over," Gretzky said. "I would have to start again in a new place with a team that had been 18th the season before." But at another press conference in Los Angeles later that day, Gretzky had regained his composure and spoke with optimism about his future with the Kings and how he and Janet looked forward to their life in Los Angeles.

HOTTEST TICKET IN HOLLYWOOD

As soon as the deal was announced, the Kings were bombarded with requests for season tickets. Hollywood is built on stars and the biggest one in hockey had just landed in town. Gretzky rewarded the Kings with a monster season, 54 goals, 168 points, second to Mario Lemieux's 85 and 199, and lifted the team to second in the Smythe Division, seven points ahead of the Oilers. The teams met in the playoffs and the Kings won the series. The jolt that Gretzky gave the NHL in Los Angeles was the inspiration for expansion in that area with the San Jose Sharks and Anaheim Mighty Ducks joining the league in the next few years. He won three scoring titles in the next five years and produced 40 points in 25 in the 1993 playoffs when the Kings lost the final to the Montreal Canadiens. Gretzky wound down his career with the St. Louis Blues and the New York Rangers while McNall wound up in jail for a variety of nefarious money schemes.

* * * * *

SHOW ME THE MONEY

"I don't know the salaries of the other players and I really don't want to know. It's the World Hockey Association, I think, that was the direct cause to all the changes in salary structures. But I think that the excesses are over and that soon, things will be back to normal."

—Yvan Cournoyer on salaries in the 1970s

"I was a multi-millionaire from playing hockey. Then I got divorced, and now I am a millionaire."

—Bobby Hull

"We've made a final offer. We hope Ziggy Palffy will come to his senses. We have NO hope his agent will."

—Islander GM Mike Milbury

"Sources also confirm that there is no one left in Canada who can remember when hockey was a simple game, played for fun."

—Ottawa journalist Roy MacGregor,
on Alexei Yashin's contract holdout

"As always, I remain hopeful that Don Cherry won't be offered the same length contract."

—broadcaster Ron MacLean, on his contract renewal

GALLIVAN-TING

Broadcaster great Danny Gallivan had a unique way of using the language in calling Canadiens games for 30 years.

Danny Gallivan, the radio and television play-by-play broadcaster of the Montreal Canadiens, described a shot by Boom-Boom Geoffrion this way: "Geoffrion creases the post with a cannonading drive." When he received a letter from an English professor who claimed that there was no such adjective as "cannonading," Gallivan's short response was "There is now."

A college English teacher himself, Gallivan's command of the language inspired his literate descriptions of the great Canadien teams he covered. He called 16 Stanley Cup championships in his 32 years behind the microphone, starting in 1952. The team advanced to the playoff final in Gallivan's first eight years on the job, the large audience exposure in the spring quickly making him a household name across Canada.

GREAT GALLIVANISMS:

"Lapointe avoids the forechecker with a slick spinnerama move."

"Dryden stymies Esposito with a scintillating save."

"Rousseau just failed to negotiate contact with that high pass."

"Bossy failed to negotiate the puck through the plethora of players in front of the net."

"Provost makes a visitation to the penalty box."

"Montreal takes the lead on a classic Robinsonian effort."

"The puck is lost in Gump Worsley's paraphernalia."

"Ferguson and Shack are in a real donnybrook, if not an outright brouhaha."

"A multiplicity of faceoffs is the overwhelmingly dominant feature in this game."

"There is an absence of sustained scintillation through the opening half period."

ARE ALL GOALIES CRACKPOTS?

The basic absurdities of the position mean that not all men who wear the pads fit the parameters of so-called "normal."

The job could be described this way: A man, his body covered with small mattresses and carrying a large wooden club, stands in front of a piece of fish net stretched over a rectangle of pipes and tries to place his body in the way of a three-inch piece of frozen rubber fired towards him at speeds in excess of 110 miles per hour. A U.S. magazine writer once called hockey goaltenders "a special breed of man, half commando and half human pincushion."

"There's only one job in sports that's worse," said Lorne "Gump" Worsley, a front-line NHL goalie for 21 seasons, "and that would be as the javelin catcher on a track team." Throughout the century or so of hockey, the men in front of the nets have been a breed apart from other players, "different" in a variety of ways; some actually, well, unusual.

THESE ARE NORMAL MEN?

Arguments claim that many goalies are ordinary chaps, level-headed guys simply trying to earn a living. Ken Dryden, the intellectual goalie of six Stanley Cup championship teams in the 1970s with the Montreal Canadiens, was viewed as normal...Sure, all "normal" folks play goal in the NHL while attending law school as a full-time student! Johnny Bower was a pleasant, easygoing man during his splendid career with four 1960s Cup-winners as a Toronto Maple Leaf. But the "normal" Bower did not start his 13-season stay with the Leafs until he was 33 and was considering retirement after years at the minor league level.

SOME PRE-GAME WARMUP

Glenn Hall was a remarkable athlete who played in a record 502 consecutive complete games. But he vomited before most of them, and often between periods. "I do think the media blew up the fact that I was throwing up," Hall said. "When I threw up, I felt like I was doing what I needed to do to prepare for the game. I felt that if I threw up, I played better."

BUT DID THEY EVER TALK BACK?

Jacques Plante was normal, except for 2,456 idiosyncrasies. Andy Brown was normal, except that he refused to wear a face mask, the last NHL goalie to play without one, and he raced stock cars in the offseason. Gump Worsley, also one of the last goalies to put on a mask, reasoned "Would it have been fair not to give the people a chance to see my beautiful face?" (Gump's antics are explored by Uncle John in more detail elsewhere in this *Reader*.) Patrick Roy, a brilliant goalie on four Stanley Cup championship teams with the Canadiens and Colorado Avalanche, often talked to the goal posts, asking them for help.

ANKLE-HACKERS

Billy Smith was the goalie on four Cup-winning teams with the New York Islanders and Ron Hextall was the Conn Smythe Trophy winner as playoff MVP with the Philadelphia Flyers even though they lost the final to the Edmonton Oilers. Both goalies created the notion that they were sadistic nuts, swinging their sticks at the ankles of opponents who ventured near their creases, and even picking fights with intruders.

PLANTE A SEED

Jacques Plante is the choice of many as the best goalie ever. Certainly he was the most innovative: A serious, intelligent man whose status as a flake was acquired unintentionally. Plante was the first goalie to wear a protective face mask regularly, the first to venture out of the net to block shoot-ins around the boards and clear the puck to teammates. He always insisted necessity was the mother of his invention: "I got sick of being hit in the face with pucks, especially deflected slapshots, so I wore a mask," Plante said. "Management opposed it and felt it showed I had lost my nerve. But it wasn't their faces that were being stitched all the time. It didn't take a genius to figure out that a mask could stop the stitches."

IT CAME TO ME IN A DREAM

"In semi-pro hockey, I played behind a defence that had two players who couldn't skate backwards and two who couldn't pivot. I skated better than any of them so I started to go out to clear loose pucks. When I did it with the Canadiens, management figured I was showboating, even when it helped us win." Canadien coach Toe Blake figured Plante was a hypochondriac who dreamed up ailments, especially asthma, that showed at strange times. Plante insisted that the team's hotel in Toronto caused asthma flare-ups and Blake allowed him to stay in a different hotel. But he appeared at Maple Leaf Gardens the next morning with his asthma in full bloom, and his explanation caused Blake to react as if he had encountered a complete nut. "I dreamed I was sleeping in the team's hotel and when I woke up the next morning, my asthma had flared up," Plante said. When the Canadiens traded Plante a year after he was named the NHL's most valuable player, Blake said, "I couldn't cope with his nonsense any more. He was driving me nuts, always something wrong with him."

"IT STILL BOTHERS ME FROM TIME TO TIME..."

Gilles Gratton was a goalie who was truly different, a pure flake, who logged time in the WHA with the Toronto Toros and in the NHL with the Rangers and St. Louis Blues. Gratton was into reincarnation, meditation, playing the piano, streaking and often stated that his ambition was to become a star in pornographic movies. He claimed that what had happened in his several previous lives influenced his current one. When he was with the Rangers and said he could not play in a game because of a leg injury, GM John Ferguson asked him when he had suffered the injury. "I was a soldier in the Franco-Prussian war and was wounded in the leg," Gratton said. "It still bothers me from time to time." Gratton had a tiger's features painted on his face mask in honor of his being a tiger in one of his previous lives on earth. The Ranger players complained to Ferguson "that Gratton growls like a bloody tiger behind the mask."

PLAY TO PAY

Walter "Turk" Broda rates at or near the top of the list of goalies who have excelled in the pressure of the Stanley Cup playoffs, a major reason why the Maple Leafs won Cups. His goals-against average during the schedule was a solid 2.53 in 629 games but in the playoffs, he lowered the mark to 1.98 in 101 games. Broda was a hearty, fun-loving man who enjoyed life and offered the "typically goalie's" explanation for his postseason brilliance. "I suppose I was too dumb to realize how serious it was in the playoffs and never let it get to me," Broda said. "Also we didn't make big salaries in the 1940s and I really needed the playoff bonuses to pay my bills."

The pressure did reach a few goalies. The wife of Wilf Cude of the Montreal Canadiens in the 1930s prepared his game-day steak and, for no reason, Cude hurled the steak against the kitchen wall. "In the time it took that steak to hit the wall, then fall to the floor, I retired," Cude said. "I had been on edge long enough."

* * * * *

"Playing goal is like being shot at."

—Jacques Plante

"Goaltenders are three sandwiches shy of a picnic. From the moment primitive man lurched erect, he survived on the principle that when something hard and potentially lethal comes toward you at great velocity, get the hell *out* of it's path."

—sports journalist Jim Taylor

"I'm not dumb enough to be a goalie."

—Brett Hull

* * * * *

Goalie Jim Stewart must have the worst goalie stats on record, and it all happened in twenty minutes. Jim's entire NHL career lasted only one period, but that was long enough for him to let in an embarrassing five goals on nine shots as his Boston Bruins lost 7–4 to the St. Louis Blues in January, 1980.

SO BE GOOD, FOR GOODNESS SAKE

Nothing throws the bah-humbug into a Christmas celebration quite like one of hockey's bitterest rivalries.

In December of 2003, when the New York Islanders offered anyone dressed as Santa Claus a free ticket to a pre-Christmas game against the Philadelphia Flyers, the idea was to add holiday spirit to—and fill a few empty seats in—Nassau Coliseum. They even invited the 1,000 faux-Santas onto the ice for a parade between periods.

WHAT'S SANTA DOING TO THAT MAN, DADDY?

What the Islanders promotions department didn't count on was a trio of Saint Nicks throwing off their red-and-white coats to reveal the red-and-blue jerseys of the hated in-state enemies, the New York Rangers. The bitter intrastate rivalry regularly features as many fights in the stands as on the ice, so it came as no surprise that the Islanders faithful responded by jumping the Rangers fans, ripping off the offending jerseys, and pummelling the intruders to the ice. Security was on the scene, but calming the escalating free-for-all wasn't easy as more fans took advantage of the chaos by sliding across the ice. It took nearly ten minutes to clear the fans from the rink, which almost forced officials to delay the start of the second period.

THE RIVALRY CONTINUES

The Islanders, who rallied in the third period for a 4–2 win, said after the game that they weren't even aware of the between-period melee. But more than a few were smiling after being debriefed. It's not surprising given the history of the rivalry between the Manhattan-based Rangers and their cousins from Long Island. Officially the two teams play for the Pat LaFontaine Trophy, awarded to the winner of the season series. Unofficially, respect, dignity and regional pride are at stake—for the fans as well as the players. In addition to the frequent fisticuffs off the ice, there have even been reports of parking lots charging Rangers fans more at Islanders home games. Brawling Santas, however, may be hard to top. Even in New York.

HOLD THAT TIGER

How a coach's quest to rescue his tough guy started a chain reaction that led all the way to the Stanley Cup finals.

Sometimes things happen that nobody can explain. Like crop circles and Stonehenge and the Bermuda Triangle. Like the 1982 Vancouver Canucks, in those garish flying-V yellow, black and orange jerseys going all the way to the Stanley Cup Finals.

FERMEZ LA BOUCHE, MONSIEUR TIGRE

Canucks head coach Harry Neale surely wasn't aware of what he was getting into when he decided to wade into the stands to prevent his rough-and-tumble forward Dave "Tiger" Williams from getting ambushed during a March 20, 1982, game at Quebec City. Williams had made some disparaging remarks about French Canadians in an interview prior to the game. Tension had been mounting and now Williams, who was being pinned to the boards by Quebec's Wilf Paiement, was also in danger of being sucker-punched by a fan reaching over the glass. Neale wasted little time in charging into the stands himself, followed by a pair of his players.

"He had been a mouthy fan," Neale recalled years later. "I'd known him from the World Hockey Association days when I coached Hartford. I ran off to try and get him. I never quite got to him and I think Marc Crawford and Doug Halward and I forget who else—three [players] came with me—so I was going to be alright if a fight started."

BUT WHO WILL PROTECT US FROM THE FANS?

Neale paid dearly for his excursion into the stands. The coach was handed a lengthy suspension by the NHL, a punishment that would carry over into the postseason. But his action would also begin a strange momentum that the Canucks rode all the way into the finals. Many from that team still point to the incident in Quebec City as the catalyst for a playoff run that would see the Canucks beat Calgary, Los Angeles and Chicago before ultimately losing to the powerful New York Islanders dynasty in four straight. It was the first trip to the finals for the Vancouver franchise, which wouldn't make it there again until a dozen years later.

Up until March 20, 1982, however, the Canucks were having a rather forgettable winter. Despite going unbeaten over the final ten games of the regular season, they still finished with three more losses than wins. Nobody expected much out of them in the postseason.

CAPTAIN VIDEO TO THE RESCUE

While Neale's suspension pushed him off the Canucks' bench it also meant that Roger Neilson, the head coach in waiting for the following season, took over a few months early. Neilson's highly prepared, systematic approach to the game proved to be the perfect fit for these Canucks, who collectively bought into his plan—for one postseason, at least. Neale, who during his suspension had scored a cozy seat as a CBC-TV *Hockey Night in Canada* analyst, was smart enough to realize that Neilson and the team had stumbled upon some kind of crazy chemistry. Neale stayed at *Hockey Night in Canada*.

"When Roger had won the last three games of the [regular] season and the first three of the playoffs, I didn't have to be [Montreal Canadiens' mastermind GM] Sam Pollock to figure out this guy's got something going with this team," Neale said. "We were going to make the [coaching] change anyway, so we made it then."

A KING IS BORN (FOR A VERY SHORT REIGN)

Canuck players from that team give a lot of credit to goaltender "King" Richard Brodeur, who was brilliant for Vancouver during those playoffs. But at least as much credit goes to the late Neilson, who managed to motivate the first- and fourth-line players with equal success and guide his unlikely group of skaters further than anybody could have imagined. "I think that run was largely due to the gentleman who was coaching—Roger Neilson," defenceman Rick Lanz would later say. "He basically took a group of players that really nobody expected a whole lot from, especially a playoff run like that. And you know, the players who came in to help because of the injuries we had did a fantastic job...Everybody got kind of caught up in the emotion of it all and subsequently were playing at the peak of their abilities. That was largely due to Roger who kind of rallied the troops."

"We got on a roll and played over our heads," Neale said. "No matter who got hurt, the guy coming in, even if he hadn't played, did a good job and we were getting some excellent goaltending...It was just a perfect example of a team that got on a roll."

ON THE TABLE

Hockey's most intense competition takes place in a gymnasium?

The reigning world champion in men's hockey is Sweden's Daniel Wallen, while in women's hockey it is the Finnish phenomenon Piia Pulliainen, as your family was no doubt discussing around the dinner table the other...What's that? *Canadian* teams won gold at the last Olympics? Please, that's old hat—we're talking about the Table Hockey World Championships.

CANADA'S GAME?

True, there are numerous table hockey tournaments held in North America, including the U.S. Nationals in Chicago and regional tourneys throughout Canada, but since 1989 the World Championships have been held in northern Europe and played without fail on Swedish-made Stiga game sets. Yet table hockey was invented by a Canadian and brought to international prominence by Canadians! The denizens of the Great White North must truly wring their hands and wonder—as they have when other nations triumphed in that version of hockey played by actual people on sheets of ice—"What happened to *our* game?"

NECESSITY IS THE FATHER OF INVENTION

In 1932, the Great Depression was in full swing in Canada. Donald H. Munro couldn't afford to buy his children Christmas gifts, so he built them the first-ever table hockey game from scraps of wood and metal he found around his Toronto neighborhood. Using a steel ball for a puck and wire-and-peg paddles for players, Munro's initial effort resembled a pinball game more than it did the table hockey of today, but his kids' enthusiasm prompted him to build several more, which the Eaton's department store then agreed to sell on consignment. They sold out immediately, and by the late 1930s Munro was selling several thousand each year at $4.95 per game. You may heave a sentimental sigh at the notion of being able to buy end-to-end hockey excitement for a handful of change, especially in light of how much a new game costs today, but keep in mind that $4.95 in 1939 dollars translates to about $85 today. With that sort of income, it's no surprise that the Munro company was able to stay in the black for decades, adapting its wooden-paddle model to the more modern tin-men version in 1955 before selling its assets to U.S. manufacturer Servotronics in 1968, when market demand prompted by NHL expansion surged to more than the humble Munro could hope to meet. Hundreds of thousands of games were being bought across the continent.

RISE OF THE TIN MEN

In 1954, the Eagle Toy Company of Montreal released the first Canadian table hockey set with game pieces resembling actual players, punched from accurately colored tin and set on rods that allowed them to turn 360 degrees. This second innovation, though, had been borrowed from the Aristospel games company of Sweden, who since 1939 had been manufacturing a table hockey game that featured long slots that allowed the players to move up and down the board. In 1956, both Eagle and Munro began selling rod-and-slot versions to the North American market, and they continued to lay low all competitors over the following decades through innovations such as clear plastic above the boards, puck-droppers, scoreboards and goal lights. Eagle was the dominant company thanks to their official NHL endorsement allowing them, to fans' delight, to clothe their tin men in exact reproductions of team uniforms. Indeed, the games most likely to induce salivation in modern-day collectors feature defunct teams like the Cleveland Barons and California Golden Seals, manufactured by U.S.-based Coleco following their absorption of Eagle in 1968.

MEANWHILE, IN STOCKHOLM

The popularity of Aristospel's game grew steadily in Sweden over two decades, with sales in the late 50s peaking at 25,000 units per year. At the same time, Stig Hjelmkvist began manufacturing games under the Stiga label in the southern town of Tranås, though his efforts made little impact on the market until Swedish superstar Sven "Tumba" Johansson—the first European to attend an NHL training camp—lent his endorsement to the game in 1959. Since then, Stiga has enjoyed unrivalled success in the European market, moving 100,000 games a year. They put upstart Alga—maker of the first game with rounded corners and three-dimensional players—out of business in the early 1960s, and gave venerable Aristospel the same treatment in 1972.

SVEN "TUMBA" JOHANSSON WOULD BE PROUD

With the rise of video games in the 1980s, the words *table hockey* vanished from Christmas lists. Radio Shack, Kevin Sports, Irwin, and Playtoy/Remco introduced new models in the early 1990s, but none could compete with Stiga's newly arrived state-of-the-art $85 model, complete with hand-painted three-dimensional players and a left-winger that could skate behind the net, making the dreaded "dead spot" a thing of the past. In 1998, Stiga acquired the exclusive NHL licence, and North American gamers can now select player uniforms from any of the 30 NHL franchises as well as six international squads. The handful of North American-made games still on the market now fall into one of two camps: flimsy tabletop models selling for $20 or deluxe table-sized games selling for around $300, though without the NHL's endorsement the best any of these models can offer is pulse-pounding action between the Red Team and the Blue Team.

WHAT IN THE WIDE, WIDE WORLD OF SPORTS IS GOING ON HERE?

Regardless of the physical quality of the Stiga game, it only seems appropriate that a Swedish company should receive the NHL's world-wide endorsement, as Swedes have won every World Championship since the tournament's inception in 1989. As we go to press, the 2005 tourney in Riga, Latvia, is still a month away, but the results of 2003's competition in Zurich, Switzerland, still ring loud in fans' ears: First, second and third place in the women's event all go to Finns—without a single Canadian so much as competing—while Sweden swept the men's event, with the highest Canadian placing 101st. How can this be? Does Stiga's version tap unfairly into some genetic propensity of the Swedish race? Could Canada hold its own if the tournament were only played on Munro's 1936 peg-and-wire model? Or is the reason for the Canadians' lacklustre showing simply that none of them wanted to fly all the way to Zurich just to play table hockey in a cold gymnasium? That might seem a convincing argument, yet the top positions at the 2005 Boston F1 Challenge—lauded as North America's toughest tournament—were swept by three jet-lagged Swedes, and *not* the same three who'd won at Zurich! "Darn it," mutters Canada…

VITAL STATISTICS

Does the value of scoring stats change over time?
Was Gretzky that much better than Newsy Lalonde?
Here are a few numbers compiled by Uncle John
for your consideration.

Wayne Gretzky's mark of 215 regular-season points in the 1985–86 season is one of hockey's most lauded statistics, a record that seems utterly untouchable today—consider that Martin St. Louis was the 2003–04 points leader with only 94! Indeed, in the 88 years since the NHL's 1917 inception, only Gretzky has hit the 200-point mark, which he did so three other times (212, 196, 205 and 208 were his totals leading up to 1985–86). But lest we imagine that goal-scoring hadn't been invented in the league's first 60 years or that the players had only been skating around for their health, keep in mind that Gretzky had the luxury of an 80-game season in which to set his record. How would his seemingly lofty numbers translate to, say, the 18-game season of 1918–19? The 36-game season of 1925–26? Could simple mathematics knock Gretzky from his pedestal like a trade to Los Angeles never could?

MULTIPLYING MALONE

The NHL's inaugural season of 1917–18 was 22 games long, and Joe Malone of the Montreal Canadiens led the league in scoring with 48 points. That's an average of 2.18 points per game—pretty good, right? And if he had managed to keep up that pace for a full 80-game season, Malone would have gone on to notch exactly 174 points, which, yes, is almost double Martin St. Louis' mark, but nowhere near Gretzky's. Only 18 games were played in the 1918–19 season when fellow Canadien Newsy Lalonde turned in 33 points to steal the scoring crown, however, his points-per-game was a less-exemplary 1.83, or 146 points over an 80-game season. Not that this flood of dainty numbers should diminish our respect for Newsy Lalonde—in those skull-crushing days any player who could lace up his skates for each game must have been tougher than leather, much less one who could expect to score 1.83 points every time he did.

The next 30 years saw the NHL lengthen its season no less than eight times, starting with five 24-game seasons from 1919–24. Now in a Quebec Bulldogs uniform, Joe Malone dominated this era as well, scoring 49 points in 1919–20 or 2.04 per game, not far below his 2.18 of two years before. The 1924–25 schedule had 30 games, and saw Babe Dye of the Toronto St. Pats put in 44 points, an average of 1.46 per contest. Did Dye know at the time that he was trying to outscore Wayne Gretzky? We can only hope he didn't, because he didn't come close. The Montreal Maroons' Nels Stewart earned 42 points over the longer 36-game season of 1925–26, 1.17 points per game or 93.6 points over an 80-game season—the lowest average, sadly, until Martin St. Louis's 1.15.

BISECTING BOSTON

From 1926 to 1931 each team played 44 games a season, and for the 1929–30 campaign Boston's Cooney Weiland led the league with a seemingly insurmountable record of 73 points, the highest of the period, though over the longer season his average was only 1.66, still well shy of Malone. Were ever-longer schedules wearing the players down? In the 48-game era of 1931–1942, another Bruin, Bill Cowley, turned in a landmark performance of 62 points over the 1940–41 season—a 1.29 average. Linemate Herb Cain earned 1.64 points per game in 1943–44, the second of four 50-game seasons, which though a marked improvement, translates to only 131 points over an 80-game season. As we climb through the years, Gretzky's 215 has yet to see much competition. The best average of the three 60-game seasons is lower still, 1.2, thanks to the 72 points Max Bentley earned for the Chicago Black Hawks in 1948–49. No disrespect to Bentley, of course, but a guy just can't argue with statistics.

MINIMIZING MIKITA

The length of the NHL season stabilized at 70 games for 18 full seasons, 1949–1967, culminating in 97-point performances from Black Hawks Bobby Hull and Stan Mikita in 1965–66 and 1966–67 respectively. Almost 100 points—impressive, right? Again, the longer season brings their average down to just 1.39, or 111.2 points over an 80-game schedule. Mikita topped the charts again over the 74 games of the 1967–68 season, scoring 87 points for an even weaker average of 1.18—the second-lowest in our survey after Stewart's 1.17 of 1925–26.

ESTIMATING ESPOSITO

For the 1968–1972 seasons the league made its least-monumental adjustment thus far, adding two games for a total of 76. Far more noteworthy was the performance of Boston's Phil Esposito during this period, racking up a staggering 152 points in 1970–71 to earn an average of 2.0. Ah, what a satisfying statistic: exactly 2 points per game! And yet simple multiplication tells us that he would have earned only 160 points had he played an 80-game season, lower than any one of Gretzky's totals between 1980–81 and 1986–87—seven campaigns with more than 160 points each! With only 30 NHL seasons left to evaluate, we've yet to see the Great One's pedestal so much as quiver. Esposito scaled the heights again in the two 78-game seasons of 1972–73 and 1973–74, earning 145 points in the latter alone. Unfortunately this is a lower figure than his previous 152, tallied during a longer season at that, though the resulting 1.86 average still tops every player who'd come before except himself and our beloved Joe Malone.

GRAPHING GRETZKY

The NHL stabilized for another 18-season run, 1974–1992, when it fixed its schedule at 80 games, and, as noted above, 1985–86 was the watershed campaign of that period as the Edmonton Oilers' Wayne Gretzky tallied 215 points. Tired of reading that number? Then try its sister statistic, a jaw-dropping 2.68 points per game. Had Gretzky played in the 1917–18 season, we can estimate, based on this average, that he would have earned exactly 58.96 points to Joe Malone's modest 48, and considering that goalies of that era had much less equipment than what Gretzky was used to shooting at, he may well have netted more still.

WE HAVE A WINNER!!! (ALMOST)

And what of the players since 1985–86? Well, Gretzky has always had a great admiration for Mario Lemieux, and for a man whose career has so often been hampered by injuries, our handy points-per-game calculations prove to be useful in showing that Super

Mario once gave the Great One a serious run for his millions. In 1988–89, Lemieux managed to log in one of his healthier seasons, with 76 games out of a possible 80 (Mario never did manage to play a full schedule). He fell just short of the 200-point mark with a spectacular 85 goals and 114 assists for 199 points. But give him another four games at his 2.61 average, and he'd have reached 209—third-best total of all-time! Heck, say Mario even manages to squeeze in an extra seven points above his average into those hypothetical four games—which isn't beyond practicality when we're talking about Mario—and the big 215 would have been demoted to second best.

SO WHAT? TRY 4 POINTS A GAME!

It would probably be going just a bit far to call one of the greatest NHL players of all-time a one-season statistical wonder, but one knock on Lemieux is that while Gretzky recorded 2 to 3 points per game for more or less a decade of his career, Lemieux only went over the 2-mark once, though leaping all the way up to 2.61. On the other hand, stepping one year out of the NHL, Mario's scoring record in his final junior season seems even more insurmountable than Gretzky's NHL mark—playing for the Laval Voisons of the Quebec Major Junior League, Lemieux recorded 133 goals, 149 assists and 282 points. Over 70 games, this makes for a 4.02 average. Imagine being the opposing goaltenders that year! Before you write it off as a junior stat, consider that to be hailed as the greatest scoring prospect in recent memory, Sidney Crosby managed a comparably measly 2.7 points a game playing in the same league that his Penguins teammate Lemieux did.

One more interesting PPG stat: Even though Mario eclipsed 2 points per game in a season only once, he's been just under the mark often enough to currently have a 1.91 career average. Gretzky sits at 1.92. Aren't numbers wonderful?

IRREPRESSIBLE ROGER

Roger Neilson brought many innovations to hockey in his long coaching career with over a dozen big-league and junior teams.

When NHL commissioner Gary Bettman announced at the 2002 entry draft in Nashville that Roger Neilson had lost his three-year battle with cancer, just about everyone in the stadium simultaneously thought of a great Roger Neilson story. Few in hockey—players, coaches or executives—achieved the legend status of the small, quick-moving man who devoted his entire life to the sport and never stopped seeking ways to test hockey's rules or inspire players to improve. In his final NHL season when he was an assistant coach with the Ottawa Senators and cancer was winning the battle, head coach Jacques Martin allowed Neilson to replace him for the concluding two games of the schedule, lifting Neilson's games total as an NHL head coach to 1,000.

THE ABSENT-MINDED PROFESSOR

"Mention Roger to hockey people and they would shake their heads, laugh and tell you a story about him that covered either some out-of-the-ordinary thing he'd tried or some goofy thing he had done, often based on his absent-mindedness," said Colin Campbell, who played junior and NHL hockey under Neilson, was his assistant coach with the New York Rangers and now is an NHL vice-president. "Many figured he was a genius one day and then talk of his nutty side the next. The one thing I never heard anyone say about Roger Neilson is that they didn't like him. He never said a bad word about anyone, even those who fired him."

WELL-TRAVELED

In his 1,000 games as a head coach, Neilson built a 460-381-159 win-loss-tie record in stays behind the bench of varying lengths with the Toronto Maple Leafs, Buffalo Sabres, Vancouver Canucks, Los Angeles Kings, New York Rangers, Florida Panthers and Philadelphia Flyers. He also logged time as an assistant (he also served as an assistant on some of the teams he went on to coach) with the St. Louis Blues, Chicago Blackhawks and Ottawa Senators, and was video analyst for the Edmonton Oilers in one of their 1980s Cup-winning springs.

CAPTAIN VIDEO

The most-used wrinkle that Neilson initiated in hockey is the use of video as a teaching and coaching tool. His devotion to the camera and screen earned the nickname "Captain Video." In his first coaching job in top-level junior hockey with the Peterborough Petes, Neilson also worked as a high school physical education teacher. He convinced the school board to purchase video equipment as a teaching aid, then "borrowed" the equipment to have a helper shoot full-ice pictures of the Petes' games. "Those early pictures were pretty grainy but I was able to use them to have an assessment of what my team was doing right and wrong," Neilson said. "By analyzing them, I could see areas of the game where our team and individual players needed work and what the opposition was doing."

THE TRUE WAY

In his first NHL job, a two-season stint with the Toronto Maple Leafs from 1977 to 1979, Neilson did an even more complex breakdown of the game tapes. When he used the phrase "scoring chances" to analyze the offence, hockey had a new phrase. "Shots on goal were an oft-used statistic but they did not really tell you much because a soft shot from the blue line that was easy to handle for the goalie counted the same as a 15-foot shot that required a difficult save," Neilson explained. "It was more useful to list the true scoring chances the teams had from the scoring areas where a good shot would produce a goal."

THEY JUST NEEDED MORE SCORING CHANCES...

The main criticism of Neilson through his long coaching career was that his clubs played dull, defensive hockey. His devotion to prevention, more than the production, of goals allowed several of his teams to achieve much more than their talent appeared capable of achieving. That he was trained as a teacher allowed him to turn hockey into a classroom, especially at the junior level. "I always thought it was a bad rap that I was totally a defensive coach," Neilson said. "Sure, I stressed that side of the game because knowing how to play without the puck was something every good player had to know. Besides, finding players with a high level of offensive skills always was difficult at every level of the game. But guys who were willing to work and learn, even if they didn't have great slickness or speed, could always find a job in hockey."

LES PAPER BOYS

Thus, it's no surprise that two of Neilson's top Petes graduates, Bob Gainey and Doug Jarvis, were the defensive anchors of the Montreal Canadiens when they won four consecutive Stanley Cup crowns in the late 1970s. Much Neilson mythology was inspired by antics during his ten seasons in junior hockey. He had coached minor hockey and baseball teams in Toronto for years and was hired by the Canadiens as a part-time scout for junior talent, then landed the Peterborough post. At one time, Neilson delivered close to 1,000 copies of a morning newspaper in Toronto, often hiring his young hockey players to help.

LOOPY LOOPHOLES

A Neilson specialty was finding small loopholes in hockey rules he could use to his advantage, his twists inspiring the rewriting of several pieces of hockey legislation. When he pulled his goaltender for an extra attacker, Neilson instructed the goalie to leave his stick across the crease to stop any sliding shots. If leading by a goal in the final minute of the game, Neilson would send out an extra skater, the too-many-men penalty eating up precious seconds. He continued to use an extra skater until the penalty box was full of Petes but the final minute was finished. The rule was changed to award a penalty shot to the opposition if a team was charged with over-use of players in the last two minutes of a game.

RON LED THE LEAGUE IN GAA

Neilson gained wide publicity when he employed a defenceman, not a goalie, to face the shooter on penalty shots. The Petes had a large backliner, Ron Stackhouse, and in a preseason game when the Toronto Marlboros were awarded a penalty shot, Neilson took his goalie out of the net and inserted Stackhouse. When the opponent skated from center with the puck, Stackhouse met him at the blue line and checked the puck away from him. The befuddled officials decreed that the rules stated the "goalie" could not leave the crease until the opponent had crossed the blue line and ordered the penalty shot repeated. Stackhouse stopped the second try plus six others that season before the rules were changed to limit the defence to the goalie.

DID MIKE EVER CRACK THE LINEUP?

Another oft-told Neilson story concerns his use of his dog Mike as a teaching aid. Because his Pete forwards were going deep too often on forechecking missions and being trapped by the opposition's breakouts, Neilson stationed Mike in front of the net while he went behind it, puck on stick. No matter what moves or fakes Neilson tried, Mike held his spot until the "puck carrier" crossed the goal-line. "I don't think the players liked the inference from me using Mike but they got the message," Neilson said.

SO LONG AND THANKS FOR THE TRAP

Perhaps Neilson's top coaching accomplishment came with the expansion Florida team from 1993 to 1995. Playing the much scorned neutral zone trap, which made the action very dull, the Panthers missed the playoff by a single point in each of their first two seasons. In their third season after Neilson was replaced as head coach, the Panthers—with the basic roster Neilson had trained—advanced to the Stanley Cup final.

JUST DON'T ASK ME DIRECTIONS TO THE RINK

A devout Christian who never married and did not use profanity or drink alcohol, Neilson was renowned for his ties, always in loud colors and weird designs. When not called Captain Video, Neilson was mentioned as "the absent-minded professor." In most of his coaching jobs, he lived close enough to the arena to take his bicycle to work. But he often forgot the route, made wrong turns and admitted that he often had to knock on strangers' doors to ask for directions. That's something his well-drilled teams never had to do on the ice.

THE DUKE AND THE TAMPA BAY LIGHTNING

How Phil Esposito used royal connections to get an NHL expansion team.

Once the NHL grants permission for a city to start a club and join its elite organization, it's customary for there to be a press conference. Preferably, amid much hullabaloo, an oversized cardboard cheque with a multi-million dollar figure is flapped around and presented by the owner(s) of the new team to the NHL commissioner. Thus, another franchise is added to the NHL. The story of the symbolic cheque which was presented to then-NHL President John Ziegler by representatives of the Tampa Bay Lightning in 1991 turned disastrous two weeks later, and hilarious with two years hindsight.

LESSON 1: DON'T TRUST YOUR BROTHER TONY

Let's go back to May 1991, when Phil Esposito and associates are scrambling to find millions of dollars for his proposed Tampa Bay expansion club's entry NHL fee. Through his brother Tony, Phil met a man named Carroll Tessier who was purported to be a close friend of the Duke of Manchester—a wealthy royal interested in U.S. investment opportunities. Phil did his research, confirming the existence of a very well-heeled Duke of Manchester living in Britain. Unfortunately, he didn't also uncover the background of Mr. Tessier, a professional confidence man who was as phony as a three-dollar bill and had no authority to spend the Duke's money. It turned out the promised expenditure was a scam to get "the Duke" a hefty bank loan.

AS PHONY AS A THREE-MILLION-DOLLAR CHEQUE?

Through a series of mishaps, Esposito needed to use a dubious three-million-dollar cheque from the Duke of Manchester as the down payment for bringing hockey to Florida. The cheque was signed *Lord Montague, the Duke of Manchester*. This cheque was, of course, worthless. This was confirmed by an alarmed phone call from NHL head office some time after the presentation. Espo later found another cheque that was—luckily for the Lightning's chance at the 2004 Stanley Cup—legitimate. An FBI manhunt ensued and—unluckily— Tessier the con man was caught, tried and later died in prison in July 2002.

* * * * *

YOU GOTTA HAVE FRIENDS

"I remember what Ron Greschner said when he retired. 'The thing I'm going to miss most is showering with 23 guys.' And that's what it's all about: camaraderie."

—New York Rangers goaltender Mike Richter

"We believe in camaraderie but that's taking it too far.

—Rick Bowness, when Ziggy Palffy kissed teammate Travis Green on the lips after a goal

* * * * *

I SPY

"When I look at the net I don't see a goalie."

—Pavel Bure, the Russian Rocket

"When I look at the net I see 2 or 3 goalies."

—Radek Dvorak, right wing, Edmonton Oilers

HYPE AND PUCKS IN NEW YORK

The boss bootlegger and the peerless promoter combined to bring hockey to the Big Apple.

Although William Dwyer and Tex Rickard earned fortunes in very different businesses, the fabled characters of Roarin' Twenties Manhattan combined to bring hockey to the "big town," New York, anchoring the game's U.S. success.

THE UNION OF BOOZE & BOXING

An associate of crime giants Legs Diamond and Dutch Schultz, Dwyer was "the king of the bootleggers" during U.S. Prohibition. In 1925, Dwyer purchased the troubled Hamilton Tigers for $75,000 and moved the team to New York as the Americans. The Hamilton players had been suspended after hockey's first strike in the 1925 Stanley Cup playoffs when they were refused a $200 bonus for the postseason. Rickard was the legendary promoter and mastermind of the career of heavyweight boxer Jack Dempsey, who generated record sports gate receipts, notably for his bouts with Gene Tunney. Rickard was president of the new Madison Square Garden in New York, where the Americans played in their first season. In 1926, Rickard was prominent in the creation of the New York Rangers, the team name produced by a Rickard pun—Tex's Rangers.

NEW YORK DRYER IF NOT FOR DWYER

When the NHL admitted the Boston Bruins for the 1924–25 season, several other U.S. cities wanted franchises—but a team in New York was necessary to give the project a truly big-league look. The challenge was locating a potential owner. Dwyer "owned" ships, trucks, warehouses, nightclubs, a Miami casino and pieces of several racetracks, including one in Montreal. Backed by the mob, he controlled the gigantic illegal liquor business in New York, a town turned "dry" by prohibition. A Canadian friend, Bill MacBeth, who worked for a New York newspaper, convinced a skeptical Dwyer that hockey would be a success in the big town. But plans for a new Madison Square Garden did not include an ice surface because the man in charge, Rickard, saw it as a big boxing and concert location.

HOCKEY'S BABE RUTH

Two Montreal men, promoter Tom Duggan and Montreal Canadiens star Howie Morenz, placed a hockey core in the Big Apple. When Duggan figured hockey had big U.S. potential, he convinced the owners of the four financially struggling Canadian teams (Montreal, Toronto, Ottawa, Hamilton) to sell him three expansion franchises for $7,000 each. Duggan moved teams to Boston and Pittsburgh interests and pitched Rickard hard to place a team in New York. Box office success in Boston caught Rickard's interest, but the promoter always insisted that he made a trip to Montreal with a group of friends, including fabled writer Damon Runyon, to see the Canadiens and their young star Morenz only "to get that pest Duggan off my back about hockey." One game with the electrifying Morenz in it was enough to sell Rickard on the game's potential as an attraction. He immediately tagged Morenz as "hockey's Babe Ruth" and an ice plant was included in suddenly revised Madison Square construction plans. On his new ice, Rickard insisted on a strong team that he did not finance.

THREATS FOR CHARITY

The NHL happened to have its first-place team from the previous season, the suspended Hamilton club, available because the players remained under suspension for their "strike." Duggan sold his third franchise to Dwyer—they were co-owners of a racetrack in Cincinnati—and talked him into buying the entire Tiger roster for $75,000. That gave the Americans such top talent as forwards Billy Burch, Red and Shorty Green, defenceman Mickey Roach and goalie Jumpin' Jake Forbes. Proceeds from the opening MSG game—against, of course, the Canadiens—went to a New York hospital. Dwyer used strong-arm tactics on potential ticket-buyers, threatening to cut the liquor supply to his booze customers if they did not purchase hockey tickets.

BIG BILL WHO?

Two weeks before the opener, Dwyer was arrested, charged as the head of a multi-million dollar illegal liquor business and wide-ranging bribery of public officials. Madison Square Garden immediately said "Big Bill who?" when Dwyer's name was mentioned. He retained ownership of the Americans but Rickard was listed as president. Although the Americans missed the playoffs in their first season, the franchise was a box office success. The players shared a Dwyer-owned hotel with various mobsters and were high-living celebrities in Manhattan. Top stars Burch and Forbes earned $10,000 for the season, a fortune compared to Morenz's $3,000 with the Canadiens.

TEX'S RANGERS

The NHL granted Rickard and MSG a franchise, the Rangers, for the 1926–27 season. The new team into its first season under team president Colonel John Hammond hired a young Toronto man named Conn Smythe, who had coached the University of Toronto team, to recruit the first roster. Smythe built an instant contender, acquiring 31 players for $32,000, including stars in goalie Lorne Chabot, defencemen Taffy Abel and Ching Johnson, and forwards Bill and Bun Cook, Frank Boucher and Murray Murdoch. But before the season opened, Hammond fired Smythe, claiming he lacked the experience to run a big-league team, and hired Lester Patrick for a job he held until 1946.That inspired a vengeful Smythe to purchase the NHL Toronto St. Patricks, change the name to Maple Leafs, build Maple Leaf Gardens and create one of the most successful teams ever in pro sport.

BIG BILL HITS THE WALL

Dwyer avoided trial for two years while controlling the Americans, then in 1927 was sentenced to two years in an Atlanta penitentiary. He served a year, then was paroled to return to an NHL Board of Governors who wished he would disappear. Dwyer also continued his other "business" until the 1931 raid on a large Manhattan brewery co-owned by Dwyer and former public enemy number one Owney Madden. In a long prosecution, the government nailed Dwyer for $3.7 million in fines and back taxes.

COOKED IN BROOKLYN

The Americans qualified for the playoffs five times in their 17 seasons, once in the last ten years. The team, called the Brooklyn Americans for its last season, folded in 1942. The Rangers thrived under Rickard's promotional genius and Patrick's leadership as general manager and coach, winning the Stanley Cup in 1928 and 1933.

THINGS NOT TO SAY TO THE BOSS' WIFE

Well-traveled masked man's wisecrack led to a one-way ticket out of Canuckville.

Look up the term "free spirit" in an NHL dictionary and you just might find a portrait of journeyman goaltender Gary Smith. They called him "Suitcase," and for good reason. Despite being a proficient puck-stopper capable of carrying an entire team's fortunes on his back, he certainly made his rounds, playing for eight different NHL teams during a 14-year career.

A NEW PLACE IN THE RECORD BOOKS

Smith did things his own way. He wore as many as 15 pairs of socks inside his goalie skates. He sometimes took showers between periods of games. He traveled stylishly on the road in a full-length lynx jacket. And he warmed to the social aspects of being a professional hockey player in the 1970s. "I led the league in hangovers," he once told a Vancouver newspaper columnist. "Fourteen years, every day."

In 1974–75, Smith was almost single-handedly responsible for the Vancouver Canucks making their first Stanley Cup playoff appearance. He recorded 32 wins, nine ties and six shutouts (that's 705 socks, 365 hangovers) and led an otherwise modestly talented team into the post-season where they gave the legendary Montreal Canadiens a tough series. But less than a year later, he was no longer a member of the organization.

WHEN THE BITE IS AS BAD AS THE BARK

During a team Christmas party in 1975, Smith was introduced to Emily Griffiths, the wife of Canucks owner Frank Griffiths. Mrs. Griffiths also happened to be the heiress to the Ballard pet-food fortune. "Gee, I see the resemblance on the can," Smith is widely reported to have said when the two were formally acquainted. The next morning, an enraged Frank Griffiths called head coach Phil Maloney and told him to get rid of Smith, no matter what the Canucks could get for him. Suitcase was on the road again. Like breaking a mirror, the Curse of the Loose-Lipped Goalie plagued the Canucks with bad luck for the next seven years. The franchise didn't make the playoffs again until 1982.

THE BODYGUARD

He grew up big and he grew up tough
He saw himself scoring for the Wings or Canucks
But he wasn't that good with a puck
Buddy's real talent was beating people up
His heart wasn't in it but the crowd ate it up

They never played a minute in the NHL, but Detroit sports columnist and author Mitch Albom and the late musician Warren Zevon teamed up nicely to capture the essence of the enforcer in their tune "Hit Somebody (The Hockey Song)." Tough guy, goon, policeman, hired muscle. Whatever the nickname, the hockey enforcer is like no other animal in professional sport.

SOMEBODY'S GOTTA DO IT

Like a cop, his job is to serve and protect, and nobody really wants to see him until his presence is urgently required. Like some sort of black market referee, he often hovers outside the normal flow of the game, meting out frontier justice when it's necessary. And unlike the image that most fans get, the enforcer is often among the most quiet, reflective and intelligent members of any professional hockey team.

It is a job. It is a chance to earn a huge paycheque in the NHL. It is a role that most tough guys realize, sometime during the meat-grinder of junior hockey, is there for the taking. It's a role that has been required, in one form or another, since the 1960s, when hockey stars, in large part, stopped fighting for themselves.

THE GOON CODE

There are some ground rules, though. The unspoken code of the NHL means enforcers seek each other out for fights, rather than picking on less worthy and perhaps more talented opponents. Unless one of those opponents delivers a cheap shot, that is. Then he can expect a visit from the policeman.

Between these hulking gladiators on skates, there is an unwritten code of conduct. In general, you don't fight dirty. Kneeing, tugging hair, or taking a bite out of somebody's ear is frowned upon.

Mike Tyson would never have made it as an NHL tough guy.

The enforcer era, by most accounts, began in the 1960s, when the Montreal Canadiens, the essence of pure-flowing, offensive hockey, enlisted John Ferguson to watch the back of star Jean Béliveau. And although the role changed significantly when the NHL brought in its instigator and third-man in regulations in 1992—essentially penalizing players who started scraps and ejecting those who joined into an ongoing dispute—the job is still out there for those who can skate a little and throw a lot.

Reggie Fleming, who came into the NHL in 1960 and watched out for Black Hawks star Bobby Hull, was one of the first goons. But he didn't care for that description. "I would rather be called the enforcer," he said, long after his career was over.

GRETZKY'S GIANT SHADOW

Fleming also rode shotgun for the likes of Bobby Clarke and Gilbert Perreault during his NHL days. But he wasn't the most famous bodyguard in hockey. That honor likely went to Dave Semenko, whose hulking presence helped keep honest anybody with thoughts of laying a glove—or anything else for that matter—on Edmonton Oilers superstar Wayne Gretzky.

When it comes to marquee bodyguards, Kevin Costner had nothing on Semenko. Big Dave's toughness and fighting ability kept him in the NHL for nine years. And although he was famous for protecting No. 99, he watched out for the multitude of skilled players on the Oilers' juggernaut of the 1980s. Grant Fuhr saved the pucks, while Semenko saved the superstars.

"If that guy wants to do that, let him face the music," Semenko said of opponents who took liberties with other Oilers. "It's called a fistfight. We've been doing this since the beginning of time. There is nothing wrong with a good old fistfight...they knew I would be coming after them and they had to fight."

THE ULTIMATE TEAMMATE

Gino Odjick was one of the most effective tough guys in the NHL during his career. Besides being the bodyguard for the Russian Rocket Pavel Bure during their time together in Vancouver, Odjick also had to be able to keep up with Bure—no easy feat. Odjick had to learn how to scrap early on in life, growing up on a First Nations reserve in Quebec where there were often tensions between the natives and the mostly white townspeople. "We learned to stick together as a family from the get-go and we thought that we would be okay if we stuck together and if anybody picked on one of us then they'd have to pick on all of us. That's how we got by, so that's where I learned how to fight," Odjick said. "It just came naturally to me [on the ice]."

Odjick's presence opened up all kinds of room for Bure and other Canucks during the early 1990s. And as a result, the "Algonquin Enforcer," as he was known in Vancouver, was loved by both fans and teammates. Whenever those at the Pacific Coliseum thought his services were needed, the chants of "Gino! Gino!" rained down from the rafters. "Gino is one of those guys you'd refer to as an ultimate teammate," former Canuck defenceman Dana Murzyn said. "He really cared about his job, which was one of the toughest jobs in the NHL. I don't think anyone can underestimate that. Gino had no problem going out there and taking on the toughest guys in the league two or three times a game. He took pride in it and, like most of the enforcers that I've known, once you take off the skates, he's one of the nicest guys you'd ever want to be around."

THE REST OF THE GOON SHOW...

Most enforcers have not been joined at the hip to one particular star with whom they were charged with protecting. In general, they have simply created mayhem, not to mention space, for their more talented, smaller teammates. The enforcer honor roll has included names such as Dave "The Hammer" Schultz, Willi Plett, Chris Nilan, Georges Laraque, Dave Brown, Joe Kocur, Link Gaetz, Donald Brashear and John Kordic. Some enforcers can play a little hockey, too. Lump Tiger Williams, Chris Simon, Tie Domi, Marty McSorley, Bob Probert and Darren McCarthy into that group. In fact, Tiger is the NHL's all-time king of the sin bin, having recorded 3,966 penalty minutes during his career, with Domi second at 3,406, and McSorley third at 3,381. If you have toughness and some talent, you're on the ice longer. That means you're in the box more often, too.

THE FABULOUS FATMAN

"The Battle of the Bulge," an order to Maple Leaf goalie Turk Broda to lose weight, was front-page news in Toronto in the 1940s.

The most famous picture of the man many regard as the greatest playoff goalie ever is not a shot of a game-saving stop or a victory celebration. In it, Turk Broda is wearing only a towel around his middle, seated Buddha-style on the platform of a set of scales—the type with the big, round dial and the words "TOLEDO. No Springs. Honest weight" on it.

MORE IMPORTANT THAN THE GREY CUP

Broda is smiling in the picture, taken early in the 1949–50 NHL season and carried on the front pages of Toronto newspapers and those of many NHL cities. The previous week, the Grey Cup game, the finale of the Canadian Football League season, had attracted much attention in Toronto, pushing the Leafs and hockey from their accustomed prominent spots in the paper. That upset Leafs owner Conn Smythe, who felt hockey should always hog the limelight, and he earned full attention with a decree that Broda had to lose seven pounds to 190 before he could return to the Leafs' net. Of course, the publicity grab happened when the club did not have a win in its previous six matches. Broda always had battled weight problems, his playoff exploits for four Stanley Cup championship teams earning him the nickname "The Fabulous Fatman."

SLOW NEWS DAY?

The stunt became huge news in Toronto where three very competitive daily newspapers got into the act, keeping Broda's portly body in the front page. He was photographed taking a steam bath, riding a bicycle, eating salads and sitting on the scales. Dozens of diets were submitted to the papers and experts in weight control offered a myriad of solutions to Turk's chubbiness. Broda missed one game, then Smythe announced that his goalie had reached the proper weight. One paper ran a two-inch-high headline that said BRODA HITS 190. The Turk returned to the net, the Leafs to the limelight. Years later, when Broda was a successful junior hockey coach, he claimed the whole exercise was a publicity stunt. "I had a lot of fun with it," Broda said, "but the truth is I never lost a single, solitary ounce of weight. Smythe must have doctored the scales."

* * * * *

SUPER MARIO

"One thing I hate is people screaming at me. If you want me to do something, talk to me. When someone screams at me to hurry up, I slow down."

—Mario Lemieux

"Nobody sleeps like Mario. He lives for sleep. He hits the bed and that's it. It irritates the hell out of me."

—Pittsburg Penguins teammate, Terry Ruskowski

"I don't order fries with my club sandwich."

—Mario Lemieux when asked what he does to stay in shape in the off season

"I'm sorry, but the NHL would not have a franchise in Pittsburgh today had Mario not come along. Think about it, no hockey in Pittsburgh."

—Wayne Gretzky

"I remember the day of his last radiation treatment. He went to Philly. He got there about four o'clock and he played. I think he gets overlooked, what he's overcome. It's ridiculous. Everybody talks about Michael Jordan coming back from baseball, but Mario came back from cancer."

—Penguins left wing, Kevin Stevens

"It had been a great career. I mean, how many guys can say they averaged two points a game in their careers? It's too bad he's retiring too soon. The league is going to miss him. The fans are going to miss him. A real classy person and a great guy."

—John Bucyk, former Bruins left wing, on Mario Lemieux

CLEAR THE TRACK!

A wild man on and off the ice, Eddie Shack certainly left a mark over 1,047 games of a rewarding career.

He was the flywheel come loose from the shaft, the human bowling ball, skating helter and skelter and other spots. Eddie Shack was a hockey original, a wild and woolly performer, who seldom saw a classroom after 12 years of age and never mastered reading and writing, although he was quite good at 'rithmetic.

WHAT'S NOT TO LIKE?

That he scored 239 goals in his career is a surprise to some who watched him with pleasure play the game whirling dervish style, seemingly with little discipline or method. But he was a member of the four Stanley Cup championship teams of the Toronto Maple Leafs in the 1960s and an extremely popular player with hockey fans. But when a guy appears to be having great fun doing his job and has a song written in his honor, "Clear the Track, Here Comes Shack," what's not to like?

WANT TO BUY SOME CHICKENS? COAL?

Players, both mates and foes, often scoffed at Shack for his illiteracy but it never bothered Eddie. A favorite trick of his on road trips was to spy the magazine his mates had purchased for the flight. Shack would then buy it himself, find a sportswriter friend to read him the stories, and then enter the players' conversation on the subject as if he had done his reading well. Money was the subject Shack had really mastered. He was selling chickens in the market in his hometown of Sudbury, Ontario, when he was 13, and when he excelled in junior hockey with the Guelph Biltmores, Shack drove a coal track to supplement his junior hockey pittance. He also bought fedoras at cost from the hat-manufacturing team sponsor and sold them at a profit.

AND HE CAN GOLF ANYTIME HE WANTS

When he first joined the Leafs in a trade from New York Rangers in 1960, Shack lived in the converted carriage house on an estate owned by one of Toronto's top mining and financial investors, who liked Shack and passed along a few investment tips. "I was living in the carriage house and he was living in the mansion," Shack said. "I would have been stupid not to listen to him." When he retired, Shack owned a golf course and considerable other property in the Toronto area, proving that not everything necessary for a good life is learned from books (except for this one).

* * * * *

Candace Cameron might be well-known for her former role as DJ Tanner on the American sitcom *Full House*. However, did you know that she is also the wife of Los Angeles Kings forward Valeri Bure?

* * * * *

FIGHT NIGHT

"If hockey fights were fixed, I'd be in more of them."

—Rod Gilbert,
former New York Rangers right wing

"If they're going to allow guys to wear helmets, they should at least force them to round the edges."

—Rick Chartraw, after punching
Paul Holmgren in the head

"I'd rather fight than score."

—former "Broad Street Bully" Flyer
Dave "The Hammer" Schultz

THE NOBLE GOALIE

A few famous keepers wax philosophical about the art of tending goal.

"Because the demands on a goalie are mostly mental, it means that for a goalie, the biggest enemy is himself. Not a puck, not an opponent, not a quirk of size or style. Him."

—Ken Dryden

"That one-hundred-foot skate to the bench after you have been pulled is the longest, slowest skate in the world. It seems likes five miles..."

—former L.A. King goaltender Kelly Hrudey

"Anyone who wears one is chicken. My face is my mask."

—former Canadien, Gump Worsley

"I'm sorry I can't put on a show like some of the other goaltenders. I can't look excited because I'm not. I can't shout at other players because that's not my style. I can't dive on easy shots and make them look hard. I guess all I can do is stop pucks."

—George Hainsworth, former Canadien

"It's pretty tough for a goalie when you look at it. You're always the last line of defence. If you let a goal in, you can't go to the bench and hide between the guys or anything."

—former Canuck Kirk McLean

"I just made up my mind that I was going to lose my teeth and have my face cut to pieces."

—Johnny Bower, after being asked why he became a goaltender

"How would you like a job where, every time you make a mistake, a big red light goes on and 18,000 people boo?"

—Jacques Plante

"My style? What do you mean *my style*? My style is to stop pucks!"

—former Flyer Roman Cechmanek

"There is no position in sport as noble as goaltending."

—Vladislav Tretiak

KEEP IT IN THE FAMILY

As a family activity, hockey can sometimes mean more than the familiar picture of parents driving kids to practices and games on cold early mornings.

From the start, hockey had brother acts galore, players of two, and even three, generations and family groups of fathers, sons, uncles and cousins. The NHL has had more than 70 father-son combinations in its playing ranks, and approximately 200 brother acts.

THE SUTTER BROTHERS

Grace and Louis Sutter of Viking, Alberta, are the most productive hockey parents. They raised seven sons on their farm and six of the boys born in a seven-year stretch from 1956 to 1963 had lengthy NHL careers. Brian, Darryl, Duane, Brent and twins Rick and Ron played a total of 4,994 games and produced 2,935 points and all had the family toughness and tenacity. All six brothers went on to successful coaching, managing and scouting careers in the NHL and Western Hockey League. An older brother, Gary, likely would have had a hockey career, too, had he not chosen to remain at home and help with the farm while his parents were driving back and forth to the rink. While the Sutters hold the record for one generation of hockey players from a family, other clans also were well populated with puck-chasers.

THE PATRICK PACK

Patrick is among the game's most illustrious names. In only a very few years in the past century has a family member or two not been involved in the top levels of hockey. Brothers Lester and Frank were top players in the formative years, founders and financial backers of the Pacific Coast League that competed with the NHL for talent and the Stanley Cup. Both managed and coached in the NHL, Lester the illustrious head of the New York Rangers for 20 years. Lester's sons Lynn and Muzz had strong NHL careers, winning the 1940 Stanley Cup with the Rangers before moving into management: Muzz with the Rangers, Lynn with the Bruins and Blues. Lynn's sons Craig (eight seasons) and Glenn (38 games) played in the NHL. Craig was the assistant GM-coach of the 1980 U.S. "Miracle On Ice" Olympic gold medal team, then became GM of the Rangers and Pittsburgh Penguins.

CONACHER CONNECTION

The Conacher clan of five boys and five girls grew up poor in downtown Toronto but that offered no roadblock to their participation in many sports, notably hockey. Three of the brothers became legendary NHL players. Charlie was the hard-shooting winger of the Toronto Maple Leafs' fabled Kid Line in the 1930s with center Joe Primeau and Busher Jackson. Roy, a winger like Charlie, played for the Chicago Black Hawks. Three-time all-star defenceman Lionel was on two Stanley Cup winners (Montreal Maroons, Chicago) and, in 1950, was named Canada's top athlete of the first half-century for his excellence in at least a half-dozen sports. Charlie's son Pete and Lionel's son Brian also had NHL careers.

THE HOWE HOWITZERS

Of all the highlights in Gordie Howe's career, one has particular distinction: He's the only father to be a teammate of his sons. Two years after he retired from a 26-year career of excellence with the Detroit Red Wings, Howe made a comeback with the Houston Aeros of the World Hockey Association, signing his biggest hockey contract in a package deal with his sons Mark and Marty. They spent four seasons in Texas winning two WHA championships and when the team folded, they played for two seasons with the New England Whalers, who moved to the NHL as the Hartford Whalers in 1979. Add up the Howes' totals in big-league hockey—Gordie always insisted that his WHA numbers be added to his NHL statistics—and the numbers are staggering: 4,197 games, 1,449 goals, 3,214 points.

THE HULL GUNNERS

Bobby Hull, his brother Dennis and Bobby's son Brett formed the highest scoring family unit in NHL history. In 3,697 games in the NHL and WHA, the Hull gang produced 1,944 goals, 3,825 points. Bobby broke Rocket Richard's record of 50 goals in a season with 54 in 1955–56. Dennis probably shot the puck as hard as his older brother, and Brett, who arrived in the mid-1980s, had a magical goal-scoring touch, collecting as many as 86 in a season, 228 in a three-season stretch, and enough to break into the top three all-time (his father is twelfth).

STAGGERING STATS

The Stastny brothers, Peter, Anton and Marian, who had all excelled with the Czechoslovakian national team, defected from their home country in the early 1980s to join the Quebec Nordiques. They played brilliantly, led by center Peter, who was the NHL's second highest scorer in the 1980s behind the great Wayne Gretzky. The Stastnys achieved the extraordinary feat of averaging more than a point per game as a family (2,169 points in 1,949 games).

AND CUPS ARE IMPRESSIVE, TOO

Among brother acts, the Richard boys, Maurice "Rocket" and Henri "Pocket Rocket," had a unique achievement with the Montreal Canadiens. The Richards could score plenty (902 goals in 2,234 games and 255 points in 313 playoff games) but their top feat is winning 19 Stanley Cups combined. Henri played on a record 11 winners while Maurice was on eight.

FAMILIES GALORE

The family trees seem un-ending in hockey, a list that includes the three gritty Hunter brothers, Dave, Mark and Dale; the slick Broten boys, Neal, Paul and Aaron; the raucous, fun-loving Plager brothers, Barclay, Bob and Bill; the high-scoring (821 goals) Mahovlich brothers, smooth six-Cup Frank and fun-loving Peter; Bill Dineen and his three sons, Kevin, Peter and Gord; Cal Gardner and offspring Dave and Paul; three generations of the Hextall family, Bryan Sr., a key member of the Rangers' 1940 Cup victory, his sons Bryan Jr. and Dennis, and grandson Ron, a fine goalie in a long career; the three Boucher brothers, stars all in the 1920s and 1930s, Frank, George, and Billy; and an unusual father-son pair of Bert Lindsay, a top goalie early in the last century, and his left-winger son Ted, a Hall of Famer.

THOMPSONS, TURGEONS, AND TWINS

Brother acts came in all shapes, sizes, and positions. Hockey's early days had the fabled rowdy Cleghorns, Odie and Sprague. Bun and

Bill Cook were keys to the Rangers' early success on the great line with Frank Boucher. Gunners and goalies teamed up with the early era tandem of stopper Tiny (2.08 average in 533 games) and scorer Paul Thompson and, later, with gunner Phil and goalie Tony Esposito. Max and Doug Bentley, Nick and Don Metz, Kevin and Derian Hatcher, Joe and Brian Mullen, Marcel and Jean Pronovost, Sylvain and Pierre Turgeon, and Russ and Geoff Courtnall were front-liner brother acts.

Twins Peter and Chris Ferraro played several games together with the New York Rangers and Pittsburgh in the 1990s, and many more in the minors. But the premier twin act is undoubtedly Daniel and Henrik Sedin, who dazzled Vancouver fans and confused the opposition with their tight teamwork and no-look passes after Canucks GM made some deals in order to draft them No. 2 and No. 3 overall in 1999 (Daniel was picked before Henrik…we think).

Dave and Ken Dryden stand out. They are the only brothers to be the opposing goalies in a game.

* * * * *

Zac Bierk is a goaltender who has played several games with the Phoenix Coyotes and Tampa Bay Lightning in the NHL as well as spending a lot of time in the American Hockey League. However, did you know that his brother, who goes by the stage name of Sebastian Bach, was the former lead singer of the rock band Skid Row?

* * * * *

"Sometimes when I make a good save I yell out, 'Woo-Hooo!' I'm not sure why, but it just feels good. I don't think I scare anyone or freak anyone out when I do it. I just like to holler when I make a tough stop."

—Wilkes-Barre Penguins goaltender,
Marc-Andre Fleury

SIEVES AND SWISS CHEESE

It may give coaches indigestion and fans heart palpitations, but bad goaltending makes for some great stories.

NO-LUCK NHL NETMINDERS

Today Greg Millen is well-known as a hockey TV commentator whose sharp tongue dissects the action for SportsNet and *Hockey Night in Canada*. But the veteran of 604 NHL games holds a dubious goaltending record. In 1982–83, he allowed a league-worst 282 goals in 60 games for the Hartford Whalers, which still stands as the all-time record. Millen also led the NHL in goals allowed in 1980–81 with Pittsburgh (258) and in 1983–84 with Hartford (221).

Darryl Sittler will always cherish the memory of February 7, 1976, when he set an NHL record by scoring ten points in one game versus the Boston Bruins. However, Dave Reece, the Boston goalie, obviously has different feelings about being on the receiving end of an 11–4 thrashing. Reece told the Hockey Hall of Fame years later, "It was beachball city. It just wasn't my night and Darryl was pure magic. The Leafs were going nuts, but I never realized he was doing all the scoring or going for a record. That's the fun of sports, but sometimes I wonder why I wasn't pulled after five or six goals." It was Reece's last NHL game. There's a joke that claims Reece went out after the loss and tried to end his life by jumping in front of a train, but the train went right through his legs.

Vancouver is sometimes dubbed the NHL's "goalie graveyard." Apart from Richard Brodeur and Kirk McLean in their peak-form days, goalies typically struggle to make their mark in the west coast city. After McLean was dealt to Carolina in 1998, the Canucks have gone through Sean Burke, Arturs Irbe, Garth Snow, Kevin Weekes, Felix Potvin and Bob Essensa (plus a few others) before finally allowing Dan Cloutier to solidify his status as the number one man between the pipes. But even though the Quebec native posted three straight seasons of 30-plus wins from 2001–02 to 2003–04, Cloutier is probably best remembered for an incident in the 2002 playoffs. The Canucks held a 2–0 lead in their first-round series with the Detroit Red Wings, and the score was tied 1–1 midway through game three. That was when Detroit's star defenceman Nicklas Lidstrom dumped in a 90-footer that got past Cloutier's glove and into the net with 24.6 seconds left in the second period. It proved to be the winning goal. Cloutier's play then took a nosedive and the Wings went on to win the series—and the Stanley Cup.

Names such as Jacques Plante, Ken Dryden and Jose Theodore have made Montreal's goaltending famous. But not every Canadiens goalie has fared well. Patrick Roy, whom some consider the best goalie of all time, surrendered nine goals in his final game in Montreal, an 11–1 loss to Detroit. He then demanded a trade and was sent to the Colorado Avalanche. Roy's erstwhile backup, Andre Racicot, earned an unfortunate nickname in his 68 NHL games: "Red Light." It's tough to prosper with that kind of reputation, though Racicot did get his name on the Stanley Cup in 1993.

Another rather hurtful nickname was assigned to Warren Skorodenski, a minor league and Canadian national team goalie who managed to post a dismal 6.89 goals-against average and .720 save percentage over 61 minutes of playing behind the powerful 1987–88 Edmonton Oilers: Warren "Score Against Me."

INTERNATIONAL ERRORS

Canadian goalie Bob Dupuis had a moment of Olympic shame in Lake Placid, New York, in a 1980 game versus Finland. From his own side of center, Finnish defenceman Kari Eloranta flipped the puck into the Canadian zone. Dupuis went to handle what should have been a straightforward play. But the slow-moving disc slid right past the goalie and into the empty net, which gave Finland a 3–1 lead. The blue-and-white team secured a spot in the medal round, while Canada, loaded with future NHLers such as Glenn Anderson, Randy Gregg and Paul MacLean, would have to settle for sixth place.

In the 1981 Canada Cup, Mike Liut picked a bad time to have a bad game for the host nation. The St. Louis Blues netminder had been named a First Team All-Star the season before and NHLers voted him the winner of the Lester Pearson most-valuable-player Award ahead of Wayne Gretzky. Liut won four games and tied one prior to facing the Soviets in the final. There, his counterpart Vladislav Tretiak shut the door in the first period, and then the Soviets simply ventilated Liut, scoring on 30 percent of their shots in an 8–1 victory. Although Liut played another ten years of quality hockey—he earned the NHL's best goals-against average in 1989–90—he never suited up again for Canada in international hockey.

Probably the most famous bad goal surrendered in international hockey history occurred in the Sweden-Belarus quarterfinal at the 2002 Olympics. Belarusian defenceman Vladimir Kopat took a long floater from the neutral zone that Swedish goalie Tommy Salo struggled to handle. The puck hit him in the mask area as he tried to glove it down, and then it bounced over his shoulder and trickled slowly into the net with 2:24 left in the game. Kopat's goal gave Belarus a 4–3 win over a squad that included Mats Sundin, Nicklas Lidstrom and Markus Naslund. Apart from the USA's "Miracle on Ice" victory over the Soviets in 1980 and Great Britain's 2–1 win over Canada in 1936, this was probably the biggest upset ever in Olympic hockey.

Canada's Marc-Andre Fleury was the victim of bad luck in the 2004 World Junior gold medal game versus the USA. The young goalie came out to clear a loose puck but chipped it off the shoulder of teammate Braydon Coburn, and it rebounded into the net to give the USA a 4–3 lead and ultimately the victory. Still, Pittsburgh's number one overall pick from the 2003 NHL Draft should have a bright future.

It's hard to know whether to laugh or cry when you look at the goaltending stats of Armen Lalayan. Who? The number one netminder for Armenia, that's who. The 29-year-old struggled at the Division III tournament of the 2005 IIHF World Championship, playing every minute as Armenia lost 33–1 to South Africa, 23–1 to Ireland, 38–3 to Luxembourg, and 48–0 to Mexico. That left him with a 35.50 GAA and a .549 save percentage. Of course, he didn't get much defensive support.

THE TINY PIONEER

Abigail Hoffman was known as "Ab" in her pioneering adventure in boys' minor hockey in the 1950s.

The times were much different in children's minor sports in the mid-1950s. Boys could play all sports. Girls? Well, there was always skipping and hopscotch...In the days before the women's movement, females played on softball teams—and a few played golf—but that was it. However, women's hockey did exist in small pockets around North America and had for the first half of the century. Such teams as the Preston (Ontario) Rivulettes, the Canadian women's champions for an entire decade from 1930 to 1940, were popular in their regions. But any hint of competition between girls and boys was regarded as impossible because the males were thought to be too rough.

LI'L AB

Abigail Hoffman had brothers who played hockey near their Toronto home. Her brother Muni progressed as far as Junior A. She was as devoted to the game as her brothers, and as skilled and determined in the family and neighborhood games. Thus at eight years of age, when she registered for a boys' team as "Ab Hoffman" with her short tomboy's haircut, no one questioned her gender.

ALL-STAR AB(IGAIL)

Hoffman played for a team called the Tee Pees, named after the well-known St. Catharines (Ontario) junior team that sent Bobby Hull and Stan Mikita to the NHL. Most of the kids in her Toronto Hockey League donned their hockey gear at home, only putting on skates and gloves at the arena, which eliminated any problem of exposing the boy-girl mix. Defenceman (defenceperson?) "Ab" turned out to be among the best players in the league: a quick, agile skater who had no fear in chasing the puck into the traffic. She was named to the league all-star team at the end of the season.

STAY AWAY FROM POOL PARTIES

But in her second season, when her team was entered in the important Timmy Tyke Tournament, part of their schedule was a swimming party after a game. Also, to play in the tournament, players had to have a birth certificate; tournament organizers noticed that one was held by "Abigail." When word of the presence of a girl in boys' hockey leaked out, Abby Hoffman became an instant celebrity: Stories on her, her family and her hockey skills attracted newspaper articles and TV and radio interviews, which she handled with surprising poise for her age. She was invited to attend NHL games in Toronto and Montreal. She continued to play for the Tee Pees, well-liked by her teammates. One lad insisted no player on the team had any idea of Abby's "secret" and that they wanted her on their team because "she's really good."

UP AND RUNNING

At the end of her second season in boys' hockey, Abby joined a girls' team but said that it wasn't as big a challenge. She tried and succeeded in other sports before devoting her athletic energy to track and field. She worked her way up through the tough ranks of middle-distance running and competed in two Olympic Games plus British Empire and Commonwealth Games. In the 1972 Games in Munich, West Germany, Hoffman won a bronze medal in the women's 800 metres event.

A BIG DIFFERENCE, ABIGAIL, A BIG DIFFERENCE...

A few years after she retired as an athlete, Hoffman was named Director Of Sport Canada, the government-backed group that supervised amateur sport, especially the allocation of government funding for Canada's Olympic athletes. At the 1988 Winter Olympics in Calgary, Hoffman reflected on her days as a hockey player in a boys' league. She said that the subject was a long way in her past and she was enthusiastic about recalling it.

"My family, and certainly myself, never thought of me as any trailblazer or a girl trying to prove that girls could play a sport as well as boys," Hoffman said. "At that age, eight and nine, there isn't a big gap between the sexes in size and strength. I was nothing except a girl who loved to play hockey and had done it with her brothers every chance there was from the time she got skates. I never wore so-called 'girlish' white figure skates; I wanted hockey skates like my brothers wore. I had a lot of fun in those two years and when my 'secret' was revealed, my teammates just shrugged as if it didn't matter. In reality, what difference did it make?"

RARE JEWEL AND KING

How Conn Smythe parlayed a bet on a slow horse named Rare Jewel into the purchase of the great King Clancy.

Norman "The Dude" Foden liked to brag that he had played a very important role in the construction of both the Toronto Maple Leafs hockey team and Maple Leaf Gardens, the famous Toronto building that was the Leafs' home. Foden was a jockey, a small man who rode at various Canadian racetracks from his teenage years until he was 55. In September 1930, he was the rider on Rare Jewel, owned by Conn Smythe, who also owned the Toronto Maple Leafs of the NHL and—in the middle of the Great Depression—was forming plans to build the Gardens.

BET ON THE HORSE, NOT WITH THE JOCKEY

Rare Jewel, a filly that had never won a race, became an integral part in one of hockey's favorite tales. Smythe bet heavily on Rare Jewel against the advice of his jockey Foden and when the horse won at odds of 107-to-1, Smythe used the money he collected as a portion of the $35,000 he paid the Ottawa Senators for defenceman King Clancy, who became a big part of the Leafs in their drive for popularity and arena-building funds.

GRAVEL, HORSES AND HOCKEY

The yarn of how Smythe reached the point of the Clancy deal is a wonderful bit of folklore about a man's angry reaction to what he felt was dreadful treatment by the New York Rangers. Born in Toronto, Smythe was captain of the University of Toronto hockey team, served in the Canadian Army in World War I, finished his degree, built a sand and gravel company, and started his thoroughbred racing stable. He coached the U of T hockey team and was an investor in the Toronto Marlboros, operated by Frank Selke, who rated among the game's best executives in his more than 40 years in hockey. "Smythe was a master at watching young players and spotting the spirit and talent that would allow them to excel at the professional levels," said Selke, himself a rare judge of talent who had frequent battles with Smythe. "He wasn't good at considering the opinions of others."

10,000 BUCKS AND A LOT OF DRIVE

When the NHL expanded into the United States in the mid-1920s with six American teams, Smythe was hired to build the first roster of the Rangers, headed by Colonel John Hammond. While the other new teams were buying established stars from the defunct Pacific Coast league, Smythe sought players from outside of the hockey mainstream, earning much skepticism from the large New York sporting press. At a total cost of $32,000, Smythe's own scouting found defencemen Ching Johnson and Taffy Abel in Minnesota, the awesome forward line of Bill and Bun Cook with Frank Boucher in western Canada, and goalie Lorne Chabot in northern Ontario.

When Smythe refused to buy top scorer Babe Dye from the Toronto St. Patricks—Smythe knew Dye was disliked by his teammates—the Manhattan media heaped such scorn on him that Hammond fired Smythe from the post, hiring Lester Patrick to run the franchise. A threat of legal action earned Smythe a $10,000 severance package from the Rangers and he returned to Toronto vowing revenge against the New York team.

OFF TO THE RACES

Smythe loved to tell the story of how he took $2,500 of his severance pay, doubled it on a college football bet, then did the same by betting $5,000 on "his" Rangers to beat the St. Pats. A Philadelphia group had bid $200,000 for the St. Patricks franchise but, armed with his $10,000 as down payment, Smythe tried to buy the Toronto team. The St. Pats majority owner, mining magnate Jack Bickell wanted a more substantial offer. Smythe's persistent and patriotic pitch—keep the team in Canada—raised enough money for Bickell to be convinced to leave money in the team but only if Smythe ran the operation. The name was changed to the Maple Leafs, the colors to blue and white, and one of the great franchises in pro sports was off to the races, precisely where Smythe made the money for a key purchase.

IRISHMAN FOR SALE

Selke became Smythe's assistant in most areas of the operation and they combined to build a strong team. Selke had recruited some exceptional young players for his Marlboro juniors—Red Horner, Busher Jackson, Charlie Conacher and Alex Levinski. Smythe handpicked Joe Primeau, Ace Bailey, Hap Day plus goalie Chabot in a trade with the Rangers. But the Leafs owner knew his club needed a top defenceman, especially a player to add spirit and zip to the club, on and off the ice. Smythe knew that Clancy could be that player. The Ottawa Senators, where Clancy had been a star for nine seasons and twice a Stanley Cup champion, had severe financial problems and spread the word that their nifty little (5-foot-7, 145 pound) Irishman was for sale.

AMAZING THE HORSE COULD RUN STRAIGHT

When the Senators turned down Smythe's offer of $25,000—all the Leafs directors would allow him to pay—the Leafs owner took another big chance. Smythe had paid $250 for Rare Jewel and when he entered the perennial loser in the Coronation Stakes, his trainer said it was a waste of money. Although Foden told Smythe that he felt the horse might have a "slim chance," he also told his wife to bet on another horse. Smythe placed $50 across the board on Rare Jewel and when Smythe's racetrack pals needled him about it, he bet another $30 on her to win. Years later, Smythe confessed to pouring a pint of brandy into the horse before the race as a stimulant. It worked because Foden rode a smart race, Rare Jewel won, and Smythe collected close to $11,000 on his bets.

LITTLE MAN HUGE FAVORITE

He added $10,000 of his earnings to the $25,000 the directors were willing to pay, threw in two players, Art Smith and Eric Pettinger, and Clancy became a Leaf. The rollicking defenceman became a huge favorite in Toronto and gave the Leafs seven big seasons plus several decades as an executive and coach after a stint as a referee. Rare Jewel, the horse that helped make a great franchise work, died a few weeks after her big win.

WHERE ARE THEY NOW?

The transition to civilian life can be difficult for retired hockey stars.

IF YOU CAN'T TAKE THE HEAT, JOIN THE FIRE DEPARTMENT

The on-the-job parallels of teamwork, emotional intensity and physical toil—heck, even the wearing of uniforms—may contribute to drawing ex-NHLers into firefighting. Gary Bromley (G, Buffalo/Vancouver, 1973–1980) joined the Vancouver Fire Department after a year in the minors, while Jack Egers (RW, NY Rangers/St Louis/Washington, 1969–1976) became not just a captain in the Kitchener-Waterloo Fire Department but president of the Kitchener Professional Firefighters' Association. The parallels multiply with the Barrett brothers, John (D, Detroit/Washington/Minnesota, 1980–1987) and Fred (D, Minnesota/Los Angeles, 1970–1984), who skated away from their respective blue lines to join fire departments in the neighbouring Ontario towns of Nepean and Gloucester.

BACK IN THE PENALTY BOX

Putting out fires more figuratively, Dennis O'Brien (D, Minnesota/Colorado/Cleveland/Boston, 1970–1980) is now a corrections officer at Brookside Youth Center in Port Hope, Ontario. And as principal of Tecumseh Public School in Mississauga, Dave Dryden (G, NY Rangers/Chicago/Buffalo/Edmonton, 1961–1979) must sometimes feel like a youth-corrections officer himself.

AN ENGINE DRIVER I WILL BE

Believe it or not, there was once a time when the average hockey player's salary wasn't enough to support him during the offseason, forcing him to take a summer job. Once Bill Juzda (D, NY Rangers/Toronto, 1940–1952) left the NHL for good, he managed to parlay his seasonal work with the Canadian Pacific Railroad into a 37-year career as engineer on the Winnipeg-to-Brandon route.

One of his opponents in the hard-fought semifinals of 1940, Frank Brimsek (G, Boston/Chicago, 1938–1950), continued to work for Juzda's competition after leaving the rink, serving many years as engineer on the Duluth, Winnipeg and Pacific branch of the Canadian National Railway.

TWO SKATES GOOD, FOUR HOOVES BETTER

Gilles Villemure (G, NY Rangers/Chicago, 1963–1977) spent his first eight years off the ice competing on the New York harness-racing circuit, while Noel Picard (D, Montreal/St Louis/Atlanta, 1964–1973) trained teams of Clydesdale horses to promote the wares of Anheiser-Busch Breweries. One variation on the horse-trainer theme: Walt Tkaczuk (C, NY Rangers, 1967–1981) owner and manager of River Valley Golf & Country Club in St. Marys, Ontario, has captured media interest from as far away as Japan by pioneering the use of llamas as caddies.

SOME SERIOUS ROAD TRIPS

Speaking of the Orient, Cliff Korill (RW, Chicago, 1969–1980) travels routinely to the Far East, South America and the Middle East—as Manager of Customer Service and Logistics for U.S.-based Cargill, Inc., he's responsible for the supply of shortening and oil to hundreds of far-flung McDonald's restaurants. Randy Manery (D, Detroit/Atlanta/Los Angeles, 1970–1980), on the other hand, racks up his own frequent-flyer points as he teaches leadership skills to third world Christian leaders at workshops in Maui and Singapore. Think that sounds exotic? Rick Martin (LW, Buffalo/Los Angeles, 1971–1982) oversaw the drilling of gold deposits in the Ivory Coast for the Eden Rock mining company, while Tim Ecclestone (RW, St Louis/Detroit/Toronto/Atlanta, 1967–1978) undertook the salvage of Spanish gold from galleons off the coast of Belize.

THESE GUYS WORE THEIR HELMETS

It may surprise some, though, to learn that the bulk of Ecclestone's treasure-hunting involved hard research rather than going toe-to-toe with smugglers and sharks. Hockey players, after all, are seldom known for their book-learning, though there are several other notable exceptions. Dave Shand (D, Atlanta/Toronto/Washington, 1976–1985) practices corporate law in Detroit, and while orches trating international bank deals often uses the fluent German he picked up while winding down his playing career in Austria. And Randy Gregg (D, Edmonton/Vancouver, 1981–1992) completed a residency in orthopedic surgery between winning the Stanley Cup in 1987 and competing for Canada in the 1988 Olympics, and after hanging up his skates for good established a successful practice in Edmonton.

THE POLITICAL GAME

But the best-known player-scholar must be Ken Dryden (G, Montreal, 1970–1979), who was known as an academic even in the midst of his NHL career—he sat out the 1973–74 season to practice law—and after retiring wrote the non-fiction bestsellers *The Game*, *Home Game*, *In School* and *The Moved and the Shaken*. In 2004, Dryden threw his face mask into the political ring and was elected Member of Parliament for York Center, at which time he was also named to the federal cabinet as Minister of Social Development. Along with his degrees in History from Cornell and Law from McGill, he's also been awarded honorary doctorates from the universities of Ottawa, Windsor, York, McMaster, St. Mary's, Niagara and UBC—enough post-NHL highlights for five or six guys!

MEEKER OF THE HOUSE

But we should not let Dryden overshadow the handful of other ex-players who have enjoyed political careers. Edgar Laprade (C, NY Rangers, 1945–1955) served 20 years as alderman in Thunder Bay, Ontario, and Fred Saskamoose (C, Chicago, 1953–54) was Band Chief of Saskatchewan's Sandy Lake Reserve from 1980 to 1987. Frank Mahovlich (LW, Toronto/Detroit/Montreal, 1956–1974) ran a Toronto travel agency before being named to the Canadian Senate by Prime Minister Jean Chrétien in 1998; at present Senator Mahovlich sits on the upper-house committee for Fisheries and Oceans as well as for Foreign Affairs. Mahovlich's former setup man and fellow Hall of Famer Red Kelly (D, Detroit/Toronto, 1947–1967) represented York South as a federal Liberal from 1962 to 1965, while performing double duty as one of the game's top defencemen. Well-known TV analyst Howie Meeker (RW, Toronto, 1946–54) also had a career in politics while still playing professionally: He was a Member of Parliament for Waterloo South from 1951 to 1953—seasons in which he totalled only 31 points in 79 games for the Leafs.

DOUGHNUT ASK WHAT YOUR COUNTRY CAN DO FOR YOU

Perhaps the NHLer with the best-known off-ice career, Tim Horton (D, Toronto/NY Rangers/Pittsburgh/Buffalo, 1949–1974) was also exploring other arenas while still an active player—tragically, both careers ended simultaneously as he was killed driving home to Toronto after a game in Buffalo. In the early 1960s Horton had opened a string of hamburger restaurants in Ontario, but when these had proven unsuccessful he opened his first Tim Hortons store in Hamilton in 1964, simply serving coffee and doughnuts, including his own creations the dutchie and apple fritter. Initial success led him to open one store after another, and following Horton's death his business partner, retired policeman Ron Joyce, bought Horton's widow's share of the 40-outlet Tim Hortons chain for $1 million. Joyce has continued the expansion, and as of 2005 there are 260 outlets in the United States and 2,482 in Canada—1,364 in Ontario alone!

TRADING COLOMBIAN GOLD FOR JUST PLAIN GOLD

One last variation on the post-hockey career: Danièle Sauvageau, former coach of the Canadian women's national team, is now a motivational speaker and TV commentator. But *before* Sauvageau went to the 2002 Olympics she worked undercover in the narcotics division of the Montreal Urban Police, busting violent drug dealers and leading her squad to extricate from deep cover any officers whose lives she deemed were in jeopardy. The coach claimed to not be the least bit nervous prior to the much-hyped Salt Lake City tournament, and we can only speculate whether her team could have captured gold with such composure had Sauvageau managed a golf course in her other life.

HOW TO MARRY A MILLIONAIRE

A handful of NHL players who have opted for a good old-fashioned celebrity marriage.

THIS YEAR'S MODEL

New York Rangers all-star forward Ron Duguay met *Sports Illustrated* swimsuit model Kim Alexis at a photo shoot in New York City, and they married in 1992. They were *both* modeling on that first day, incidentally, which should come as no surprise to anyone who fondly remembers Duguay's magnificent head of hair and high-cheekboned good looks. In 2005, 16 years after his last NHL shift, Ron Duguay is firmly grounded in hockey, coaching the Jacksonville Barracudas to the championship of the Souther Professional Hockey League 2003–04. His wife has also distanced herself from her more superficial past, arguing against unrealistic diets, skimpy outfits and loose morals in her book *A Model for a Better Future*, as well as recording the exercise audio-tapes *Victory Chant*, *All Things Are Possible* and *I Walk by Faith*.

THE PRIDE OF GOODSOIL

And in case you'd imagined that Alexis was unique in her role of model-turned-actress-turned-author-and-hockey wife, we turn our heads to look at Carol Alt. Appearing on the cover of the *Sports Illustrated* swimsuit issue in 1982, the next year she would—just like Kim Alexis would nine years later—marry a Rangers all-star who'd skated against the Canadiens in the 1979 finals. Ron Greschner, hailing from Goodsoil, Saskatchewan, and a down-to-earth guy if there ever was one, stands behind only Harry Howell, Rod Gilbert and Brian Leetch for most games played as a Ranger—982! The celebrity marriage proved too much for even his vaunted staying power, though, and in 1996 he and Alt parted ways; she was keen on furthering her acting career while he was ready to start a family. Greschner has since remarried, had "a few children," and moved into the title insurance business in Florida.

RUSSIAN TO THE ALTAR

Alexei Yashin, the current Ottawa Senators' first-ever draft selection, was Carol Alt's second-round selection for marriage. They were introduced at the 1999 NHL Awards, where Alt was a presenter. He was 25 at the time, Alt 38. Alt said, "He's so sweet. He'll say, 'Why do you wear your hair in your face like you're hiding?' He'll put it in a ponytail and say, 'Good, now I can see your beautiful face.' When a guy says that to you, all of a sudden you don't feel 40 anymore."

Similar gallantry, on or off the ice, might have kept Ottawa's front office equally enamoured with Yashin, but in 2001 he was traded to the New York Islanders. The couple married a year later, and in 2004 Alt published *Eating in the Raw: A Beginner's Guide to Getting Slimmer, Feeling Healthier, and Looking Younger the Raw-Food Way*. Despite her commitment to uncooked cuisine, Alt assured the Russian media that she would prepare pancakes and borscht for Yashin, while his mother defended her son and daughter-in-law's age difference by pointing out that, with 65 films and counting, Alt can thank hard work for everything she's gained in life. Hockey fans in both Long Island and Ottawa wish that they could say as much for her husband, who continues to perform below expectations.

HOCKEY WAS HIS FIRST LOVE—MR. HOCKEY

Rumors of runaway spending prior to the wedding of Wayne Gretzky and movie actress Janet Jones—predictions of a million-dollar ceremony were rampant—prompted Gretzky to retort to the media that Ms. Jones's dress did not cost $40,000, as they had reported, but merely had 40,000 sequins. Even so, the big day just oozed glitz. Millions of TV viewers watched as the Edmonton Symphony played the happy couple up the aisle, the pews of St. Joseph's Basilica filled with a who's-who of the NHL, and the reception that followed didn't lack for star power either. Those proceedings were overseen by Gretzky's best man, goaltender Eddie Mio, who asked all of the Great One's former girlfriends to please come forward and return their keys to his apartment. As the CBC reported, "People were laughing as Paul Coffey's mom and the very pregnant wife of one of Gretzky's teammates joined the procession." When all but one of the keys had been returned, Mio pleaded for the last girlfriend to please make herself known, and at last Gordie Howe rose sheepishly to his feet.

CZECHMATES

Sounds like a pretty classy reception, eh? But compare it to the proceedings in Prague orchestrated by then-Oiler Petr Nedved. In 2004, the same year that she graced the cover of the *Sports Illustrated* swimsuit issue, he married model Veronica Varekova in St. Vitus Cathedral, the centuries-old coronation site of Czech royalty. The couple then rode in a white Rolls-Royce to the Hergetova Cihelna restaurant, its floor strewn with rose petals, and after dinner strolled onto the balcony to watch a fireworks display, set off in their honor, burst over the river Vltava and the twelfth-century Charles Bridge. In fact, Nedved had gone down on one knee and proposed to Varekova on that same bridge one year before, when he'd still been playing for—which team? Yes, the New York Rangers.

RUSSIA: "A RIDDLE WRAPPED IN A MYSTERY INSIDE AN ENIGMA."

Tennis sensation Anna Kournikova and Detroit Red Wings all-star forward Sergei Fedorov raised several million more eyebrows by beginning their relationship when she was 16 and he was 28, waving to the crowds together in the 1997 Stanley Cup parade. "People didn't realize we have parents," Fedorov said recently. "She has parents, I have parents. Everything was normal as far as I'm concerned." In 1999 Kournikova sported a diamond ring at Wimbledon, sparking rumors that she and Fedorov were engaged. By the next year her tennis career had peaked with a number eight ranking—she never won a professional singles tournament—while her status as a sex symbol continued to ascend. She began to spend as much time at photo shoots as on the tennis court, and in 2002 was proclaimed "Sexiest Woman in the World" by *For Him* Magazine.

Fedorov's mother, meanwhile, claimed that her Sergei and the tennis star had been married in a Moscow registry office in 2001, while at the same time Kournikova appeared in a music video with Latin pop singer Enrique Iglesias and her publicist confirmed that she and the singer were dating. The *Hockey News* asked Fedorov to dispel the rumors. "We were married, albeit briefly," he admitted, "and we are now divorced." Kournikova has also been romantically linked to Fedorov's former Russian national-team linemate (and New York Ranger!) Pavel Bure, but we're not going to speculate when she would've had time for that relationship...

CHERCHEZ DES FEMMES AUX JEUX OLYMPIQUES

In the marriage of Bret Hedican and Kristi Yamaguchi we also achieve a two-athlete union, though this one is shrouded in no mystery whatsoever: They met at the 1992 Olympics in Albertville, France—where Hedican's Team USA finished without a medal and Yamaguchi took gold in women's figure skating—and were married on July 8, 2000. Hedican has played for St. Louis, Vancouver, Florida and Carolina in his professional career, contributing mightily to the Hurricanes' run to the finals in 2002, while Yamaguchi, who retired from competitive skating in 1997, now works full-time with the Always Dream Foundation, which she founded to benefit children in need. The couple's first child, Keara Kiyomi Hedican, was born October 1, 2003. Doesn't it all sound nice and straightforward?

MODEL BEHAVIOR

Which makes this as good a time as any to wrap things up, though believe it or not we haven't covered all of the couples that we might have. Former Ottawa Senators' first-overall pick Alexandre Daigle has scored off the ice more than on it, dating rock stars Alanis Morisette and Sheryl Crow and ex-*Baywatch* superstar Pamela Anderson. Montreal Canadiens star defenceman Sheldon Souray is married to another *Baywatch* alumnus, Angelica Bridges. Former Canucks winger Russ Courtnall is married to actress (and singer Sarah Vaughan's daughter) Paris Vaughan, Islanders winger Mariusz Czerkawski is divorced from *Goldeneye* actress and model Izabella Scorupco, and Mighty Ducks center Rob Niedermayer was long linked with *Sports Illustrated* swimsuit model Niki Taylor. Los Angeles Kings pest Sean Avery split up in the summer of 2005 from supermodel and Rod Stewart's ex-wife Rachel Hunter (who is 11 years Avery's senior).

Can there be any explanation for the eternal attraction between hockey players (particularly, as we've noticed, New York Rangers) and models? "It's because they have the same type of life, on the road all the time, moving from place to place," Carol Alt explains. "Also, it seems that they're the only people we meet."

FATHER HOCKEY

Les Costello abandoned an NHL career with the Maple Leafs to become a priest, but the "Flying Father" did not give up hockey.

PORCUPINE PRODIGY

Les Costello was a winner in hockey: twice with St. Michael's College in Toronto as Memorial Cup Canadian junior champions, and then with the 1948 Stanley Cup champions Toronto Maple Leafs. From the hockey-crazed mining area of South Porcupine, Ontario, Costello was a star with St. Michael's at only 16, producing 15 goals and 30 points in 23 playoff games as the team won the 1945 Memorial Cup, a feat they repeated two seasons later. Costello scored 32 American Hockey League goals in 1947–48, and then put up four points in five playoff games with the Cup-bound Leafs.

GOING OUT A WINNER

At age 21, he appeared to have started a solid NHL career. But despite the boundless enthusiasm he showed for hockey and life in general, Costello had serious doubts about his career choice. At the end of the 1949–50 season, he made a big decision, leaving hockey to enter the seminary and become a Catholic priest. Costello graduated four years later and was ordained, serving in parishes in the northern Ontario area where he grew up.

A CALL TO THE BIGS

But Father Costello was far from finished with hockey. He formed a team of priests from all parts of Ontario called the Flying Fathers. The team, which played the game well but also added hilarious comedy routines, played a busy schedule of games across Canada, raising millions of dollars for various charities. The Flying Fathers also played games in Europe and had a Vatican audience with Pope Paul VI. "Being a priest was a thought I had from a young age but I loved hockey, too, and the game got me to St. Mike's where several priests were a big influence on me and many others," Costello said. "I loved my time in hockey, both junior and pro, and playing on a Stanley Cup winner is a rare happening for any player. But my 'other' career possibility never went away. In the Catholic faith, we believe that God selects the ones he wants to be priests and we don't know why he makes his choices."

* * * * *

"Hockey captures the essence of Canadian experience in the New World. In a land so inescapably and inhospitably cold, hockey is the chance of life, and an affirmation that despite the deathly chill of winter we are alive."

—Canadian humorist Stephen Leacock

* * * * *

"I don't understand the deliberate intent to injure. I played this game for a long time and never deliberately tried to hurt anyone—except the Russians."

—Phil Esposito as NY Rangers General Manager, after sending the tape of an incident where Dave Brown of the Flyers cross-checked Rangers forward Thomas Sandstrom in the face, April 1987

* * * * *

DOH!

"You've got to go to the net if you want to score."

—Tom McVie, former coach, Washington Capitals

"When we've got the puck, they can't score."

—Paul Coffey, former Oilers defenceman

THE INCREDIBLE GOODBYES

Howie Morenz and Rocket Richard, major figures in two Montreal sports/political eras, had funerals that rivaled those of royalty.

Writer Andy O'Brien used a side entrance of the Montreal Forum on a March day in 1937 and was puzzled by the total silence in the building. He had expected a large crowd for the funeral of Howie Morenz, the great star of the Montreal Canadiens and an important player in the successful U.S. expansion of the NHL. "Morenz had lay in state at center ice in the Forum and nonstop for more than two days, the stream of people never eased, and many of the game's biggest stars were in a guard of honor around his casket," O'Brien said. "When I entered under the seats for the funeral and the building had this almost eerie silence, I couldn't believe it because I expected a full house. When I could see the stands, every seat in the building was being used but not a sound was made." Similarly memorable images marked the departure of another Canadien icon, Maurice "Rocket" Richard in May, 2000: four-deep lines of people stretching around the new Molson (now Bell) Center and nearby Windsor Station, part of the 115,000 who viewed the Rocket's casket over 24 hours.

FERVENTLY IDOLIZED

The two great players were idolized in Montreal with a fervor usually reserved for religious leaders or great politicians. Morenz was of Swiss descent and from Ontario, but his extraordinary talent, charisma and the spark he gave Les Habitants made him as popular as if his name were Quelque Chose. Richard was the greatest goal-scorer of his time, a member of eight Stanley Cup championship teams, and a player who always had an on-ice war going with an opponent with a non-French name: Lindsay, Laycoe, Ezinicki…His suspension late in the 1954–55 season that led to the St. Patrick's Day riot at the Forum is viewed by many historians as the start of the Quiet Revolution in which the French slowly took control of their economy and culture. The Rocket's funeral was attended by a multitude of politicians and sports figures and estimations of the crowd in the streets for his funeral procession range as high as two million.

Morenz had died at 35 in hospital for a broken leg. Concerned about his future and the likely end to his playing the game he loved, close friends claimed he died of a broken heart. More than 200,000 lined the streets as his body went to the cemetery.

* * * * *

CHERRY PICKING

Don Cherry doesn't pull his punches—he either loves ya or hates ya. Here are some of his best digs and honours.

"When I compared one of my players to Blue, it was like nominating him for knighthood."

"Even a poultry expert wouldn't buy some of the turkeys we had on our roster."

"He [Bobby Orr] was the greatest hockey player I have ever seen, Gordie Howe and Wayne Gretzky included."

"I'm just me. I'm like bagpipes—either you like them or you hate them."

HAIRY TIMES IN HOCKEY

From the buzzcut to the mullet, hockey hair has its own history.

Today, the term "hockey hair" usually conjures up images of a "mullet," the style favored by men who yearn for the days when Bon Jovi topped the charts and the Edmonton Oilers dominated the NHL. In the golden era of the Original Six, though, hockey's standard issue haircut was the military buzzcut, which kept everybody looking pretty similar. The 1960s Toronto Maple Leafs occasionally used this fact to their advantage. Let's say a certain Leaf was summoned to traffic court for a driving violation. He would get a teammate to appear in the dock in his stead. When the policeman was asked to identify the culprit, he'd point to the wrong guy, and the case would be dismissed.

THE 1970s AND 1980s: UNLOCKING THE LOCKS

Only in the Styling Seventies did players start to introduce a little madness into their manes.

Derek Sanderson of the Boston Bruins was the perfect example. The forward's long hair, big sideburns, and Fu Manchu moustache gave him a rebellious glamor only rivaled in contemporary pro sports by NFL superstar Joe Namath. Retrospectively, however, Sanderson looks like nothing more than an extra from *Boogie Nights*.

Another forward of lesser talent had his hairdo immortalized in the classic 1970s hockey film *Slap Shot*. Bill Goldthorpe was the model for the fictional goon Ogie Oglethorpe, and both were instantly recognizable due to their huge blond afros. The look seemed to accentuate the ferocity of this career minor league battler, whose record included throwing a phone at a referee, biting a linesman, and jail time.

Mel Bridgman was a bit of a rough-and-tumble character himself, but you wouldn't have known it from the nickname his Philadelphia Flyers teammates gave the 1975 No. 1 overall draft pick. When Bobby Clarke stepped down as the captain of the Broad Street Bullies in 1979, Bridgman took over the "C." According to Andrew Podnieks' book *Players*, however, Bridgman "quickly lost the respect of his teammates, who dubbed him 'Captain Shampoo,' because, it seems, his greatest concern was ensuring there was enough hair wash in the showers.'"

This was the sort of problem Bobby Hull would have loved to have had during the 1978 WHA playoffs. With his Winnipeg Jets facing the goon-heavy Birmingham Bulls in a first round matchup, The Golden Jet engaged in fisticuffs with another *Slap Shot* alumnus, Dave Hanson. At first it was a normal fight, but then a hush fell over the Winnipeg crowd when Hanson pulled off Hull's toupee! Shocked, Hanson dropped the lustrous rug to the ice. He was only assessed a minor and a major for fighting, rather than the usual match penalty for hair-pulling, since he hadn't tugged Hull's real hair. Hanson apologized when he saw Hull returning for the second period in a JOFA helmet. Hull said, "Don't worry about it, kid, I needed a new one anyway."

Ron Duguay cut a more glamorous figure with the New York Rangers in the early 1980s. The forward was noted for three things: his on-ice scoring panache, his relationship with supermodel Kim Alexis, and his long, curly brown locks. He maintained the latter with great care. One night, Duguay was serving a two-minute minor, and the penalty timekeeper noticed a peculiar odour. Continuing to sniff the air, the official finally realized it was the coconut hair oil with which Duguay had anointed himself.

Wayne Gretzky was anointed as hockey's savior around the same time, and the Great One also adopted a series of distinctive hairdos in the 1980s. In fact, merely by glancing at a Gretzky photo, an astute observer can tell which year it is: "Duguay-style perm? The 1981 Canada Cup. Short spiky blond look? Married to Janet and traded to L.A. in 1988."

THE 1990s AND BEYOND: HAIR TODAY, GONE TOMORROW

The 1990s had their share of hairy glory, too. Enforcer Chris Simon and scrappy center Mike Ricci were teammates for four seasons with the Colorado Avalanche franchise, but they were simultaneously competing for the title of NHL's Longest Hairdo. Ricci would eventually triumph after Simon abandoned his stance that long hair honored his native Indian heritage and got it chopped off.

But the most famous hockey hair of the 1990s unquestionably

belonged to Jaromir Jagr. The Czech superstar of the Pittsburgh Penguins was the first player not named Gretzky or Lemieux to win the NHL scoring title since 1981, and the powerful right-winger performed his wizardry with a spectacular set of black curls streaming from beneath his helmet. Jagr reputedly has strong faith in the Bible, but perhaps he forgot to read the story of Samson and Delilah. Much like Samson, Jagr seemed to lose his strength after he got his hair cut in 1999. In fairness, he won a couple more scoring titles, yet his passion for the game waned, and he would make a lot of people's hair fall out with his indifference after moving on to Washington and New York.

Hockey people tend to be conservative. If it works, keep on doing it. That's why Toronto defenceman Bryan McCabe took some heat for his flight of follicular fancy in 2003 when his play fell off concurrently. "If Jaromir Jagr can wear a mullet for eight years, why can't I wear a mohawk?" McCabe griped. "As long as I can go home and my wife likes it, that's the most important thing."

* * * * *

BAD HAIR DAY?

"I remember taking a look at him and saying 'Anyone who perms his hair has got to go.' So we sent him to Fort Worth."

—Don Cherry, March 1987, on Don Saleski, who he coached in Colorado

"I think I'm old enough to have short hair now. No more of that girl stuff."

—Jaromir Jagr